ACT®
Reading Mastery
Level 1

(2014-15 Edition)

The ultimate workbook to help you succeed on the ACT Reading test

Craig Gehring
Ring Publications

ACT® is the registered trademark of ACT, Inc. Ring Publications, LLC has no affiliation with ACT, Inc., and the ACT Mastery program is not approved or endorsed by ACT, Inc.

Copyright © 2014 by Craig Gehring.

All Rights Reserved. No part of this publication may be reproduced or transmitted in any form or by any means, electronic or mechanical, including photocopy, recording, or any information storage or retrieval, without permission in writing from Craig Gehring.

This publication, its author, and its publisher, are in no way affiliated with or authorized by ACT, Inc. or by College Board. ACT and SAT are copyrights and/or trademarks of ACT, Inc. and College Board, respectively.

Inquiries concerning this publication should be mailed to:

Ring Publications
7117 Florida Blvd.
Baton Rouge, LA 70806

Printed in the United States of America.

ISBN-10: 1500699020
ISBN-13: 978-1500699024

LR-083014

Contents

Lesson 1: Overview 5
Lesson 2: Pace 7
Lesson 3: How to Read the Passages 9
Lesson 4: Intro to Vocabulary 15
Lesson 4.1-4.4: Vocabulary 17-63
Lesson 4.5: Vocabulary Review 65
Lesson 5: Finding Exact Details 75
Lesson 6.1-6.4: Vocabulary 89-135
Lesson 6.5: Vocabulary Review 137
Lesson 7: Finding and Interpreting Details 149
Lesson 8.1-8.4: Vocabulary 165-211
Lesson 8.5: Vocabulary Review 213
Lesson 9: Reading Comprehension 223
Lesson 10.1-10.4: Vocabulary 241-287
Lesson 10.5: Vocabulary Review 289
Lesson 11: Making Inference 301
Lesson 12.1-12.4: Vocabulary 311-357
Lesson 12.5: Vocabulary Review 359
Lesson 13: Decoding Vocabulary 387
Reading Mini-Practice Tests 395
About the Author / More Information 444

🛑 *Have You Registered Your Book Yet?*

With your purchase of *ACT Reading Mastery, Level 1*, you have gained access to a special series of videos on prepping for the ACT Reading test by the workbook's author, Craig Gehring, who made perfect scores on both the ACT and the SAT. These videos are not available anywhere. You'll also have the option to receive Craig's free newsletter designed to give you the edge you need before your exams. The entire registration process is free and takes less than 1 minute.

Visit
www.actmastery.org/reading

Lesson 1
Overview

The ACT Reading test is a reading comprehension test. Above all, it checks your ability to read. Strong readers will score better than poor readers on this test.

No number of reading strategies can overcome weak reading skills. Improving your reading skills takes practice. You have to read a lot, and you have to actively work on building your vocabulary as you read. Bookworms definitely have the upper hand on this section of the test.

In this course, you'll read through a wide variety of practice reading tests and become familiar with the most common question types that can come up. You'll learn essential strategies for working through the passages and questions.

You'll also review the meanings of the words used most frequently by the ACT, and in the process learn the tools for improving your vocabulary and reading level.

There are no shortcuts to a higher ACT Reading score, but if you learn the strategies provided in this book and take every opportunity to read and improve your reading level as this course suggests, your score can improve.

Lesson 2
Pace

On the ACT Reading test, the easy questions aren't stacked in the front. The questions don't gradually become more difficult. As a matter of fact, it's totally possible for the last question on the test to be easier than the first one! That's because ACT Reading questions are distributed randomly in terms of difficulty.

This is the reason why you must pace yourself on the ACT Reading test. Every single passage on the test has questions that you can answer. Every single one. If you don't give yourself time to consider each and every question, you are leaving points on the table.

You are given 35 minutes to complete the ACT Reading test. The test contains 4 passages. Each passage is followed by 10 questions, which means that there are a total of 40 questions on the test.

I am going to share with you a simple tip for never running out of time on the Reading test. Give yourself 8 minutes per passage and question set. That means 8 minutes for the passage as well as the 10 questions which go with it.

Think of each passage as a container with 8 minutes. Don't let yourself borrow time from another passage in order to answer the questions for this passage. Once the 8 minutes are gone, they're gone. Move on to the next passage.

Using this pace, you'll have at least 3 minutes at the end of the test to double back, check your answers, and reconsider any questions you weren't sure about.

In this course, I want you to practice at the correct pace. That means that you need to time yourself 8 minutes for each practice passage that we provide. Once the 8 minutes are up, check your answers and read through the explanations.

Lesson 3
How to Read the Passages

Each ACT Reading passage contains an 800-word narrative along with questions and answers, which are an additional 500 to 600 words. This means that in order to get through the entire reading passage at the correct pace, you'd have to be able to read at least 1,300 words in 8 minutes.

As you've probably guessed, there is a problem with this. The average adult reads comfortably at around 200 words per minute, meaning if you read at a normal pace, you'll only just be finished reading the passages and questions when you run out of time. You won't even have time to answer the questions!

On the ACT Reading test, I want you to spend only 3 minutes on each passage; just skim it. When skimming, you are reading too fast to remember every detail but can still comprehend the main idea and tone of a passage.

In order to do this, you have to finish the reading passage and begin on its questions within 3 minutes. However, it takes practice to skim at this pace. If you have a hard time reading that quickly, try the technique of reading only the first and last sentence of each paragraph. Under no circumstances should you skip a passage altogether. There are questions included in the test specifically designed to punish you for skipping a passage.

In the practice questions that follow, give yourself 3 minutes to read each passage. Once the timer hits 3 minutes, begin answering the questions. These questions are not ACT-level but are intended to simply check your understanding of the overall meaning of each passage. The overall point is to improve your reading speed.

Remember that the most important element in the ACT Reading test is *"where."* **The answer to every ACT Reading question is contained in the content of the passages, meaning that you need to remember *where* things are**. By mentally indexing the location of information as you read, it will be much easier to find those answers later.

"Where" is much more important than *"who," "what," "when," "why,"* or *"how."* You don't need to remember all the details in a passage. If you know where to find the details, then you can simply go looking for them; that's how you'll be able to get through each passage in only 3 minutes.

Skim through the passage before reading its questions, paying attention only to the general idea of what is being said, the tone of the passage, and where everything is situated. Understanding the main idea and tone of a passage while you are reading it will save you some time; those questions can cause you to re-read entire passages if you aren't prepared.

Passage

Instructions: Skim the passage in 3 minutes, then answer the 10 practice questions that appear below. Use a timer to keep track of when you should start answering the questions. Just like on the ACT, you are allowed to refer to the passage in order to find the correct answers.

LITERARY NARRATIVE: This passage is adapted from the essay "Some Nonsense About a Dog" by Harry Esty Dounce, which appeared in Christopher Morley's *Modern Essays* in 1921.

The day he came was a beautiful bright, cool one in an August. A touring car brought him. They put him down on our corner, meaning to lose him, but he crawled under the car, and they had to prod him out
5 and throw stones before they could drive on—I carried him over the railroad tracks. That night he got chop bones and she got a sensible homily on the unwisdom of feeding strays, and he was left outdoors. He slept on the mat. The second morning we thought he had gone.
10 The third, he was back, wagging approval of us and intent to stay, which seemed to leave no choice but to take him in. We had fun over names. "Jellywaggles," "Rags," or "Toby"; finally we called him "Nibs" and soon his tail would answer to it.

15 Cleaned up—scrubbed, the insoluble matted locks clipped from his coat, his trampish collar replaced with a new one bearing a license tag—he was far from being unpresentable. A vet once opined that for a mongrel he was a good dog. Always, depending on the moment's
20 mood, he was either terrier or spaniel, the snap and scrap and perk of the one alternating with the gentle snuggling indolence of the other.

As terrier he would dig furiously by the hour after a field mouse; as spaniel he would "read" the
25 breeze with the best nose among the dog folk of our neighborhood, or follow a trail quite well. I know there was retrieving blood. A year ago May he caught and brought me, not doing the least injury, an oriole that probably had flown against a wire and was struggling
30 disabled in the grass.

Nibbie was shabby-genteel black, sunburnt as to the mustache, grizzled as to the raggy fringe on his haunches. He had a white stock and shirt-frill and a white fore paw. The brown eyes full of heart were his
35 best point. His body coat was rough Scottish worsted, the little black pate was cotton-soft like shoddy, and the big black ears were genuine spaniel silk. As a terrier he held them up smartly and carried a plumy fishhook of a tail; as a spaniel the ears drooped and the tail swung
40 meekly as if in apology for never having been clipped. The other day when we had to say good-by to him each of us cut one silky tuft from an ear, very much as we had so often when he'd been among the burdocks in the field where the garden is.

45 In flea time it seemed hardly possible that a dog of his size could sustain his population. We finally found a true flea bane, but, deserted one day, he was populous again the next. They don't relish every human; me they did; I used to storm at him for it, and he used, between
50 spasms of scratching, to listen admiringly and wag. We think he supposed his tormentors were winged insects, for he sought refuge in dark clothes-closets where a flying imp wouldn't logically come.

He was willful, insisted on landing in laps when
55 their makers wanted to read. He would make advances to visitors who were polite about him. He would get up on the living room table, why and how, heaven knows, finding his opportunity when we were out of the house, and taking care to be upstairs on a bed by the time we
60 had the front door open; I used to slip up to the porch and catch through a window the diving flourish of his sinful tail.

One of his faults must have been a neurosis really. He led a hard life before we took him in, as witnessed
65 the game hind leg that made him sit up side-saddle fashion, and two such scars on his back as boiling hot grease might have made. And something especially cruel had been done to him when asleep, for if you bent over him napping or in his bed he would half rouse and
70 growl, and sometimes snap blindly.

He was spoiled. That was our doing. We babied him abominably—he was, for two years, the only subject we had for such malpractice. He had conscience enough to be sly. I remember the summer evening we
75 stepped outside for just an instant, and came back to find a curious groove across the butter, on the dining table, and an ever-so-innocent Nibbie in a chair in the next room.

It was lucky that the big dogs in our neighborhood
80 were patient. And he never would learn about automobiles. Usually tried to tackle them head on, often stopped cars with merciful drivers. When the car wouldn't stop, luck would save him by a fraction of an inch. I couldn't spank that out of him either. We had
85 really been expecting what finally happened for two years.

That's about all. Too much, I am afraid. A decent fate made it quick the other night, and clean and close at hand, in fact, on the same street corner where once a car
90 had left the small scapegrace for us. We tell ourselves we couldn't have had him forever in any event; that some day, for the junior member's sake, we shall get another dog. We keep telling ourselves these things, and talking with animation on other topics. The muzzle,
95 the leash, the drinking dish are hidden, the last muddy paw track swept up, the nose smudges washed off the favorite front window pane.

But the house is full of a little snoofing, wagging, loving ghost. I know how the boy Thoreau felt about
100 a hereafter with dogs barred. I want to think that somewhere, some time, I will be coming home again, and that when the door opens Nibbie will be on hand to caper welcome.

Lesson 3 - How to Read the Passages

1. This passage is about a:
   A. cat.
   B. dog.
   C. human.
   D. bird.

2. It is most accurate to say that the narrator:
   F. enjoys having fleas.
   G. is planning on buying a house.
   H. wishes his dog was still around.
   J. hates his dog.

3. In which paragraph does the narrator describe giving his dog a new collar?
   A. Paragraph 2 (lines 15-22)
   B. Paragraph 4 (lines 31-44)
   C. Paragraph 6 (lines 54-62)
   D. Paragraph 8 (lines 71-78)

4. In which paragraph does the narrator describe Nibbie getting up on the living room table?
   F. Paragraph 3 (lines 23-30)
   G. Paragraph 4 (lines 31-44)
   H. Paragraph 5 (lines 45-53)
   J. Paragraph 6 (lines 54-62)

5. In which paragraph does the narrator describe Nibbie as being spoiled?
   A. Paragraph 6 (lines 54-62)
   B. Paragraph 7 (lines 63-70)
   C. Paragraph 8 (lines 71-78)
   D. Paragraph 9 (lines 79-86)

6. What brought the dog to the narrator's family?
   F. A touring car
   G. A stork
   H. A vet
   J. A ghost

7. Which of the following statements is true about Nibbie's life before he came to live with the narrator?
   A. Nibbie had a hard life.
   B. Nibbie had an easy life.
   C. Nibbie used to live in a touring car.
   D. Nibbie always wore a muzzle.

8. In which paragraph does the narrator describe Nibbie's flea problems?
   F. Paragraph 2 (lines 15-22)
   G. Paragraph 5 (lines 45-53)
   H. Paragraph 9 (lines 79-86)
   J. Paragraph 11 (lines 98-103)

9. The narrator's tone is best described as:
   A. grief.
   B. anger.
   C. hatred.
   D. fond remembrance.

10. In which paragraph does the narrator discuss the dog digging for mice?
    F. Paragraph 1 (lines 1-14)
    G. Paragraph 2 (lines 15-22)
    H. Paragraph 3 (lines 23-30)
    J. Paragraph 4 (lines 31-44)

Reading Mastery - Level 1

1. This passage is about a:
   A. cat.
   B. dog.
   C. human.
   D. bird.

   In the header, we see that the title of the essay is "Some Nonsense About a Dog," so "dog" is our best choice.

2. It is most accurate to say that the narrator:
   F. enjoys having fleas.
   G. is planning on buying a house.
   H. wishes his dog were still around.
   J. hates his dog.

   In the last paragraph, the narrator says that he wants "to think that somewhere, some time, I will be coming home again, and that when the door opens Nibbie will be on hand to caper welcome." This means that he wishes his dog were still around.

3. In which paragraph does the narrator describe giving his dog a new collar?
   A. Paragraph 2 (lines 15-22)
   B. Paragraph 4 (lines 31-44)
   C. Paragraph 6 (lines 54-62)
   D. Paragraph 8 (lines 71-78)

   In paragraph 2 (lines 15-22), the narrator describes his dog's "trampish collar" being "replaced with a new one bearing a license tag."

4. In which paragraph does the narrator describe Nibbie getting up on the living room table?
   F. Paragraph 3 (lines 23-30)
   G. Paragraph 4 (lines 31-44)
   H. Paragraph 5 (lines 45-53)
   J. Paragraph 6 (lines 54-62)

   In paragraph 6 (lines 54-62), the narrator says "he would get up on the living room table," so choice J is the best answer.

5. In which paragraph does the narrator describe Nibbie as being spoiled?
   A. Paragraph 6 (lines 54-62)
   B. Paragraph 7 (lines 63-70)
   C. Paragraph 8 (lines 71-78)
   D. Paragraph 9 (lines 79-86)

   In paragraph 8 (lines 71-78), it says "he was spoiled," so choice C is the best answer.

6. What brought the dog to the narrator's family?
   F. A touring car
   G. A stork
   H. A vet
   J. A ghost

   In paragraph 1 (lines 1-14), the narrator says that "a touring car brought him." For that reason, choice F is the best answer.

Lesson 3 - How to Read the Passages

7. Which of the following statements is true about Nibbie's life before he came to live with the narrator?
   A. **Nibbie had a hard life.**
   B. Nibbie had an easy life.
   C. Nibbie used to live in a touring car.
   D. Nibbie always wore a muzzle.

In paragraph 7 (lines 63-70), the narrator says that "he led a hard life before we took him in," so choice A is the most accurate answer.

8. In which paragraph does the narrator describe Nibbie's flea problems?
   F. Paragraph 2 (lines 15-22)
   G. **Paragraph 5 (lines 45-53)**
   H. Paragraph 9 (lines 79-86)
   J. Paragraph 11 (lines 98-103)

In paragraph 5 (lines 45-53), the narrator says that "in flea time it seemed hardly possible that a dog of his size could sustain his population," so choice G is the best answer.

9. The narrator's tone is best described as:
   A. grief.
   B. anger.
   C. hatred.
   D. **fond remembrance.**

While it's sad that his dog passed away, the passage doesn't have an overall emotion of grief or sadness, so we can eliminate choice A. Choices B and C can also be eliminated because the narrator does not come off as being truly mad about the dog or about anything he is describing. That leaves us with choice D: fond remembrance. Fond means "having affection or liking," and remembrance means "the action of remembering something." Throughout the passage, the narrator is recalling memories about his dog in a fond sort of way.

10. In which paragraph does the narrator discuss the dog digging for mice?
    F. Paragraph 1 (lines 1-14)
    G. Paragraph 2 (lines 15-22)
    H. **Paragraph 3 (lines 23-30)**
    J. Paragraph 4 (lines 31-44)

In paragraph 3 (lines 23-30), it says "he would dig furiously by the hour after a field mouse," so choice H is the best answer.

Lesson 4
Intro to Vocabulary

When students improve their reading level, the ACT Reading and Science tests get easier. The key to improving your reading level (and improving your reading comprehension abilities) is *vocabulary*. If you don't understand the individual words being used in a sentence, you can't comprehend the sentence. And if you can't comprehend the sentence, then you'll have difficulty with the paragraph!

In this workbook we'll be teaching you and reviewing with you 200 key vocabulary terms that are most likely to show up and be misunderstood on the ACT. By learning these terms, you can improve your score.

IMPORTANT INSTRUCTIONS:

In each vocabulary lesson there are 10 vocabulary words to learn—one per page. The definition that appears at the top of the page is the most common (or most commonly misunderstood) definition. You'll need to read that as well as the example sentences. Then read the words that are similar to it and the words listed that are opposite to the word's definition.

When you read the words that are similar and opposite, put a check mark over each word that you know at least one definition for. If you don't know what the word means, circle it. Look up the definition of each word you've circled in your dictionary. After you look it up, then close your dictionary and make sure you remember what the word meant. Then check it off, too.

After you do that, you'll be asked to look up the top word in the dictionary and make up your own sentences in your mind using each definition until you feel totally confident about using the word in your vocabulary. Finally, you write five sentences using the word correctly.

It's important not to speed through this. You'll only be cheating yourself. By really taking the time to look up the words, as well as reviewing the synonyms (words that are like it), you'll literally be improving your vocabulary level by thousands of words!

This is the make-or-break point of doing well on the ACT.

Note: words have many different definitions. To gain a thorough understanding of the word so that it doesn't trip you up on the test, be sure to go over each definition as it appears in the dictionary. Each definition has its own meaning and you will need to make up sentences for each of these separate definitions.

Make sure that if you are learning a word in this workbook and don't understand a word in the definition, look that word up, too! Otherwise, there's no way you'll learn the word well enough for it to help you on the ACT. The more words you learn, the better chance you have of scoring well.

Lesson 4.1
Vocabulary

scheme

_{noun} an elaborate or sophisticated plan or plot; ALSO a sophisticated drawing or representation

example sentences

He spent all day working on a **scheme** to get out of the house without his babysitter noticing.

The police uncovered an elaborate **scheme** to defraud the bank.

The architect's **scheme** of the new house was far too complicated for me to understand.

also written in this form **schemes, scheming, schemed**

words that are similar **plan, sketch, drawing, arrangement, diagram, strategy, tactics, system, outline**

Look up the full definition of "scheme" in the dictionary and use each definition in sentences of your own creation until you feel you fully understand the word and can use it in conversation.

Write five sentences using the noun and verb "scheme":

_____

_____

_____

_____

_____

_____

_____

keen

adjective **intense or sharp**

example sentences

Ever since he saw the presentation by the chemical engineer, Allan has had a **keen** interest in chemistry.

William had a **keen** desire to win the part, and that saw him through his auditions.

Quinton described a **keen** pain behind his left eye to the doctor.

also written in this form **keenly**

words that are similar **enthusiastic, alert, avid, eager, spirited, intense, earnest, zealous**

words that are opposite **reluctant, unenthusiastic, uninterested**

Look up the full definition of "keen" in the dictionary and use each definition in sentences of your own creation until you feel you fully understand the word and can use it in conversation.

Write five sentences using the adjective "keen":

_____

_____

_____

_____

_____

_____

_____

_____

liberal

adjective having political or social views tending in favor of reform and progress; ALSO tending toward open-mindedness

example sentences

The **liberal** philosophers of the time believed that definite progress needed to be made in our culture.

The teacher had a **liberal** policy about conduct and wouldn't flunk you just because you talked too much in class.

I wish my parents would be a little more **liberal** when it comes to curfew.

also written in this form **liberally**

words that are similar **progressive, enlightened, flexible, free, indulgent, humanistic, humanitarian, left, reasonable, tolerant, unbiased, unconventional, unorthodox**

words that are opposite **conservative, narrow, narrow-minded**

Look up the full definition of "liberal" in the dictionary and use each definition in sentences of your own creation until you feel you fully understand the word and can use it in conversation.

Write five sentences using the adjective "liberal":

_____

_____

_____

_____

_____

_____

_____

_____

despair

noun a feeling of hopelessness; the state of lost hope

example sentences

The student felt **despair** when he saw that his test score wasn't high enough to pass the class.

Some psychologists receive special training on how to help their clients deal with **despair**.

In the movie, the protagonist reached a point of **despair** when he thought his family had disappeared forever.

also written in this form despair, despaired, despairing

words that are similar depression, hopelessness, anguish, dejection, desperation, despondency, discouragement, gloom, misery, sorrow

words that are opposite cheer, cheerfulness, confidence, faith, happiness, hopefulness, joy

Look up the full definition of "despair" in the dictionary and use each definition in sentences of your own creation until you feel you fully understand the word and can use it in conversation.

Write five sentences using the noun "despair":

_____

_____

_____

_____

_____

_____

_____

tide

noun the daily rise and fall of sea level; ALSO something that may increase or decrease

example sentences

They forgot to account for the **tide** and built their sandcastle too close to the sea.

The **tide** washes in seaweed every night.

The **tide** of public interest in the film seemed like it would never wane.

words that are similar **flow, current, ebb, stream, trend**

*Look up the full definition of "**tide**" in the dictionary and use each definition in sentences of your own creation until you feel you fully understand the word and can use it in conversation.*

Write five sentences using the noun "tide":

_____

_____

_____

_____

_____

_____

_____

_____

attitude

noun one's beliefs, acts, feelings and one's tendency to act or react in certain ways

example sentences

In the Olympics, the athletes with positive **attitudes** were better able to deal with disappointments and continue to compete.

The speaker emphasized that a negative **attitude** toward school can keep students from being able to benefit from it.

Michael wanted to know why the politician developed his specific **attitude** about immigration.

words that are similar outlook, belief, disposition, demeanor, character, frame of mind, inclination, mindset, mood, opinion, perspective, point of view, sentiment, temperament

Look up the full definition of "attitude" in the dictionary and use each definition in sentences of your own creation until you feel you fully understand the word and can use it in conversation.

Write five sentences using the noun "attitude":

_____

_____

_____

_____

_____

_____

_____

_____

justify

verb to show why or how someone or something is right by providing reasons or proof

example sentences

You'll need to **justify** that expense before the board approves it in the budget.

The professor did not try to **justify** his mistakes, but rather spent his time helping his research students to learn from them.

The leader was finally **justified** in the tough decisions he had made when, at long last, the economy started coming back to life.

also written in this form **justify, justified, justifying, justification**

words that are similar **contend, confirm, defend, excuse, exonerate, explain, maintain, rationalize, show cause, validate, verify, vindicate, warrant**

words that are opposite **assail, attack, criticize, impugn, oppose, protest**

Look up the full definition of "justify" in the dictionary and use each definition in sentences of your own creation until you feel you fully understand the word and can use it in conversation.

Write five sentences using the verb "justify":

_____

_____

_____

_____

_____

_____

_____

_____

Lesson 4.1 - Vocabulary

humble

adjective **not arrogant, prideful or boastful; meek or modest**

example sentences

The movie star was surprisingly **humble** when Elise had a chance to talk with him.

Although his parents spent a large amount of time teaching him to be **humble**, the lessons apparently didn't work.

It is increasingly rare to find a **humble** politician.

also written in this form **humility**

words that are similar **meek, unassuming, modest, courteous, mild, obliging, ordinary, reserved, self-effacing, soft-spoken, unobtrusive, unpretentious**

words that are opposite **assertive, boasting, conceited, egotistical, insolent, pretentious, proud, showy**

Look up the full definition of "humble" in the dictionary and use each definition in sentences of your own creation until you feel you fully understand the word and can use it in conversation.

Write five sentences using the adjective "humble":

_____

_____

_____

_____

_____

_____

_____

_____

flag

verb to become less intense; ALSO to droop, sink or settle from pressure or loss of tautness

example sentences

His energy **flagged** until finally he fell asleep.

One graduate stated that his secret to getting through college was finding ways to prevent his interest from **flagging** in his junior year and getting more involved on campus.

The football team got off to a great start, but the intensity of their defensive players **flagged** after the first quarter.

also written in this form **flagged, flagging**

words that are similar **bend, break, cave in, deflate, give in, keel over, subside, weaken, weary**

words that are opposite **build, increase, rise**

Look up the full definition of "flag" in the dictionary and use each definition in sentences of your own creation until you feel you fully understand the word and can use it in conversation.

Write five sentences using the verb "flag":

_____

_____

_____

_____

_____

_____

_____

merit

<small>noun</small> the quality of being deserving of something; ALSO any positive or admirable quality

example sentences

Fewer colleges are offering **merit**-based scholarships, these days.

Becoming valedictorian **merits** special recognition.

Your idea has a lot of **merit** and will be fully considered at our next board meeting.

words that are similar goodness, excellence, credit, value, virtue, talent

words that are opposite demerit, disadvantage, fault, weakness

Look up the full definition of "merit" in the dictionary and use each definition in sentences of your own creation until you feel you fully understand the word and can use it in conversation.

Write five sentences using the noun "merit":

_____

_____

_____

_____

_____

_____

_____

_____

Lesson 4.2
Vocabulary

manifest

adjective **clearly visible or revealed**

verb **to become clearly visible or to make an appearance**

example sentences

His intentions became **manifest** when he told the girl he loved her.

Their animosity towards the other school became **manifest** when they stole Istrouma High's mascot.

Once a year, the groundhog **manifests** above ground to announce the end of winter.

also written in this form **manifesting, manifested, manifestation**

words that are similar **clear, obvious, apparent, bold, conspicuous, evident, noticeable, prominent, revealed, unmistakable, visible**

words that are opposite **concealed, obscure, unclear, vague, ambiguous**

Look up the full definition of "manifest" in the dictionary and use each definition in sentences of your own creation until you feel you fully understand the word and can use it in conversation.

Write five sentences using the adjective and verb "manifest":

_____

_____

_____

_____

_____

_____

_____

notion

noun an idea, often a vague or fanciful one, or concept

example sentences

Frank had a spur-of-the-moment **notion** to go see the movie.

She wanted to know where he got the **notion** that she liked him.

The upper class's **notion** of equality differed greatly from the lower class's ideas about the same.

words that are similar belief, idea, concept, conception, imagination, judgment, insight, opinion, sentiment, thought, view, understanding

Look up the full definition of "notion" in the dictionary and use each definition in sentences of your own creation until you feel you fully understand the word and can use it in conversation.

Write five sentences using the noun "notion":

_____

_____

_____

_____

_____

_____

_____

scale

noun a series of things arranged in levels for comparison or reference

verb to climb

example sentences

She wanted to know how Julie liked the boy on a **scale** of one to ten.

Most movie critics rate their movies on a **scale** of one to five stars.

Josie held the distinction of being the youngest female to ever **scale** that mountain.

also written in this form **scaled, scaling**

words that are similar **graduated system, gradation, degrees, extent, spectrum, spread, ascend, climb**

Look up the full definition of "scale" in the dictionary and use each definition in sentences of your own creation until you feel you fully understand the word and can use it in conversation.

Write five sentences using the verb and noun "scale":

_____

_____

_____

_____

_____

_____

_____

Lesson 4.2 - Vocabulary

formal

adjective following the established conventions or requirements; ALSO characteristic of or befitting a person in authority

example sentences

The committee member did not feel that her dress was sufficiently **formal** for the interview.

It is **formal** to submit a two-week notice before leaving a job.

The accountant said that a **formal** review of their accounts needed to be completed before they could turn in their taxes.

also written in this form formality

words that are similar established, orderly, approved, conventional, formalistic, rigid, proper, solemn, set, strict

words that are opposite disorderly, informal, relaxed

Look up the full definition of "formal" in the dictionary and use each definition in sentences of your own creation until you feel you fully understand the word and can use it in conversation.

Write five sentences using the adjective "formal":

_____

_____

_____

_____

_____

_____

_____

_____

resource

noun **an available source of support, aid, or wealth that can be used when needed**

example sentences

Although Kelly was a senior in college, she still called her old middle school English teacher and used her as a **resource** when life got difficult.

The **resources** of the country were sufficient to get it through the long drought in its farmlands.

The librarian was a major **resource** for me as I was researching my term paper.

words that are similar **assets, capital, fortune, means, property, reserve, stock, stockpile, support**

Look up the full definition of "resource" in the dictionary and use each definition in sentences of your own creation until you feel you fully understand the word and can use it in conversation.

Write five sentences using the noun "resource":

_____

_____

_____

_____

_____

_____

_____

_____

Lesson 4.2 - Vocabulary

persist

verb to continue despite resistance, to follow through, endure, or persevere

example sentences

Her guidance counselor told her that she has to **persist** in order to get anywhere in life.

My brother **persists** in annoying me by popping gum.

If gas prices **persist** in climbing in the United States, we may see the beginnings of a recession.

also written in this form **persisted, persisting, persistent**

words that are similar **carry on, carry through, be resolute, be stubborn, continue, endure, follow through, insist, persevere, pursue**

words that are opposite **cease, give up, leave, quit, stop**

Look up the full definition of "persist" in the dictionary and use each definition in sentences of your own creation until you feel you fully understand the word and can use it in conversation.

Write five sentences using the verb "persist":

_____

_____

_____

_____

_____

_____

_____

_____

contempt

noun disrespect and intense dislike

example sentences

Police officers often have **contempt** for criminals; criminals often feel likewise about the men and women in blue.

The teacher's **contempt** for cheaters caused him to flunk three students in his class.

The reporter asked the politician his questions with thinly veiled **contempt** in his voice.

also written in this form **contemptible, contemptuous**

words that are similar **disdain, disrespect, antipathy, aversion, derision, despisal, hatred, repugnance, ridicule, scorn**

words that are opposite **admiration, affection, approval, endorsement, love, regard, respect**

Look up the full definition of "contempt" in the dictionary and use each definition in sentences of your own creation until you feel you fully understand the word and can use it in conversation.

Write five sentences using the noun "contempt":

_____

_____

_____

_____

_____

_____

_____

_____

tour

noun a journey or route all the way around a certain place or area

verb to travel along such a journey

example sentences

For a summer job, David conducted **tours** of Italy.

The guests took a **tour** of the grand house.

I've always wanted to **tour** England and see the English countryside with my own eyes.

also written in this form **toured, touring**

words that are similar **journey, trip, course, travel, trek, voyage**

Look up the full definition of "tour" in the dictionary and use each definition in sentences of your own creation until you feel you fully understand the word and can use it in conversation.

Write five sentences using the noun and verb "tour":

_____

_____

_____

_____

_____

_____

_____

_____

plead

verb to appeal, request, or beg earnestly

example sentences

Erin **pleaded** with her friends to save her a seat at the concert.

She **pleaded** with her brother to stop bothering her and pulling her hair while they were on the road trip.

The principal argued that teachers shouldn't have to **plead** with parents to get them involved in their children's educations.

also written in this form **pleaded, pleading, plea**

words that are similar **appeal, ask, beseech, beg, request, entreat, implore, petition, pray, solicit**

words that are opposite **answer, reply**

Look up the full definition of "plead" in the dictionary and use each definition in sentences of your own creation until you feel you fully understand the word and can use it in conversation.

Write five sentences using the verb "plead":

_____

_____

_____

_____

_____

_____

_____

_____

weigh

verb to judge or consider; ALSO to determine the heaviness of something, or to experience the heaviness of something

example sentences

Gus **weighed** his options before finally choosing to purchase the used car.

Eric felt like he shouldn't have such an intensive schedule **weighing** on him, so he decided to drop one of his college courses that semester.

Carefully **weigh** the consequences before you make your decision.

also written in this form **weighed, weighing**

words that are similar **measure heaviness, scale, be heavy, be important, burden, apprise, assess, estimate, evaluate, size up, valuate**

Look up the full definition of "weigh" in the dictionary and use each definition in sentences of your own creation until you feel you fully understand the word and can use it in conversation.

Write five sentences using the verb "weigh":

_____

_____

_____

_____

_____

_____

_____

_____

Lesson 4.3
Vocabulary

mode

_{noun} style or manner of doing something; how something is done; ALSO a particular functioning condition or arrangement

example sentences

He was in a partying **mode** and did not want to hear anything about the test coming up next week.

The car was able to switch between an automatic and manual **mode**.

In less than one week of school, I was fully into a learning **mode** and much less distracted.

That **mode** of dress hasn't been in style in more than a decade.

words that are similar **manner, way, approach, custom, method, plan, practice, process, quality, style**

Look up the full definition of "mode" in the dictionary and use each definition in sentences of your own creation until you feel you fully understand the word and can use it in conversation.

Write five sentences using the noun "mode":

_____

_____

_____

_____

_____

_____

_____

_____

distinction

noun a distinguishing quality; something that sets you apart from others; ALSO a telling of the difference between two things or people

example sentences

The school has the **distinction** of being the first in Mississippi to receive a Blue Ribbon Award.

The worker had the misfortune of being singularly without **distinction** in all things but one.

The board member felt it was important to make a **distinction** between operating budget and what was set aside for profits that would be divided amongst the shareholders.

words that are similar **differentiation, feature, characteristic, difference, discernment, dissimilarity, divergence, individuality, judgment, mark, quality, separation, tact, unlikeness**

Look up the full definition of "distinction" in the dictionary and use each definition in sentences of your own creation until you feel you fully understand the word and can use it in conversation.

Write five sentences using the noun "distinction":

_____

_____

_____

_____

_____

_____

_____

_____

inclined

adjective to like to do something, to want to do something, and/or to be naturally skilled at doing something

example sentences
Since she had done the same thing to me last week, I was **inclined** to let the waiter know that my sister's birthday was this very day.

Harry was **inclined** toward baseball much more than soccer and became a state league all-star at a very early age.

The teacher was **inclined** to give a pop quiz that day because it seemed this his students were not paying enough attention to the lesson.

also written in this form inclination

words that are similar tend toward, be disposed, influenced, swayed, on the verge of, gravitated toward

Look up the full definition of "inclined" in the dictionary and use each definition in sentences of your own creation until you feel you fully understand the word and can use it in conversation.

Write five sentences using the adjective "inclined":

_____

_____

_____

_____

_____

_____

_____

_____

attribute

noun a quality or characteristic that belongs to a person, place or thing

example sentences

Bob had the **attribute** of being extremely trustworthy and reliable, and his employers were glad they hired him.

The counselor found that if he focused on his patients' positive **attributes** rather than berating them about their negative ones, he usually got better results.

The old graveyard's spooky **attributes** made it a perfect site for a Halloween party.

words that are similar aspect, character, feature, characteristic, facet, property, quality, mark, sign, trait, virtue

Look up the full definition of "attribute" in the dictionary and use each definition in sentences of your own creation until you feel you fully understand the word and can use it in conversation.

Write five sentences using the noun "attribute":

_____

_____

_____

_____

_____

_____

_____

_____

exert

<small>verb</small> **to put forth effort; ALSO to push or use power**

<small>example sentences</small>

Timothy **exerted** himself when he pulled the wagon up the hill.

She had to **exert** considerable concentration to not be distracted by the television.

Having to move furniture into the house required great **exertion** on part of the movers.

<small>also written in this form</small> **exert, exerted, exerting, exertion**

<small>words that are similar</small> **apply, strain, strive, struggle, sweat it, toil, try hard, use, work, wield**

Look up the full definition of "exert" in the dictionary and use each definition in sentences of your own creation until you feel you fully understand the word and can use it in conversation.

Write five sentences using the verb "exert":

_____

_____

_____

_____

_____

_____

_____

oppress

verb to use authority to keep someone or something down; to cause to suffer

example sentences

The summer heat was so **oppressive** that the family decided not to go for a walk.

Having to work a twelve hour day made the man feel **oppressed**.

The boss would **oppress** his workers with unpaid overtime.

also written in this form **oppression, oppressed**

words that are similar **subdue, abuse, afflict, annoy, overpower, overthrow, overwhelm, persecute, pick on**

words that are opposite **aid, boost, delight, gladden, help, make happy**

Look up the full definition of "oppress" in the dictionary and use each definition in sentences of your own creation until you feel you fully understand the word and can use it in conversation.

Write five sentences using the verb "oppress":

_____

_____

_____

_____

_____

_____

_____

_____

contend

<small>adjective</small> compete for something; ALSO to assert or maintain (a belief or idea)

<small>example sentences</small>

The two philosophers both **contended** that their viewpoints were correct.

Jodie would **contend** with her friend Alana that pop is better than country music.

At the pie baking competition there was much **contention** among the judges on whether to vote for the apple or cherry pie.

<small>also written in this form</small> contended, contending, contention

<small>words that are similar</small> argue, battle, clash, confront, contest, dispute, oppose, resist, rival, stand, strive, struggle

<small>words that are opposite</small> abandon, desert, give up, leave, retreat

Look up the full definition of "contend" in the dictionary and use each definition in sentences of your own creation until you feel you fully understand the word and can use it in conversation.

Write five sentences using the verb "contend":

_____

_____

_____

_____

_____

_____

_____

_____

stake

noun a stick or post with a pointed end so it can be driven into the ground; ALSO money or the equivalent risked in a gamble

example sentences

The director was nervous about the debut because his entire career was at **stake**.

The **stakes** were high when the super hero had to choose between saving his love and saving the city.

He needed one more **stake** to anchor the tent in the bad weather.

also written in this form **stakes, staked, staking**

words that are similar **pole, picket, post, spike, stick, share, gamble, bet, prize**

Look up the full definition of "stake" in the dictionary and use each definition in sentences of your own creation until you feel you fully understand the word and can use it in conversation.

Write five sentences using the noun "stake":

_____

_____

_____

_____

_____

_____

_____

_____

toil

verb **to work hard**

noun **hard work**

example sentences

The knight **toiled** for many years to bring peace to the land.

The lights often went out in the mine, so the laborers would have to **toil** in pitch black.

It took the **toils** of countless workers to complete the construction project.

also written in this form **toils, toiled, toiling**

words that are similar **hard work, application, drudgery, effort, exertion, industry, labor, travail, occupation**

words that are opposite **entertainment, fun, pastime**

Look up the full definition of "toil" in the dictionary and use each definition in sentences of your own creation until you feel you fully understand the word and can use it in conversation.

Write five sentences using the verb and noun "toil":

_____

_____

_____

_____

_____

_____

_____

Lesson 4.3 - Vocabulary

perish

verb to die

example sentences

The monster that plagued the town would soon **perish** if the hero was as strong as he claimed.

The father worried that he wouldn't make it to his daughter's baseball game in time, but he **perished** the thought and focused on driving.

Many sailors **perished** during Ferdinand Magellan's voyage around the world.

also written in this form perished, perishing, perishable

words that are similar die, decay, decline, be destroyed, break down, cease, demise, depart, disappear, disintegrate, end, expire, fall, pass, pass away, pass on, rot, succumb

words that are opposite give birth, revive

Look up the full definition of "perish" in the dictionary and use each definition in sentences of your own creation until you feel you fully understand the word and can use it in conversation.

Write five sentences using the adjective "perish":

_____

_____

_____

_____

_____

_____

_____

Lesson 4.4
Vocabulary

disposition

noun **one's mood or general attitude**

example sentences

The teacher had a grim **disposition** and would often slap her desk with a ruler if the children were not paying attention.

The boy didn't have an outgoing **disposition** and preferred to stay inside and read rather than socialize.

Grandfather Joe had a kind **disposition** and often bought his grandchildren candy.

also written in this form **disposed**

words that are similar **temperament, being, character, emotions, humor, identity, inclination, make-up, mind-set, mood, nature, personality, predisposition, temper, tendency**

Look up the full definition of "disposition" in the dictionary and use each definition in sentences of your own creation until you feel you fully understand the word and can use it in conversation.

Write five sentences using the noun "disposition":

_____

_____

_____

_____

_____

_____

_____

_____

rail

verb **to criticize severely or complain bitterly**

example sentences

The studio was told that film critics would **rail** against the movie's story unless it was changed.

You shouldn't **rail** on like that about our work unless you're willing to help.

Tim's friends were **railing** against him for his failure in the football game.

also written in this form **railed, railing**

words that are similar **abuse, attack, bawl out, complain, rant, revile, scold, tongue-lash**

words that are opposite **compliment, praise**

Look up the full definition of "rail" in the dictionary and use each definition in sentences of your own creation until you feel you fully understand the word and can use it in conversation.

Write five sentences using the verb "rail":

_____

_____

_____

_____

_____

_____

_____

_____

cardinal

adjective being an essential component to something

example sentences

He broke a **cardinal** rule by entering the restaurant without shoes on.

A textbook is **cardinal** for any class if a student wants to study.

The keyboard and mouse are the **cardinal** instruments for using a computer.

words that are similar important, key, central, chief, essential, first, foremost, fundamental, greatest, highest, indispensable, leading, main, overriding, vital

words that are opposite inessential, insignificant, minor, negligible, secondary, unimportant

Look up the full definition of "cardinal" in the dictionary and use each definition in sentences of your own creation until you feel you fully understand the word and can use it in conversation.

Write five sentences using the adjective "cardinal":

_____

_____

_____

_____

_____

_____

_____

_____

boast

verb **to brag or show off**

example sentences

The athlete **boasted** to his friends about breaking the world record.

The shop **boasted** all the latest fashions from Paris.

Professor Blum began every class with a **boast** about his achievements.

also written in this form **boasted, boasting, boastful**

words that are similar **brag, bombast, bravado, pretension, pride, self-satisfaction, swank, treasure, vaunt**

words that are opposite **deprecation, modesty**

Look up the full definition of "boast" in the dictionary and use each definition in sentences of your own creation until you feel you fully understand the word and can use it in conversation.

Write five sentences using the verb "boast":

_____

_____

_____

_____

_____

_____

_____

advocate

noun a person who pleads or speaks for a cause or idea

verb to speak, plead, or argue in favor of

example sentences

As an **advocate** for his friend George, Li argued that George had not stolen the bike.

Most doctors **advocate** against smoking because it is bad for your health.

The representative was an **advocate** for the people of his state.

also written in this form **advocate, advocating, advocated**

words that are similar **backer, champion, counsel, defender, lawyer, pleader, promoter, proponent, proposer, speaker, supporter**

words that are opposite **antagonist, assailant, enemy, opposition**

Look up the full definition of "advocate" in the dictionary and use each definition in sentences of your own creation until you feel you fully understand the word and can use it in conversation.

Write five sentences using the noun and verb "advocate":

bestow

verb **to give as a gift**

example sentences

The Queen of England has **bestowed** the title of Knight to many people.

Medals will be **bestowed** to winners at the Olympics.

The faculty will **bestow** an honorary title to the student with the highest grades.

also written in this form bestowing, bestowed

words that are similar give, allot, apportion, award, bequeath, commit, gift, grant, hand out, honor with, impart, offer

words that are opposite deprive, refuse, take

Look up the full definition of "bestow" in the dictionary and use each definition in sentences of your own creation until you feel you fully understand the word and can use it in conversation.

Write five sentences using the verb "bestow":

allege

verb to report or maintain that something is true or has occurred

example sentences

His sister **alleged** that he was responsible for breaking the lamp.

The prosecutor was to **allege** that the defendant was guilty of the crime.

Dr. Scott took credit for the new discovery, but his apprentice made the **allegation** that the research was stolen.

also written in this form **alleged, alleging, allegation**

words that are similar **affirm, charge, declare, maintain, plead, profess, testify, state**

words that are opposite **contradict, deny, disagree, dissent, object, protest, repudiate**

Look up the full definition of "allege" in the dictionary and use each definition in sentences of your own creation until you feel you fully understand the word and can use it in conversation.

Write five sentences using the verb "allege":

_____

_____

_____

_____

_____

_____

_____

_____

Lesson 4.4 - Vocabulary

notwithstanding

adverb **despite anything to the contrary (in spite of something)**

example sentences

A good diet and exercise **notwithstanding**, the man still had a heart attack.

The excellent sales of their printers **notwithstanding**, the electronics company still lost money this year.

The other excellent films **notwithstanding**, the group of friends decided to see the film with the most explosions.

words that are similar although, however, at any rate, despite, in any case, in any event, in spite of, nevertheless, nonetheless, regardless of, though, to the contrary

Look up the full definition of "notwithstanding" in the dictionary and use each definition in sentences of your own creation until you feel you fully understand the word and can use it in conversation.

Write five sentences using the adjective "notwithstanding":

lofty

adjective **elevated, high above the ground; ALSO displaying dignity or nobility**

example sentences

The mountain reached such **lofty** heights that it touched the clouds.

Gas reached **lofty** prices, with a single gallon costing four dollars.

The scientist had the **lofty** ambition of discovering something that would change the world.

also written in this form **loftiness**

words that are similar **high, elevated, airy, lifted, raised, sky-high, skyward, soaring, spiring, tall, towering**

words that are opposite **below, beneath, low**

Look up the full definition of "lofty" in the dictionary and use each definition in sentences of your own creation until you feel you fully understand the word and can use it in conversation.

Write five sentences using the adjective "lofty":

_____

_____

_____

_____

_____

_____

_____

multitude

noun a large number or big crowd

example sentences

In every anthill there is a **multitude** of the small insects.

John had to examine a **multitude** of parts before he found what was broken in the car.

Being in a new country gave the business man a **multitude** of new opportunities.

words that are similar large group, assembly, collection, congregation, crowd, drove, horde, people, slew, swarm, throng

words that are opposite handful, portion, single, zero

Look up the full definition of "multitude" in the dictionary and use each definition in sentences of your own creation until you feel you fully understand the word and can use it in conversation.

Write five sentences using the adjective "multitude":

_____

_____

_____

_____

_____

_____

_____

_____

Lesson 4.5
Vocabulary Review

Lesson 4.5 - Vocabulary Review

Draw a line matching each word to its definition. If you miss one, go back to the lesson that you missed and review by going through the steps of learning the definition of the word again.

attitude •	• a feeling of hopelessness
despair •	• an elaborate or sophisticated plan or plot
flag •	• having political or social views tending in favor of reform and progress
humble •	• intense or sharp
justify •	• not arrogant, prideful or boastful
keen •	• one's beliefs, acts, feelings and one's tendency to act or react in certain ways
liberal •	• something that may increase or decrease
merit •	• the quality of being deserving of something
scheme •	• to become less intense
tide •	• to show why or how someone or something is right by providing reasons or proof

Reading Mastery - Level 1

attitude	a feeling of hopelessness
despair	an elaborate or sophisticated plan or plot
flag	having political or social views tending in favor of reform and progress
humble	intense or sharp
justify	not arrogant, prideful or boastful
keen	one's beliefs, acts, feelings and one's tendency to act or react in certain ways
liberal	something that may increase or decrease
merit	the quality of being deserving of something
scheme	to become less intense
tide	to show why or how someone or something is right by providing reasons or proof

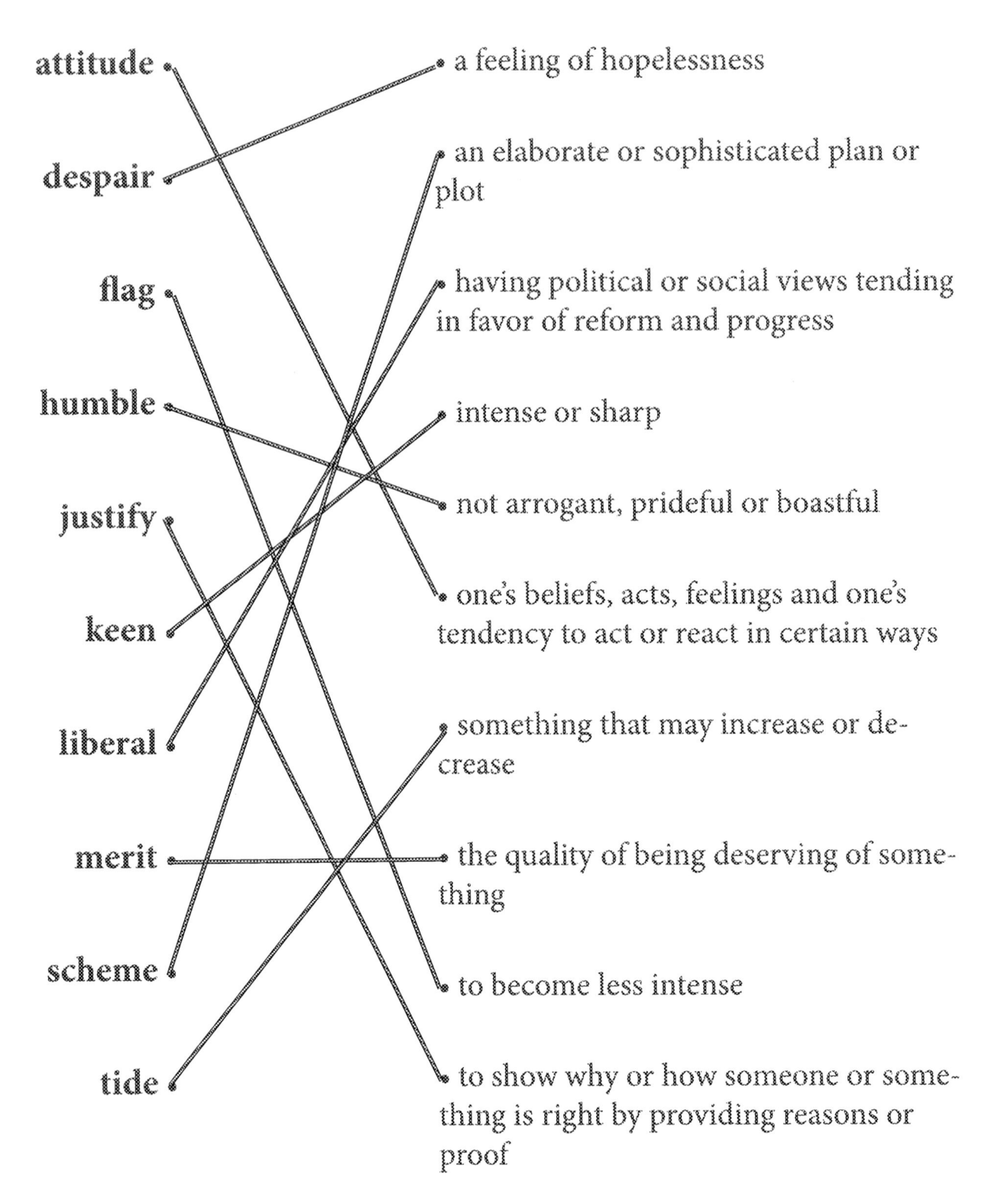

Missed one? Review Lesson 4.1.

Draw a line matching each word to its definition. If you miss one, go back to the lesson that you missed and review by going through the steps of learning the definition of the word again.

contempt •   • a journey or route all the way around a certain place or area

formal •   • a series of things arranged in levels for comparison or reference

manifest •   • an available source of support, aid, or wealth that can be used when needed

notion •   • an idea, often a vague or fanciful one, or concept

persist •   • clearly visible or revealed

plead •   • disrespect and intense dislike

resource •   • following the established conventions or requirements

scale •   • to appeal, request or beg earnestly

tour •   • to continue despite resistance, to follow through, endure, or persevere

weigh •   • to judge or consider; ALSO to determine the heaviness of something, or to experience the heaviness of something

Reading Mastery - Level 1

contempt	a journey or route all the way around a certain place or area
formal	a series of things arranged in levels for comparison or reference
manifest	an available source of support, aid, or wealth that can be used when needed
notion	an idea, often a vague or fanciful one, or concept
persist	clearly visible or revealed
plead	disrespect and intense dislike
resource	following the established conventions or requirements
scale	to appeal, request or beg earnestly
tour	to continue despite resistance, to follow through, endure, or persevere
weigh	to judge or consider; ALSO to determine the heaviness of something, or to experience the heaviness of something

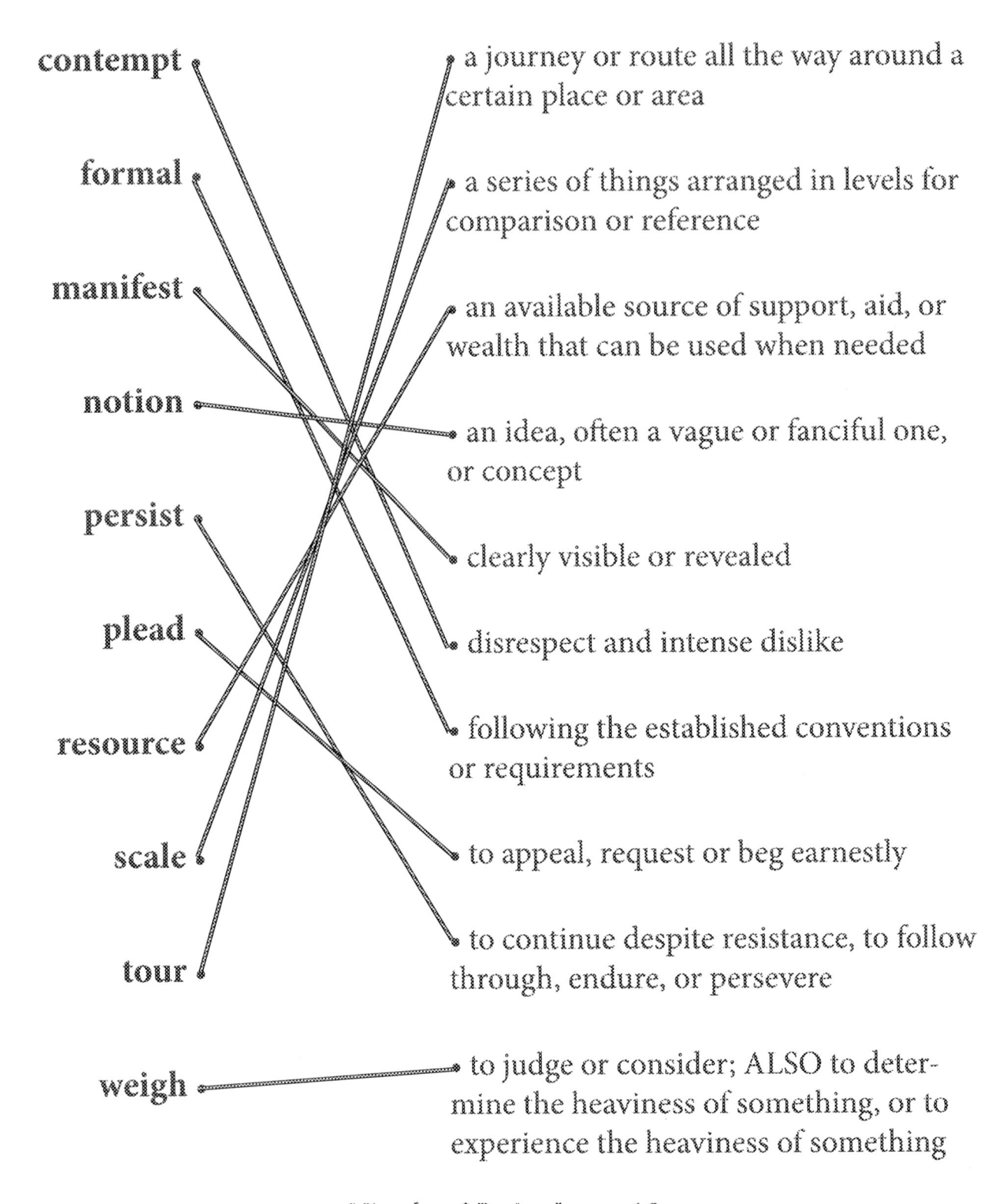

Missed one? Review Lesson 4.2.

Draw a line matching each word to its definition. If you miss one, go back to the lesson that you missed and review by going through the steps of learning the definition of the word again.

attribute •

contend •

distinction •

exert •

inclined •

mode •

oppress •

perish •

stake •

toil •

• a distinguishing quality; something that sets you apart from

• a legal share of something or money risked in a gamble

• a quality or characteristic that belongs to a person, place or thing

• compete for something

• style or manner of doing something; how something is done

• to die

• to like to do something, to want to do something, and/or to be naturally skilled at doing something

• to put forth effort; ALSO to push or use power

• to use authority to keep someone or something down; to cause to suffer

• to work hard

Reading Mastery - Level 1

attribute	a distinguishing quality; something that sets you apart from
contend	a legal share of something or money risked in a gamble
distinction	a quality or characteristic that belongs to a person, place or thing
exert	compete for something
inclined	style or manner of doing something; how something is done
mode	to die
oppress	to like to do something, to want to do something, and/or to be naturally skilled at doing something
perish	to put forth effort; ALSO to push or use power
stake	to use authority to keep someone or something down; to cause to suffer
toil	to work hard

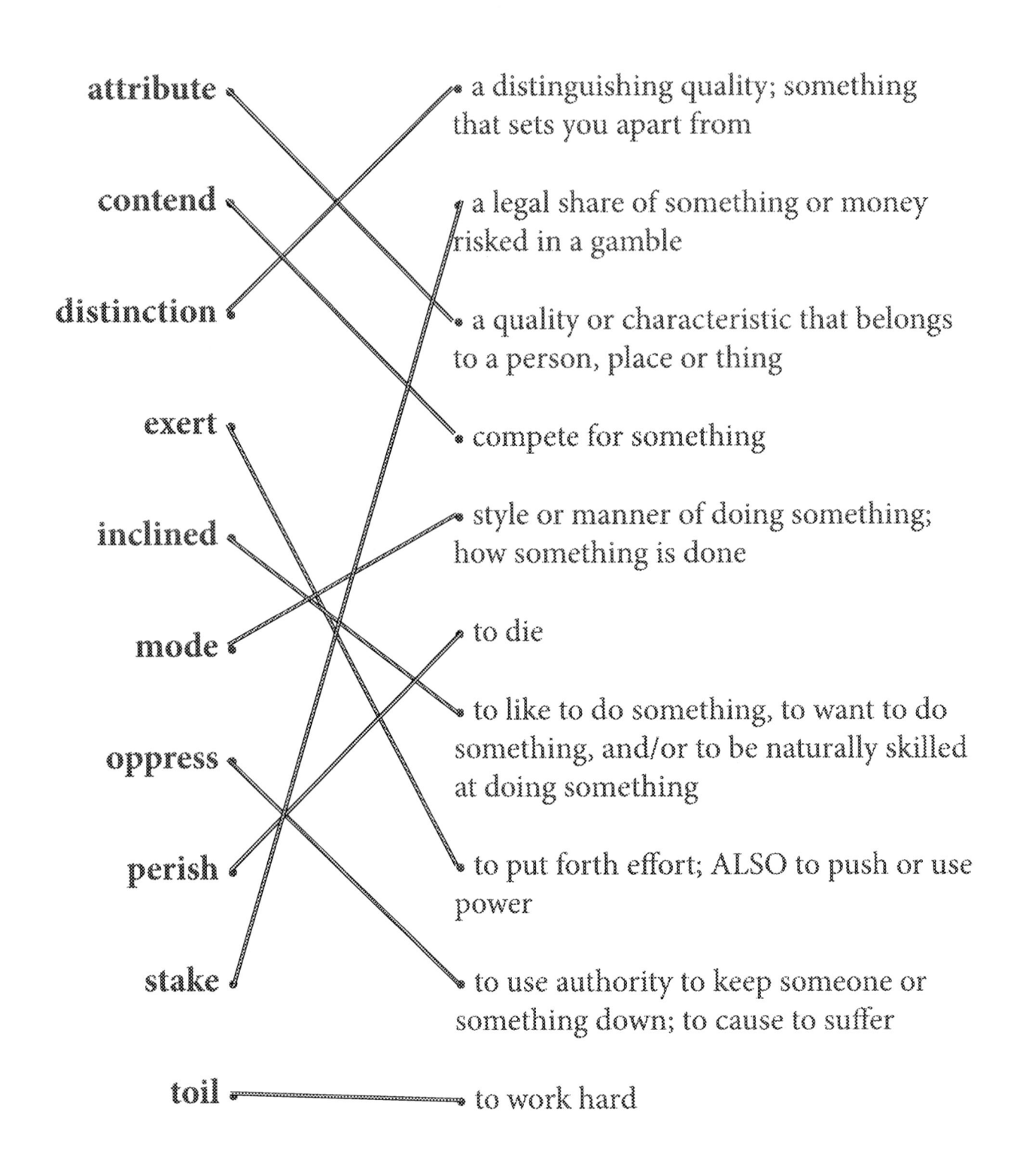

Missed one? Review Lesson 4.3.

Lesson 4.5 - Vocabulary Review

Draw a line matching each word to its definition. If you miss one, go back to the lesson that you missed and review by going through the steps of learning the definition of the word again.

advocate •   • a large number or big crowd

allege •   • a person who pleads or speaks for a cause or idea

bestow •   • being an essential component to something

boast •   • despite anything to the contrary (in spite of something)

cardinal •

• elevated, high above the ground; ALSO displaying dignity or nobility

disposition •

• one's mood or general attitude

lofty •

• to brag or show off

multitude •   • to criticize severely or complain bitterly

notwithstanding •   • to give as a gift

rail •   • to report or maintain that something is true or has occurred

Reading Mastery - Level 1

advocate	a large number or big crowd
allege	a person who pleads or speaks for a cause or idea
bestow	being an essential component to something
boast	despite anything to the contrary (in spite of something)
cardinal	elevated, high above the ground; ALSO displaying dignity or nobility
disposition	one's mood or general attitude
lofty	to brag or show off
multitude	to criticize severely or complain bitterly
notwithstanding	to give as a gift
rail	to report or maintain that something is true or has occurred

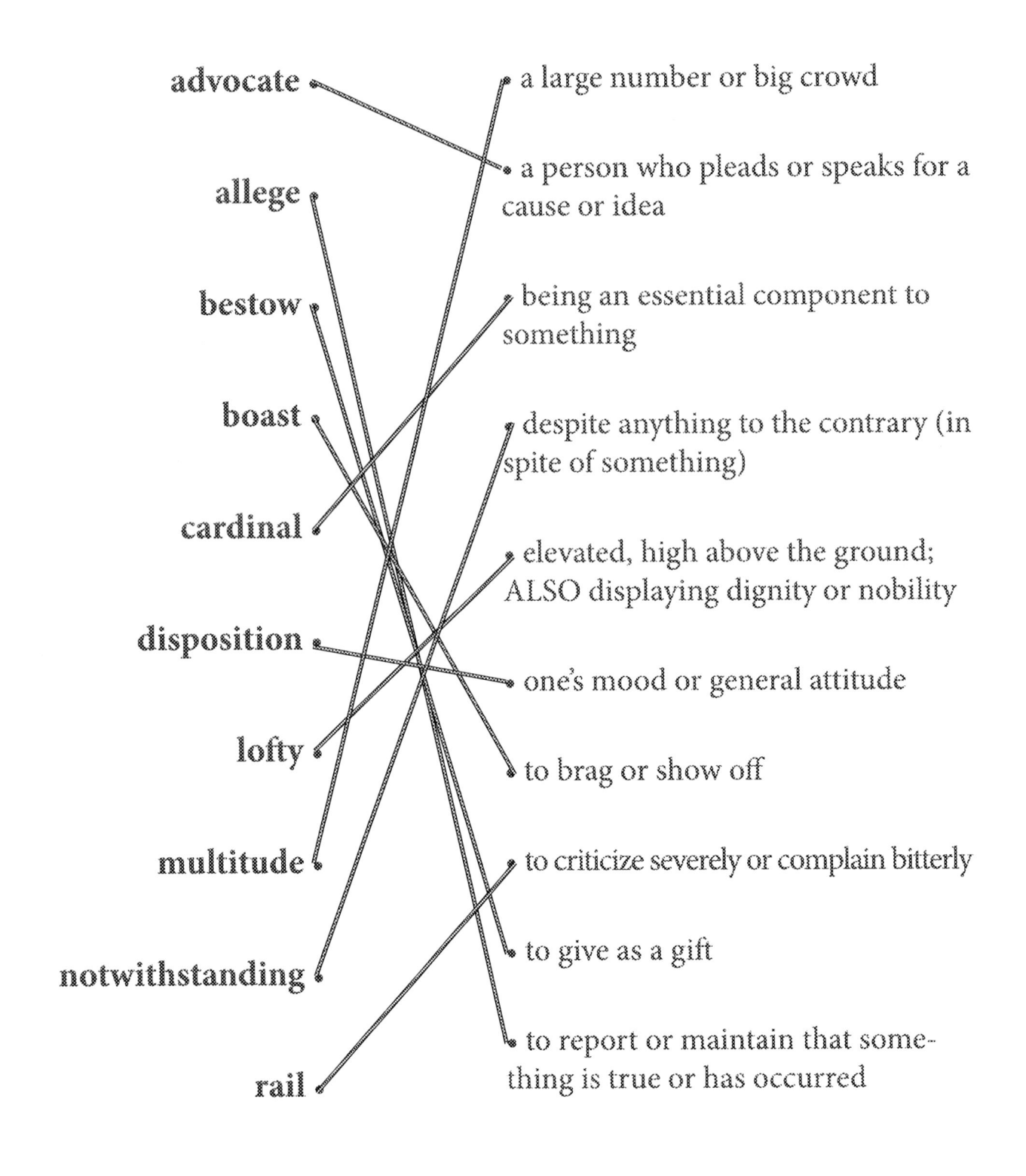

Missed one? Review Lesson 4.4.

Lesson 5
Finding Exact Details

There is a certain type of question that appears frequently on the ACT Reading test and it is also the easiest. For this question type, the answer is spelled out for you within its passage; all you have to do is find it.

Following this, I'll give you a passage with 10 questions of this kind. Be sure to practice your pace: 3 minutes for the passage, then 5 minutes for the questions. Stick with this and you'll find the time limit becomes much easier.

After answering each question, review the explanations. Once you're done, we'll discuss in more detail the important points about this question type and round the lesson off with one last set of practice questions.

Passage

Instructions: Skim the passage in 3 minutes, then answer the 10 practice questions that appear below. Use a timer to keep track of when you should start answering the questions. Just like on the ACT, you are allowed to refer to the passage in order to find the correct answers.

SOCIAL SCIENCE: This passage is adapted from *Mysticism and Logic* by Bertrand Russell, published in 1917 by George Allen & Unwin. Faraday, Maxell and Hertz refers to Michael Faraday, James Maxwell, and Heinrich Hertz, famous physicists of the 19th century.

Science, to the ordinary reader of newspapers, is represented by a varying selection of sensational triumphs, such as wireless telegraphy and airplanes, radioactivity and the marvels of modern alchemy. It is not of this aspect of science that I wish to speak. Science, in this aspect, consists of detached up-to-date fragments, interesting only until they are replaced by something newer and more up-to-date, displaying nothing of the systems of patiently constructed knowledge out of which, almost as a casual incident, have come the practically useful results which interest the man in the street. The increased command over the forces of nature which is derived from science is undoubtedly an amply sufficient reason for encouraging scientific research, but this reason has been so often urged and is so easily appreciated that other reasons, to my mind quite as important, are apt to be overlooked. It is with these other reasons, especially with the intrinsic value of a scientific habit of mind in forming our outlook on the world, that I shall be concerned in what follows.

The instance of wireless telegraphy will serve to illustrate the difference between the two points of view. Almost all the serious intellectual labor required for the possibility of this invention is due to three men—Faraday, Maxwell, and Hertz. In alternating layers of experiment and theory these three men built up the modern theory of electromagnetism, and demonstrated the identity of light with electromagnetic waves. The system which they discovered is one of profound intellectual interest, bringing together and unifying an endless variety of apparently detached phenomena, and displaying a cumulative mental power which cannot but afford delight to every generous spirit. The mechanical details which remained to be adjusted in order to utilize their discoveries for a practical system of telegraphy demanded, no doubt, very considerable ingenuity, but had not that broad sweep and that universality which could give them intrinsic interest as an object of disinterested contemplation.

From the point of view of training the mind, of giving that well-informed, impersonal outlook which constitutes culture in the good sense of this much-misused word, it seems to be generally held indisputable that a literary education is superior to one based on science. Even the warmest advocates of science are apt to rest their claims on the contention that culture ought to be sacrificed to utility. Those men of science who respect culture, when they associate with men learned in the classics, are apt to admit, not merely politely, but sincerely, a certain inferiority on their side, compensated doubtless by the services which science renders to humanity, but nonetheless real. And so long as this attitude exists among men of science, it tends to verify itself: the intrinsically valuable aspects of science tend to be sacrificed to the merely useful, and little attempt is made to preserve that leisurely, systematic survey by which the finer quality of mind is formed and nourished.

But even if there be, in present fact, any such inferiority as is supposed in the educational value of science, this is, I believe, not the fault of science itself, but the fault of the spirit in which science is taught. If its full possibilities were realized by those who teach it, I believe that its capacity of producing those habits of mind which constitute the highest mental excellence would be at least as great as that of literature, and more particularly of Greek and Latin literature. In saying this I have no wish whatever to disparage a classical education. I have not myself enjoyed its benefits, and my knowledge of Greek and Latin authors is derived almost wholly from translations. But I am firmly persuaded that the Greeks fully deserve all the admiration that is bestowed upon them, and that it is a very great and serious loss to be unacquainted with their writings. It is not by attacking them, but by drawing attention to neglected excellences in science, that I wish to conduct my argument.

One defect, however, does seem inherent in a purely classical education—namely, a too exclusive emphasis on the past. By the study of what is absolutely ended and can never be renewed, a habit of criticism towards the present and the future is engendered. The qualities in which the present excels are qualities to which the study of the past does not direct attention, and to which, therefore, the student of Greek civilization may easily become blind. In what is new and growing there is apt to be something crude, insolent, even a little vulgar, which is shocking to the man of sensitive taste; quivering from the rough contact, he retires to the trim gardens of a polished past, forgetting that they were reclaimed from the wilderness by men as rough and earth-soiled as those from whom he shrinks in his own day. The habit of being unable to recognize merit until it is dead is too apt to be the result of a purely bookish life, and a culture based wholly on the past will seldom be able to pierce through everyday surroundings to the essential splendor of contemporary things, or to the hope of still greater splendor in the future.

Lesson 5 - Finding Exact Details

1. The passage notes all of the following as accomplishments of Faraday, Maxwell, and Hurst, EXCEPT that they:

   A. developed the modern theory of electromagnetism.
   B. demonstrated the identity of light.
   C. discovered the experimental method of physics.
   D. brought together a variety of apparently detached phenomena.

2. In the passage, the author indicates that he believes that one inherent defect of classical education is that it:

   F. has too exclusive an emphasis on the past.
   G. can be too difficult for some students to learn.
   H. is crude, insolent, and vulgar.
   J. can be shocking to someone who is sensitive.

3. According to the narrator, an ordinary reader of newspapers considers that science is represented by:

   A. a gradually increasing understanding of the world around us.
   B. a varying selection of sensational triumphs.
   C. a mad scientist in a lab coat.
   D. a sophisticated system of carefully assembled knowledge.

4. The author indicates that it is a generally held belief that, compared to an education based on science, a literary education is:

   F. superior.
   G. inferior.
   H. elaborate.
   J. under-appreciated.

5. In paragraph 1 (lines 1-20), the author cites all of the following as examples of sensational scientific triumphs EXCEPT:

   A. airplanes.
   B. wireless telegraphy.
   C. radioactivity.
   D. electromagnetic theories.

6. The author calls the habit of being unable to recognize merit until it is dead the consequence of:

   F. a polished past.
   G. a purely bookish life.
   H. studying Greek civilization.
   J. researching electromagnetic phenomena.

7. Which of the following is NOT listed in the passage as an element that a man of sensitive taste might find shocking in that which is new and growing?

   A. Crudeness
   B. Wildness
   C. Insolence
   D. Vulgarity

8. The author describes which of the following as possessing an essential splendor?

   F. Contemporary things
   G. Unrecognized merit
   H. Classical education
   J. Alternating layers of experiment and theory

9. According to the passage, the author believes that all of the following are reasons that science is valuable EXCEPT that science:

   A. provides an increased command over the forces of nature.
   B. renders helpful services to humanity.
   C. allows for the development of a scientific habit of mind in forming a world outlook.
   D. causes men to respect culture.

10. The author believes that the primary cause of any inferiority in the educational value of science is the fault of:

    F. the spirit in which science is taught.
    G. the biases of college professors.
    H. the lack of classical literature that scientists study.
    J. the focus on knowledge for knowledge's sake.

1. The passage notes all of the following as accomplishments of Faraday, Maxwell, and Hurst, EXCEPT that they:

   A. developed the modern theory of electromagnetism.
   B. demonstrated the identity of light.
   C. discovered the experimental method of physics.
   D. brought together a variety of apparently detached phenomena.

In lines 26-28, the author states that the "three men built up the modern theory of electromagnetism, and demonstrated the identity of light with electromagnetic waves," which eliminates choices A and B. A little later in the paragraph, it describes their system as "bringing together and unifying an endless variety of apparently detached phenomena," which allows us to eliminate choice D. Choice C is not supported by the passage, so this is the correct answer. Note that the question says EXCEPT, which means that we are looking for the one choice that ISN'T supported by the passage.

2. In the passage, the author indicates that he believes that one inherent defect of classical education is that it:

   F. has too exclusive an emphasis on the past.
   G. can be too difficult for some students to learn.
   H. is crude, insolent, and vulgar.
   J. can be shocking to someone who is sensitive.

In lines 78-80, the author states that "One defect, however, does seem inherent in a purely classical education—namely, a too exclusive emphasis on the past," so choice F is the best choice. Choice G is not supported anywhere in the passage. Later in lines 86-88, the passage mentions that "In what is new and growing there is apt to be something crude, insolent, even a little vulgar, which is shocking to the man of sensitive taste," but this line is not referring to classical education (which is by definition a study of the past, not what is new) so choices H and J are not correct. The word "indicates" in this sense means "states briefly."

3. According to the narrator, an ordinary reader of newspapers considers that science is represented by:

   A. a gradually increasing understanding of the world around us.
   B. a varying selection of sensational triumphs.
   C. a mad scientist in a lab coat.
   D. a sophisticated system of carefully assembled knowledge.

Lines 1-3 state that "Science, to the ordinary reader of newspapers, is represented by a varying selection of sensational triumphs," so choice B is the correct answer. Choice C is not supported by anything in the passage. Later in paragraph 1, in lines 5-12, the author makes the point that "Science, in this aspect, consists of detached up-to-date fragments, interesting only until they are replaced by something newer and more up-to-date, displaying nothing of the systems of patiently constructed knowledge out of which, almost as a casual incident, have come the practically useful results which interest the man in the street," which contradicts choices A and D. The phrase "according to" in this question has the sense "as stated by."

Lesson 5 - Finding Exact Details

4. The author indicates that it is a generally held belief that, compared to an education based on science, a literary education is:

   F. **superior.**
   G. inferior.
   H. elaborate.
   J. under-appreciated.

   Lines 44-45 state that "a literary education is superior to one based on science," so choice F is the best answer. Superior in this sense means "better." Inferior is the opposite of superior and so choice G is incorrect. Choices H and J are not supported by the passage. The passage does not state that literary education is more elaborate or less appreciated than a science-based education. The word "indicates" in this sense means "points out or shows."

5. In paragraph 1 (lines 1-20), the author cites all of the following as examples of sensational scientific triumphs EXCEPT:

   A. airplanes.
   B. wireless telegraphy.
   C. radioactivity.
   D. **electromagnetic theories.**

   Lines 2-4 provide examples of "sensational triumphs, such as wireless telegraphy and airplanes, radioactivity," so choices A, B, and C are all cited as examples in the passage and so are not the correct choices. While electromagnetic theories are mentioned in paragraph 2 (lines 21-39), they are not used as examples in paragraph 1 (lines 1-20), so choice D is the best answer. Since the question uses the word EXCEPT, we are looking for the example that ISN'T cited. The word "cite" in this sense means to "mention as an example."

6. The author calls the habit of being unable to recognize merit until it is dead the consequence of:

   F. a polished past.
   G. **a purely bookish life.**
   H. studying Greek civilization.
   J. researching electromagnetic phenomena.

   The author states in lines 93-95 that "The habit of being unable to recognize merit until it is dead is too apt to be the result of a purely bookish life," so choice G is the best answer. The sentence that comes before mentions a polished past, but not in reference to being unable to recognize merit. Just because someone studies Greek civilization doesn't mean they have a purely bookish life, so choice H doesn't work. While paragraph 2 (lines 21-39) discusses three scientists who researched electromagnetic phenomena, this is not mentioned in relation to not being able to recognize merit.

7. Which of the following is NOT listed in the passage as an element that a man of sensitive taste might find shocking in that which is new and growing?

   A. Crudeness
   B. **Wildness**
   C. Insolence
   D. Vulgarity

   In lines 86-88, the author states that "In what is new and growing there is apt to be something crude, insolent, even a little vulgar, which is shocking to the man of sensitive taste," which means that choices A, C, and D are incorrect. While a later sentence mentions the "wilderness," the quality of "wildness" is not discussed in the passage. For that reason, choice B is the best answer.

8. The author describes which of the following as possessing an essential splendor?

   F. **Contemporary things**
   G. Unrecognized merit
   H. Classical education
   J. Alternating layers of experiment and theory

In paragraph 5, the last sentence (lines 95-98) states that "a culture based wholly on the past will seldom be able to pierce through everyday surroundings to the essential splendor of contemporary things," so choice F is the best answer. Unrecognized merit, classical education, and alternating layers of experiment and theory are all phrases which appear in the passage, but they are not referred to as possessing an "essential splendor," so we can eliminate choices G, H, and J. In this sense, "essential" means "the fundamental characteristics of something," and splendor means "beautiful or magnificent."

9. According to the passage, the author believes that all of the following are reasons that science is valuable EXCEPT that science:

   A. provides an increased command over the forces of nature.
   B. renders helpful services to humanity.
   C. allows for the development of a scientific habit of mind in forming a world outlook.
   D. **causes men to respect culture.**

In lines 12-15, it states that "increased command over the forces of nature which is derived from science is undoubtedly an amply sufficient reason for encouraging scientific research," so we can eliminate choice A. Lines 51-52 mention "the services which science renders to humanity," so choice B does not work. Lines 18-20 also mentions the "intrinsic value of a scientific habit of mind in forming our outlook on the world," so we can eliminate choice C. Lines 47-48 mention "men of science who respect culture," but does not specifically say that science causes men to respect culture, so choice D is the best answer. Since the question includes the word EXCEPT, we are looking for the one answer which ISN'T supported by the passage. In the sense that it is used here, "renders" means "supplies or makes available."

10. The author believes that the primary cause of any inferiority in the educational value of science is the fault of:

    F. **the spirit in which science is taught.**
    G. the biases of college professors.
    H. the lack of classical literature that scientists study.
    J. the focus on knowledge for knowledge's sake.

Paragraph 4 states in lines 59-62 that "any such inferiority as is supposed in the educational value of science, this is, I believe, not the fault of science itself, but the fault of the spirit in which science is taught," so choice F is the best answer. Choices G, H, and J are not supported by the passage.

Lesson 5 - Finding Exact Details

HOW TO FIND EXACT DETAILS

The key to finding an exact detail is to recognize it and then immediately go digging through the passage.

If you followed my advice to remember where the different parts of a passage are located, it will take much less time to accomplish this.

When you recognize that a question is asking for a specific detail, look for the unique word or phrase mentioned within the question. This is the key to finding the answer. Once you've found this unique word or phrase, look for where it appears in the passage. Typically, the correct answer choice will be found in or near the same sentence as the unique phrase.

To make this even quicker, look over the answer choices before hunting through the passage. Try to predict what choice it will be.

Don't try to answer this type of question based on memory alone. Your goal is to find the answer in the passage; think of it like a treasure hunt.

There are many different ways the ACT can ask you for a specific detail, but when a question uses words like *except, according to,* or *indicates,* chances are that it is a question of this type.

According to, as in "according to the passage," or "according to the author," or "according to lines 57-72," means "as stated by or in" or "as said by or in." When a question says, "according to the passage," it means, "as it is said in the passage."

Indicates means "states briefly," "says briefly," or "points out, shows." When a question says, "the narrator indicates that..." it is saying, "the narrator says that..."

"EXCEPT" is a clue that three of the answer choices will appear in the passage, and one will not. You need to choose the answer choice that doesn't fit. When a question includes "EXCEPT," first find each answer choice in the passage. The one that does not work or cannot be found in the passage is your answer.

One common phrase that comes up on ACT questions is "the following." In the phrase, "which of the following," *the following* means "what comes after," referring to the answer choices. It's saying "which of these answer choices..." When the question uses the word "EXCEPT," it's usually in the format "all of the following, EXCEPT..." which means that all of the answer choices but one fit what the question is describing.

On the test, the word "NOT" is used in a similar way.

Sometimes, a question might tell you where to look by referencing specific line numbers. Use these line numbers as a clue to help limit your search and save time.

It's important to note that sometimes, particularly when a question asks for details that appear throughout the passage, there won't be a unique phrase in the question. Don't let this throw you off. In this case, go hunting for the answer choices instead.

Let's walk through answering one of the questions for the passage you've just worked through.

> **5.** In paragraph 1 (lines 1-20), the author cites all of the following as examples of sensational scientific triumphs EXCEPT:
>
> **A.** airplanes.
> **B.** wireless telegraphy.
> **C.** radioactivity.
> **D.** electromagnetic theories.

Our first step is to size up the question. It is clear the question is asking us to find three details listed by the author as "sensational scientific triumphs."

If you're not clear on exactly what "sensational, scientific triumphs" means, don't worry; you can still find where the words appear in the passage. This question makes it easy for us because we only need to look as far as paragraph 1.

To narrow our search further, we can find at what place the author mentions the unique phrase "sensational scientific triumphs." The answer choices shouldn't be too far from that. "Sensational triumphs" appears in the first sentence, which is the best match. Often, the question won't say exactly the same thing as the passage, but don't let that throw you off.

Now, look near the found phrase for the first answer choice offered: airplanes. Airplanes comes right after the mention of "sensational triumphs" in the phrase "such as wireless telegraphy and airplanes, radioactivity…" This one phrase alone allows us to cross off choices B and C as well. This leaves us with choice D as the best answer.

You can check your answer if you have time by verifying that no mention of "electromagnetic theories" is made in the first paragraph.

In the passage to follow, try to apply these tips in order to move through the questions with greater speed and accuracy.

Passage

Instructions: Skim the passage in 3 minutes, then answer the 10 practice questions that appear below. Use a timer to keep track of when you should start answering the questions. Just like on the ACT, you are allowed to refer to the passage in order to find the correct answers.

NATURAL SCIENCE: This passage is adapted from *Getting Acquainted with the Trees* by J. Horace McFarland, published in 1914 by The Macmillan Company.

The old saw has it, "Great oaks from little acorns grow," and all of us who remember the saying have thus some idea of what the beginning of an oak is. But what of the beginning of the acorn? In a general way, one inferentially supposes that there must be a flower somewhere in the life-history of the towering white oak that has defied the storms of centuries and seems a type of everything sturdy and strong and masculine; but what sort of a flower could one imagine as the source of so much majesty? We know of the great magnolias, with blooms befitting the richness of the foliage that follows them. We see, and some of us admire, the exquisitely delicate blossoms of that splendid American tree, the tulip or whitewood. We inhale with delight the fragrance that makes notable the time when the common locust sends forth its white racemes of loveliness. But we miss, many of us, the flowering of the oaks in early spring, and we do not realize that this family of trees, most notable for rugged strength, has its bloom of beginning at the other end of the scale, in flowers of delicate coloring and rather diminutive size.

The reason I missed appreciating the flowers of the oak—they are quite new to me—for some years of tree admiration was because of the distracting accompaniment the tree gives to the blooms. Some trees—most of the maples, for instance—send out their flowers boldly ahead of the foliage, and it is thus easy to see what is happening above your head, as you stroll along drinking in the spring's nectar of spicy air. Others, again, have such showy blooms that the mass of foliage only accentuates their attractiveness, and it is not possible to miss them.

But the oak is different; it is as modest as it is strong, and its bloom is nearly surrounded by the opening leaves in most seasons and in most of the species I am just beginning to be acquainted with. Then, too, these opening leaves are of such indescribable colors—if the delicate chromatic tints they reflect to the eye may be so strongly named—that they harmonize, and do not contrast, with the flowers. It is with them almost as with a fearless chipmunk whose acquaintance I cultivated one summer—he was cheerful with stripes of soft color, yet he so fitted any surroundings he chose to be in that when he was quiet he simply disappeared! The oak's flowers and its exquisite unfolding of young foliage combine in one effect, and it is an effect so beautiful that one easily fails to separate its parts, or to see which of the mass of soft pink, gray, yellow and green is bloom and which of it is leafage.

The white oak leaf is the most familiar and characteristic, perhaps, of the family; but other species, close to the white oak in habit, show foliage of a very different appearance. The live oak, by the way, has a leaf very little like the typical oak—it is elliptical in shape and smooth in outline. The curious parasitic moss that so frequently covers the tree obscures the really handsome foliage. The English oak, grand tree that it is, grows well in America, as everything English should by right, and there are fine trees of this Quercus Robur on Long Island. The acorns are of unusual elegance, as the photograph which shows them will prove.

The red oak, the black oak, the scarlet oak, all splendid forest trees of the Northeast, are in the group of confusion that can be readily separated only by the timber-cruiser, who knows every tree in the forest for its economic value, or by the botanist, with his paperback Gray's Manual in hand. I confess to bewilderment in five minutes after the differences have been explained to me, and I enjoyed, not long ago, the confusion of a skillful nurseryman who was endeavoring to show me his young trees of red oak which the label proved to be scarlet! But the splendidly effective trees themselves can be fully appreciated, and the distinctions will appear as one studies carefully the features of these living gifts of nature's greenness. The trees wait on one, and once the habit of appreciation and investigation is formed, each walk afield, in forest or park, leads to the acquirement of some new bit of tree-lore, that becomes more precious and delightful as it is passed on and commented upon in association with some other member of the happily growing fraternity of nature-lovers.

These oak notes are not intended to be complete, but only to suggest some points for investigation and appreciation to my fellows in the brotherhood. I have never walked between Trenton and New York, and therefore never made the desired acquaintance with the scrub oaks along the way. Nor have I dipped as fully into the oak treasures of the Arnold Arboretum as I want to someday. But my camera is yet available and the trees are waiting; the tree love is growing and the tree friends are inviting, and together we will add to the oak knowledge and to that thankfulness for God and life and love and friends that the trees do most constantly cause to flourish.

Lesson 5 - Finding Exact Details

1. The passage mentions all of the following as splendid forest trees in the Northeast, EXCEPT:

    A. red oaks.
    B. live oaks.
    C. black oaks.
    D. scarlet oaks.

2. According to the passage, all of the following characteristics of oak blooms make them different from trees with showy blooms, EXCEPT that:

    F. they are surrounded by opening leaves in most seasons.
    G. their opening leaves are of colors that harmonize with the flowers.
    H. the flowers and foliage combine into one beautiful effect.
    J. the foliage only accentuates the attractiveness of the blooms.

3. According to paragraph 4 (lines 51-62), the acorns of which type of tree possess atypical elegance?

    A. English oak
    B. White oak
    C. Live oak
    D. Red oak

4. Information in the passage indicates that between Trenton and New York can be found a population of which of the following types of oak?

    F. Scrub oak
    G. Red oak
    H. White oak
    J. English oak

5. According to the passage, the oak family of trees is most notable for its:

    A. towering height.
    B. rugged strength.
    C. unique adaptations.
    D. ability to shelter wildlife.

6. According to the passage, which of the following types of oak is the most familiar and characteristic of the oak family?

    F. English oak
    G. White oak
    H. Live oak
    J. Red oak

7. The author indicates that he for some time missed admiring oak flowers because:

    A. he was distracted by the blooms of trees of other families.
    B. he spent too much time observing chipmunks.
    C. he had never seen a scrub oak before.
    D. oak trees provide a distracting accompaniment to the flowers.

8. According to the passage, the live oak is often covered by:

    F. red leaves.
    G. acorns of unusual elegance.
    H. parasitic moss.
    J. yellow fungus.

9. The phrase "diminutive size" in the last sentence of the first paragraph refers most specifically to the oak tree's:

    A. flowers.
    B. acorns.
    C. wildlife.
    D. colorful moss.

10. The passage indicates that English oak trees are present at:

    F. Trenton.
    G. Long Island.
    H. the Arnold Arboretum.
    J. the Northeast.

Reading Mastery - Level 1

1. The passage mentions all of the following as splendid forest trees in the Northeast, EXCEPT:

   A. red oaks.
   B. live oaks.
   C. black oaks.
   D. scarlet oaks.

Look for the unique phrase "splendid forest trees in the Northeast," which appears almost word for word in the first sentence of paragraph 5, line 64. In this sentence, we find that it mentions, "The red oak, the black oak, the scarlet oak, all splendid forest trees of the Northeast," so we can eliminate choices A, C, and D. Live oaks are mentioned in paragraph 4 (lines 51-62) but not as "splendid forest trees in the Northeast," so choice B is our best answer. The word EXCEPT clues us in that we are looking for the one tree that is NOT listed as a splendid forest tree in the Northeast.

2. According to the passage, all of the following characteristics of oak blooms make them different from trees with showy blooms, EXCEPT that:

   F. they are surrounded by opening leaves in most seasons.
   G. their opening leaves are of colors that harmonize with the flowers.
   H. the flowers and foliage combine into one beautiful effect.
   J. the foliage only accentuates the attractiveness of the blooms.

The words "different from trees with showy blooms," give us a clue as to where we should look. The end of paragraph 2, in lines 31-32, says that "Others, again, have such showy blooms that the mass of foliage only accentuates their attractiveness..." and paragraph 3, line 34, begins with "But the oak is different..." so it is likely we'll find our answers in paragraph 3 (lines 34-50). The paragraph says that "its bloom is nearly surrounded by the opening leaves in most seasons" (choice F), that "these opening leaves are of such indescribable colors—if the delicate chromatic tints they reflect to the eye may be so strongly named—that they harmonize, and do not contrast, with the flowers" (choice G), and that "The oak's flowers and its exquisite unfolding of young foliage combine in one effect, and it is an effect so beautiful that one easily fails to separate its parts" (choice H), so we can eliminate those three choices. Choice J is the best answer. In lines 31-33, trees with showy blooms are described as having "such showy blooms that the mass of foliage only accentuates their attractiveness, and it is not possible to miss them." So this confirms that choice J is correct.

3. According to the paragraph 4 (lines 51-62), the acorns of which type of tree possess atypical elegance?

   A. English oak
   B. White oak
   C. Live oak
   D. Red oak

First we search for where we can find our answer by looking for the unique phrase "atypical elegance." The word atypical in this sense means "not typical, not usual." A similar phrase appears in the last sentence of paragraph 4, in line 61: "acorns of unusual elegance." If we backtrack a bit, we find that the "English oak, grand tree that it is," is being discussed, so choice A is correct.

Lesson 5 - Finding Exact Details

4. Information in the passage indicates that between Trenton and New York can be found a population of which of the following types of oak?

   F. Scrub oak
   G. Red oak
   H. White oak
   J. English oak

The unique phrase "between Trenton and New York" is found in the second sentence of paragraph 6 (line 87). In that same sentence, in lines 88 and 89, the author states that he "never made the desired acquaintance with the scrub-oaks along the way," so choice F is our best answer.

5. According to the passage, the oak family of trees is most notable for its:

   A. towering height.
   B. rugged strength.
   C. unique adaptations.
   D. ability to shelter wildlife.

The unique phrase "most notable," appears in line 19 as part of the phrase "this family of trees, most notable for rugged strength..." so choice B is our best answer.

6. According to the passage, which of the following types of oak is the most familiar and characteristic of the oak family?

   F. English oak
   G. White oak
   H. Live oak
   J. Red oak

Find where the unique phrase "familiar and characteristic" appears in the passage. It is found word for word in line 51 and 52, which state that "The white oak leaf is the most familiar and characteristic, perhaps, of the family," so choice G is the best answer.

7. The author indicates that he for some time missed admiring oak flowers because:

   A. he was distracted by the blooms of trees of other families.
   B. he spent too much time observing chipmunks.
   C. he had never seen a scrub oak before.
   D. oak trees provide a distracting accompaniment to the flowers.

The phrase "missed admiring oak flowers" does not appear word for word in the passage, but a similar phrase, "missed appreciating the flowers of the oak," does. This appears at the beginning of paragraph 2, in lines 23-24. Later in the sentence, in lines 25-26, he gives the reason: "because of the distracting accompaniment the tree gives to the blooms." Choice D is, therefore, the best answer.

8. According to the passage, the live oak is often covered by:

   F. red leaves.
   G. acorns of unusual elegance.
   H. parasitic moss.
   J. yellow fungus.

First search for mention of "live oak." This is discussed on line 54, which is part of paragraph 4. After mention of the live oak, the passage states in lines 56-58, that "the curious parasitic moss that so frequently covers the tree obscures the really handsome foliage," so choice H is the best answer.

9. The phrase "diminutive size" in the last sentence of the first paragraph refers most specifically to the oak tree's:

   A. flowers.
   B. acorns.
   C. wildlife.
   D. colorful moss.

We look for where the phrase "diminutive size" is used and see that the complete phrase is "in flowers of delicate coloring and rather diminutive size," so choice A is the best answer. Even if we aren't sure about the meaning of "diminutive size," we can still find where it is used in the passage and what the phrase is being used to describe.

10. The passage indicates that English oak trees are present at:

    F. Trenton.
    G. Long Island.
    H. the Arnold Arboretum.
    J. the Northeast.

"English oaks" are mentioned in lines 58-62. The two sentences concerning the English oak only mention one location: "The English oak, grand tree that it is, grows well in America, as everything English should by right, and there are fine trees of this Quercus Robur on Long Island. The acorns are of unusual elegance, as the photograph which shows them will prove." Even though we don't really know what the author means by Querces Robur, we can guess that Quercus Robur is just another name for an English oak. The other locations listed in choices F, H, and J are nowhere near the mention of the English oak. Therefore, choice G is the best answer.

Lesson 6.1
Vocabulary

steep

adjective **sharply angled; ALSO high**

example sentences

The mountain was so **steep** that it had to be climbed instead of hiked.

The father thought the playground slide looked far too **steep** to be safe for his children to play on.

A vacation had been planned but the ticket prices were far too **steep** for the family to afford.

words that are similar **high, erect, lofty, perpendicular, precipitous, sheer, sharp, straight-up**

words that are opposite **gentle, mild, moderate**

Look up the full definition of "steep" in the dictionary and use each definition in sentences of your own creation until you feel you fully understand the word and can use it in conversation.

Write five sentences using the adjective "steep":

_____

_____

_____

_____

_____

_____

_____

_____

Lesson 6.1 - Vocabulary

heed

verb **to listen to and follow**

example sentences

Julius Caesar did not **heed** the Soothsayer's warnings about the ides of March.

The driver should have **heeded** the warnings about the roadwork ahead.

Grandmother always told her grandchildren that they should **heed** the words of their elders.

also written in this form **heeded, heeding**

words that are similar **conform, abide by, comply, follow, fulfill, mind, obey, attention, care, concern, study**

words that are opposite **disregard, ignore**

Look up the full definition of "heed" in the dictionary and use each definition in sentences of your own creation until you feel you fully understand the word and can use it in conversation.

Write five sentences using the verb "heed":

_____

_____

_____

_____

_____

_____

_____

_____

modest

_{adjective} **having a humble opinion about oneself; ALSO sufficient but not large**

_{example sentences}

The artist had won numerous awards but in her **modesty** never boasted.

Modest and mild-mannered, no one could have imagined that the simple reporter was in fact a superhero.

The three hundred room mansion was far from being a **modest** home.

_{also written in this form} **modesty**

_{words that are similar} **shy, bashful, humble, meek, moderate, nice, simple, unpretentious**

_{words that are opposite} **arrogant, bold, conceited, egotistical, proud, self-confident, unabashed, unashamed**

Look up the full definition of "modest" in the dictionary and use each definition in sentences of your own creation until you feel you fully understand the word and can use it in conversation.

Write five sentences using the adjective "modest":

_____

_____

_____

_____

_____

_____

_____

_____

Lesson 6.1 - Vocabulary

partial

adjective **showing favoritism; ALSO a part or portion, not whole**

example sentences

The test asked for five main points, but the student could only provide a **partial** answer with three points.

The teacher was **partial** to Juan because he always paid attention in class.

In the wake of the hurricane many buildings had **partially** collapsed.

also written in this form **partially**

words that are similar **attached, fond, friendly, soft on**

words that are opposite **antagonistic, cold, cool, disliking, unfriendly**

Look up the full definition of "partial" in the dictionary and use each definition in sentences of your own creation until you feel you fully understand the word and can use it in conversation.

Write five sentences using the adjective "partial":

_____

_____

_____

_____

_____

_____

_____

_____

apt

adjective **extremely appropriate, clever, or pertinent**

example sentences

The king thought he was the most **apt** choice for his political position but his people thought otherwise.

The fantasy series Conan the Barbarian, by Robert E. Howard, is an **apt** example of the sword and sorcery genre.

Having never failed a single test, the student proved that he was the most **apt** choice for leading a study group.

also written in this form **aptly**

words that are similar **suitable, applicable, appropriate, fitting, germane, pertinent, proper, relevant, seemly, suitable, timely**

words that are opposite **incorrect, unsuitable**

Look up the full definition of "apt" in the dictionary and use each definition in sentences of your own creation until you feel you fully understand the word and can use it in conversation.

Write five sentences using the adjective "apt":

_____

_____

_____

_____

_____

_____

_____

_____

esteem

verb to respect or admire

example sentences

Other writers held the author in high **esteem** because his work had won many awards and had deep meaning.

The politician was once an **esteemed** official, but since the scandal, people have started to look at him in a new light.

There are many universities with reputations as excellent schools; because of this the public holds them in high **esteem**.

also written in this form **esteemed**

words that are similar **admire, appreciate, be fond of, regard, honor**

words that are opposite **abuse, dislike, disregard, disrespect, hate, insult, mock, ridicule**

Look up the full definition of "esteem" in the dictionary and use each definition in sentences of your own creation until you feel you fully understand the word and can use it in conversation.

Write five sentences using the verb "esteem":

_____

_____

_____

_____

_____

_____

_____

_____

credible

adjective **honest and believable**

example sentences

He had a history of telling lies, so the police knew he was not the most **credible** source of information.

Having kept her word on every occasion she had proven herself a **credible** person.

There were many ideas about how the building collapsed, but there was no **credible** evidence to support any of the suspicions.

also written in this form **credibility**

words that are similar **believable, conceivable, creditable, plausible, possible, probable, sound, trustworthy, valid**

words that are opposite **implausible, impossible, improbable, inconceivable, incredible, unbelievable, unimaginable, unlikely, untenable**

Look up the full definition of "credible" in the dictionary and use each definition in sentences of your own creation until you feel you fully understand the word and can use it in conversation.

Write five sentences using the adjective "credible":

_____

_____

_____

_____

_____

_____

_____

Lesson 6.1 - Vocabulary

provoke

verb **to bring about a strong reaction (frequently anger)**

example sentences

The bull charged the men after it had been **provoked** by their shouting.

The cat stuck in a tree **provoked** the neighborhood to act to save it.

The old couple had been reading quietly when their dog started to bark without being **provoked**.

also written in this form **provoking, provoked, provocation**

words that are similar **aggravate, anger, annoy, gall, get on one's nerves, insult, irk, perturb, rile, upset, evoke, arouse, elicit**

words that are opposite **delight, make happy, please**

Look up the full definition of "provoke" in the dictionary and use each definition in sentences of your own creation until you feel you fully understand the word and can use it in conversation.

Write five sentences using the verb "provoke":

_____

_____

_____

_____

_____

_____

_____

_____

tread

verb to step or walk on something

example sentences

Before the hikers reached the peak of the mountain, they had to **tread** a lot of ground.

To make sure no one would hear them, the spies had to **tread** lightly on the floor of the secret facility.

The soldiers had to **tread** for five miles every day if they were going to get to their destination on time.

also written in this form **treading, treaded**

words that are similar **walk, footstep, march, pace, step, stride, tramp**

Look up the full definition of "tread" in the dictionary and use each definition in sentences of your own creation until you feel you fully understand the word and can use it in conversation.

Write five sentences using the verb "tread":

_____

_____

_____

_____

_____

_____

_____

_____

Lesson 6.1 - Vocabulary

ascertain

verb to find out something (with certainty)

example sentences

The detective had **ascertained** who the criminal was through the examination of evidence.

In order to **ascertain** how much money was in his bank account, John had to go to the bank.

The engineer needed to **ascertain** the structural integrity of the bridge.

also written in this form **ascertained, ascertaining**

words that are similar **make sure, check out, confirm, determine, establish, find out, make certain, make sure, see, settle, verify**

Look up the full definition of "ascertain" in the dictionary and use each definition in sentences of your own creation until you feel you fully understand the word and can use it in conversation.

Write five sentences using the verb "ascertain":

_____

_____

_____

_____

_____

_____

_____

_____

Lesson 6.2
Vocabulary

fare

noun the payment for transportation

verb to proceed or get along

example sentences

To ride the bus, she had to pay a **fare** of a few dollars.

The **fare** for crossing the river by boat cost more than the man had.

I'd say I'm **faring** pretty well, considering the circumstances.

also written in this form **fared, faring**

words that are similar **charge, expense, price, tariff, toll**

Look up the full definition of "fare" in the dictionary and use each definition in sentences of your own creation until you feel you fully understand the word and can use it in conversation.

Write five sentences using the noun and verb "fare":

_____

_____

_____

_____

_____

_____

_____

Lesson 6.2 - Vocabulary

cede

verb **to give up or surrender**

example sentences

The candidate **ceded** the race to her competitor once it was clear that she could not get enough votes to win.

The athlete had to **cede** her position in the race after a knee injury.

Her brother was **ceding** responsibility when he told her to watch the dogs while he went out with friends.

also written in this form **ceded, ceding**

words that are similar **abandon, surrender, concede, give in, give up, grant, relinquish, sign over, transfer, yield**

words that are opposite **defend, fight, gain, guard, win**

Look up the full definition of "cede" in the dictionary and use each definition in sentences of your own creation until you feel you fully understand the word and can use it in conversation.

Write five sentences using the verb "cede":

_____

_____

_____

_____

_____

_____

_____

_____

perpetual

adjective **continuing forever or indefinitely**

example sentences

The winter seemed **perpetual,** as snow fell every day.

After the first three hours, the movie seemed like a **perpetual** experience.

Jim, a **perpetual** procrastinator, never accomplished any of his daily goals.

also written in this form **perpetually**

words that are similar continual, lasting, abiding, ceaseless, continued, continuous, permanent, recurrent, repeated, unceasing, unending

words that are opposite brief, ephemeral, fleeting, momentary, temporary, transient

Look up the full definition of "perpetual" in the dictionary and use each definition in sentences of your own creation until you feel you fully understand the word and can use it in conversation.

Write five sentences using the adjective "perpetual":

_____

_____

_____

_____

_____

_____

_____

_____

Lesson 6.2 - Vocabulary

decree

noun a formal and authoritative order, especially one having the force of law

verb to make such an order

example sentences

Much to the people's dismay, the king made a **decree** that taxes would be doubled.

After a holiday meal, Bert made a **decree** that green beans would no longer be served in his house.

The court proceedings were to determine whether or not the governor's **decree** was legally binding.

also written in this form decreed, decreeing

words that are similar mandate, order, announcement, command, declaration, direction, directive, edict, law, order, pronouncement

Look up the full definition of "decree" in the dictionary and use each definition in sentences of your own creation until you feel you fully understand the word and can use it in conversation.

Write five sentences using the noun and verb "decree":

_____

_____

_____

_____

_____

_____

_____

_____

contrive

verb to make a plan or plot

example sentences

The villain **contrived** a scheme to kidnap the princess.

The mathematicians had to **contrive** a new formula to explain their theory.

The engineers **contrived** a plan for a skyscraper over four hundred stories tall.

also written in this form **contrived, contriving, contrivance**

words that are similar **invent, design, come up with, concoct, cook up, create, formulate**

words that are opposite **disorganize**

Look up the full definition of "contrive" in the dictionary and use each definition in sentences of your own creation until you feel you fully understand the word and can use it in conversation.

Write five sentences using the verb "contrive":

_____

_____

_____

_____

_____

_____

_____

_____

derived

adjective **coming from or being formed from something else**

example sentences

Ground beef is **derived** from cows.

Coins are **derived** from various metals.

Through trial and error, a person can usually **derive** the solution to a problem.

also written in this form **derive, derivative, derivation**

words that are similar **acquired, arrived at, assumed, determined, developed, drawn, educed, formulated, gained, gathered, procured, worked out**

words that are opposite **created, invented**

Look up the full definition of "derived" in the dictionary and use each definition in sentences of your own creation until you feel you fully understand the word and can use it in conversation.

Write five sentences using the adjective "derived":

_____

_____

_____

_____

_____

_____

_____

elaborate

adjective **complex, full of details**

verb **to add details to clarify a statement or idea**

example sentences

The palace had **elaborate** tapestries which hung from its walls.

The painting was **elaborate** in its use of many colors and technical detail.

The surprise party was an **elaborate** event that required everyone to follow detailed instructions.

also written in this form **elaborated, elaborating, elaborately**

words that are similar **complicated, intricate, involved, extravagant, luxurious, ornate, refined, thorough**

words that are opposite **general, normal, plain, regular, simple, uncomplicated, unelaborate**

Look up the full definition of "elaborate" in the dictionary and use each definition in sentences of your own creation until you feel you fully understand the word and can use it in conversation.

Write five sentences using the adjective "elaborate":

_____

_____

_____

_____

_____

_____

_____

substantial

adjective **large in size or amount; ALSO having a firm basis in reality**

example sentences

He spent a **substantial** amount of money to purchase his house.

The red team had a **substantial** lead over the blue team.

The piano weighed such a **substantial** amount that it took four movers to lift it.

words that are similar **important, ample, abundant, big, considerable, heavy, massive, material, meaningful, momentous, sizable, solid, sound, stable, steady**

words that are opposite **insignificant, little, minor, small, unimportant, unsubstantial**

Look up the full definition of "substantial" in the dictionary and use each definition in sentences of your own creation until you feel you fully understand the word and can use it in conversation.

Write five sentences using the adjective "substantial":

_____

_____

_____

_____

_____

_____

_____

_____

frontier

noun **an undeveloped field of study; ALSO a place at or beyond the outer limits**

example sentences

In past centuries the American continent was a **frontier** yet to be explored.

The forest at the edge of the town marked the beginning of the **frontier** that surrounded the populated area.

The jungles of the world remain largely unexplored **frontiers**.

words that are similar **outer limit, borderland, borderline, bound, confines, edge, limit, perimeter**

Look up the full definition of "frontier" in the dictionary and use each definition in sentences of your own creation until you feel you fully understand the word and can use it in conversation.

Write five sentences using the noun "frontier":

_____

_____

_____

_____

_____

_____

_____

facile

adjective **moving, acting, or working with ease (sometimes superficially); ALSO easy or easily mastered**

example sentences

The boy was **facile** in the cleaning of his room, as was made evident by the dirty clothes he left on the floor.

She was clearly **facile** with text messaging because she cooked dinner while doing it.

Despite the student's **facile** approach to homework he always got perfect scores.

words that are similar **child's play, easy, effortless, obvious, simple, uncomplicated**

words that are opposite **arduous, complicated, confusing, difficult, hard, involved, laborious, profound**

Look up the full definition of "facile" in the dictionary and use each definition in sentences of your own creation until you feel you fully understand the word and can use it in conversation.

Write five sentences using the adjective "facile":

_____

_____

_____

_____

_____

_____

_____

Lesson 6.3
Vocabulary

cite

verb to make reference to

example sentences

The teacher made it clear that all reference sources for the essay had to be **cited** in the bibliography.

He would often **cite** quotes from famous intellectuals to make himself seem more intelligent.

The game show champion could **cite** facts from over a dozen different subjects on demand.

also written in this form cited, citing, citation

words that are similar excerpt, refer to, name, mention, point out, reference, specify, note, quote

Look up the full definition of "cite" in the dictionary and use each definition in sentences of your own creation until you feel you fully understand the word and can use it in conversation.

Write five sentences using the verb "cite":

_____

_____

_____

_____

_____

_____

_____

Lesson 6.3 - Vocabulary

warrant

noun a reason or justification for something; ALSO formal and specific approval

example sentences

The bad call during the game was enough to **warrant** the coach's anger.

Her son winning first place in the talent show **warranted** her joy.

The forest fire **warranted** immediate action from the firefighters.

words that are similar **commission, go-ahead, green light, authorization, okay, permission, permit, right, verification**

Look up the full definition of "warrant" in the dictionary and use each definition in sentences of your own creation until you feel you fully understand the word and can use it in conversation.

Write five sentences using the adjective "warrant":

sob

verb **to weep**

noun **a weeping sound or cry**

example sentences

The child fell off her bike and began to **sob** loudly when she scraped her knee.

Romeo **sobbed** in grief when he found Juliet dead.

The man let out a **sob** as he tried to restrain his sadness.

also written in this form **sobbed, sobbing, sobs**

words that are similar **bawl, blubber, cry, shed tears, wail, whimper**

Look up the full definition of "sob" in the dictionary and use each definition in sentences of your own creation until you feel you fully understand the word and can use it in conversation.

Write five sentences using the verb and noun "sob":

_____

_____

_____

_____

_____

_____

_____

_____

Lesson 6.3 - Vocabulary

rider

noun an addition to a legislative bill; ALSO someone who is in motion on a vehicle or animal

example sentences

Cowboys are traditionally known as expert horse **riders**.

Bikers are people who are **riders** of motorcycles.

The governor would not sign the bill unless they removed the **rider** that increased spending.

words that are similar **addendum, appendage, supplement, extension, attachment**

Look up the full definition of "rider" in the dictionary and use each definition in sentences of your own creation until you feel you fully understand the word and can use it in conversation.

Write five sentences using the noun "rider":

_____

_____

_____

_____

_____

_____

_____

_____

dense

adjective **compressed, thick**

example sentences

The vegetation was so **dense** that the explorers had to use machetes to clear a path.

Not even the car's brightest light settings could pierce the **dense** fog that covered the road.

The neighborhood was so **dense** with houses that there was no room for backyards.

also written in this form **density**

words that are similar **condensed, crowded, heavy, impenetrable, jammed, opaque, solid, close**

words that are opposite **open, scattered, sparse, thin, uncompressed**

Look up the full definition of "dense" in the dictionary and use each definition in sentences of your own creation until you feel you fully understand the word and can use it in conversation.

Write five sentences using the adjective "dense":

_____

_____

_____

_____

_____

_____

_____

afflict

verb to cause physical pain or suffering

example sentences

The plants were **afflicted** with a blight that caused them to wither and die.

Muscle problems are bound to **afflict** athletes.

The child was **afflicted** with the symptoms of asthma every spring.

also written in this form **afflicted, afflicting, affliction**

words that are similar **agonize, annoy, burden, distress, harass, wound, rack, strike, torment, torture, wound**

words that are opposite **aid, comfort, help, solace, take care of**

Look up the full definition of "afflict" in the dictionary and use each definition in sentences of your own creation until you feel you fully understand the word and can use it in conversation.

Write five sentences using the verb "afflict":

flourish

verb **to grow a lot or rapidly**

example sentences

Plants will **flourish** if given plenty of water, sunlight, and good soil.

The restaurant has been packed with customers every day, and as a result the business is **flourishing**.

An economy will **flourish** when there are new jobs and high demand for products.

also written in this form **flourished, flourishing**

words that are similar **grow, exist in abundance, be alive with, overflow, swell, teem, thrive**

words that are opposite **deficient, fail, lack, need, short, want**

Look up the full definition of "flourish" in the dictionary and use each definition in sentences of your own creation until you feel you fully understand the word and can use it in conversation.

Write five sentences using the verb "flourish":

_____

_____

_____

_____

_____

_____

_____

_____

ordain

verb to issue an order; ALSO to give priestly authority

example sentences

The leaders **ordained** the new constitution would come into effect in three weeks.

The older brother **ordained** that it was time for his television show, and he snatched the television remote from his sister.

The father **ordained** that it was time for bed.

also written in this form **ordained, ordaining**

words that are similar **establish, install, appoint, bless, commission, institute, legislate**

words that are opposite **cancel, disallow, retract, void**

Look up the full definition of "ordain" in the dictionary and use each definition in sentences of your own creation until you feel you fully understand the word and can use it in conversation.

Write five sentences using the verb "ordain":

_____

_____

_____

_____

_____

_____

_____

pious

adjective being deeply religious, showing reverence for a deity

example sentences

I wish she wouldn't act so **pious** as she's pointing out my faults.

The **pious** advocate worked tirelessly to promote his church's views.

She was a **pious** supporter of the hospital and prayed for the patients each evening.

also written in this form piety

words that are similar devoted, devout, divine, ecclesiastical, prayerful, godly, spiritual, saintly

words that are opposite atheist, impious, irreligious, sinful, wicked

Look up the full definition of "pious" in the dictionary and use each definition in sentences of your own creation until you feel you fully understand the word and can use it in conversation.

Write five sentences using the adjective "pious":

_____

_____

_____

_____

_____

_____

_____

_____

vex

verb **to cause annoyance, trouble or difficulty**

example sentences

The kids ran back and forth in front of the football game on television and began to **vex** their father with their behavior.

The diplomat made the issue even more **vexing** by not compromising in the negotiations.

The terrible acts of super villains often lead to great **vexation** for their super hero foes.

also written in this form **vexed, vexing, vexation**

words that are similar **bother, annoy, distress, agitate, exasperate, irritate, infuriate, irk, pique, provoke, tease, torment, trouble, upset, worry**

words that are opposite **aid, assist, help, soothe, please**

Look up the full definition of "vex" in the dictionary and use each definition in sentences of your own creation until you feel you fully understand the word and can use it in conversation.

Write five sentences using the verb "vex":

_____

_____

_____

_____

_____

_____

_____

Lesson 6.4
Vocabulary

gravity

noun **solemnity or seriousness**

example sentences

Everyone's somber mood reflected the **gravity** of the situation.

The soccer coach had an air of **gravity** more suited to a professional coach than a little league coach.

When the other team scored, one player acted as if he had lost the game, but with another quarter to go the situation didn't merit such dire **gravity**.

words that are similar **grimness, coldness, formality, formalness, seriousness, solemnity, sternness**

words that are opposite **levity, easy-going, lightness**

Look up the full definition of "gravity" in the dictionary and use each definition in sentences of your own creation until you feel you fully understand the word and can use it in conversation.

Write five sentences using the noun "gravity":

_____

_____

_____

_____

_____

_____

_____

_____

suspended

adjective **seeming to float in liquid; ALSO delayed temporarily**

example sentences

The sand was **suspended** in the cup of water.

The bridge was **suspended** over the canyon by metal cables.

She had to mix her coffee to dissolve the **suspended** particles of sugar.

words that are similar **hang, dangle**

words that are opposite **rise**

Look up the full definition of "suspended" in the dictionary and use each definition in sentences of your own creation until you feel you fully understand the word and can use it in conversation.

Write five sentences using the adjective "suspended":

_____

_____

_____

_____

_____

_____

_____

_____

conspicuous

adjective **obvious or attracting attention**

example sentences

The detective kept his eye on the **conspicuous** man in the trench coat.

The woman wore a **conspicuous** and magnificent red dress that got everyone's attention.

Toby drank a **conspicuous** amount of sodas, as was evidenced by the mountain of cans on the kitchen counter.

words that are similar **apparent, clear, discernible, distinct, evident, obvious, plain, visible**

words that are opposite **concealed, hidden, imperceptible, inconspicuous, unseen, unnoticeable**

Look up the full definition of "conspicuous" in the dictionary and use each definition in sentences of your own creation until you feel you fully understand the word and can use it in conversation.

Write five sentences using the adjective "conspicuous":

_____

_____

_____

_____

_____

_____

_____

… Lesson 6.4 - Vocabulary

retort

noun a quick reply to a question or comment (usually clever or critical)

example sentences

When accused of a scandal in the middle of a debate the politician replied with a sharp and angry **retort**.

In a formal debate one side will present an argument and the other will offer a **retort**.

There was little time to convey information so the firefighter replied with quick **retorts**.

also written in this form **retorted, retorting**

words that are similar **answer, comeback, quip, reply, respond, response, retaliation, return, revenge, snappy comeback**

words that are opposite **question, request**

Look up the full definition of "retort" in the dictionary and use each definition in sentences of your own creation until you feel you fully understand the word and can use it in conversation.

Write five sentences using the noun "retort":

_____

_____

_____

_____

_____

_____

_____

_____

jet

verb **to move quickly**

noun **a sudden or rapid spray of water or air**

example sentences

The **jets** in the hot tub shot with enough force to ripple the surface of the water.

Dishwashers clean dishes with **jets** of water.

The pressure washer cleaned the concrete with a powerful **jet** of water.

She told us that we needed to **jet** to the grocery store and pick up the last ingredient to the soup.

also written in this form **jetted, jetting**

words that are similar **fly, race, move**

Look up the full definition of "jet" in the dictionary and use each definition in sentences of your own creation until you feel you fully understand the word and can use it in conversation.

Write five sentences using the verb and noun "jet":

_____

_____

_____

_____

_____

_____

_____

Lesson 6.4 - Vocabulary

bolt

verb to move or jump quickly

example sentences

The hunting dog **bolted** after the fox as soon as it showed itself.

As soon as the starting pistol fired, the racers **bolted** across the track.

When Susan jumped out and surprised John he gave a **bolt** to the next room in fear.

also written in this form **bolted, bolting**

words that are similar **dart, dash, leap, run, rush, scamper, sprint**

words that are opposite **stay, wait**

Look up the full definition of "bolt" in the dictionary and use each definition in sentences of your own creation until you feel you fully understand the word and can use it in conversation.

Write five sentences using the verb "bolt":

_____

_____

_____

_____

_____

_____

_____

_____

assent

verb **to agree or to express agreement**

example sentences

When his son asked if he could go to the concert the father **assented**.

The parents of the students had to **assent** by signing a permission slip before they could go on a field trip.

The candidate plans to **assent** to rumors of his defeat

also written in this form **assenting, assented**

words that are similar **agreement, acceptance, accord, admission, affirmation, approval, concurrence, nod, permission, sanction**

words that are opposite **disagreement, dissent, rejection**

Look up the full definition of "assent" in the dictionary and use each definition in sentences of your own creation until you feel you fully understand the word and can use it in conversation.

Write five sentences using the verb "assent":

_____

_____

_____

_____

_____

_____

_____

_____

purse

<small>verb</small> to contract (one's lips) into a round shape

<small>noun</small> a sum of money offered as a prize

<small>example sentences</small>

The **purse** for the race was so large that nearly everyone in Greene County had entered a horse.

Ingrid **pursed** her lips to apply her lipstick.

She had a closet of **purses**, one for each outfit.

<small>words that are similar</small> press together, close, contract, knit, pucker, wrinkle

<small>words that are opposite</small> open

Look up the full definition of "purse" in the dictionary and use each definition in sentences of your own creation until you feel you fully understand the word and can use it in conversation.

Write five sentences using the noun and verb "purse":

_____

_____

_____

_____

_____

_____

_____

plus

noun **something that is advantageous or good**

example sentences

Having a sturdy front door is definitely a home security **plus**.

You may look at the condition as a handicap, but I look at what I've had to go through as a **plus**.

Getting the first pick for the baseball team is a **plus** that could win us the game.

words that are similar **additional, increased, positive, supplementary, surplus**

words that are opposite **detrimental, minus, negative**

Look up the full definition of "plus" in the dictionary and use each definition in sentences of your own creation until you feel you fully understand the word and can use it in conversation.

Write five sentences using the adjective and noun "plus":

_____

_____

_____

_____

_____

_____

_____

Lesson 6.4 - Vocabulary

sanction

noun a threatened penalty for disobeying a law or rule
verb to provide official permission or approval

example sentences

The concert was going to use a large public space so the event had to be **sanctioned** by local officials.

He had to get **sanctions** before he could build a pool in his backyard.

No one was willing to **sanction** the new trade agreement between the two countries.

also written in this form sanctioned, sanctioning

words that are similar allowance, approval, assent, authority, consent, endorsement, permission, permit, support

words that are opposite disapproval, prevention, refusal, veto

Look up the full definition of "sanction" in the dictionary and use each definition in sentences of your own creation until you feel you fully understand the word and can use it in conversation.

Write five sentences using the verb and noun "sanction":

_____

_____

_____

_____

_____

_____

_____

_____

Lesson 6.5
Vocabulary Review

As a review, **write one sentence using each of the words that you've learned so far in this workbook.** Write a sentence that demonstrates your understanding of the word, not just its part of speech. For example, "It is substantial," is not a good demonstration of the word "substantial!" Try to make a sentence that you would give as an example if you were helping someone else to understand the word. This will deepen your understanding of the vocabulary and help you remember it more easily.

If you don't remember the meaning of the word, have no fear! Look it up in your dictionary. This is an OPEN BOOK REVIEW! Look up what you need to help you make the sentences. It takes a lot of repetition to get this information down—nobody can remember it all just by looking at the vocabulary once.

advocate

_____

_____

afflict

_____

_____

allege

_____

_____

apt

_____

_____

ascertain

_____

_____

assent

_____

_____

attitude

_____

_____

attribute

_____

_____

bestow

_____

_____

boast

_____

_____

bolt

_____

_____

cardinal

_____

_____

cede

_____

_____

cite

_____

_____

conspicuous

_____

_____

contempt

_____

_____

contend

_____

_____

contrive

_____

_____

credible

_____

_____

decree

_____

_____

dense

_____

_____

Lesson 6.5 - Vocabulary Review

derived

despair

disposition

distinction

elaborate

esteem

exert

facile

fare

_____

_____

flag

_____

_____

flourish

_____

_____

formal

_____

_____

frontier

_____

_____

gravity

_____

_____

heed

_____

_____

humble

_____

_____

inclined

jet

justify

keen

liberal

lofty

manifest

merit

mode

modest

multitude

notion

notwithstanding

oppress

ordain

partial

Lesson 6.5 - Vocabulary Review

perish

---

perpetual

---

pious

---

plead

---

plus

---

provoke

---

purse

---

rail

---

resource

_____

_____

retort

_____

_____

rider

_____

_____

sanction

_____

_____

scale

_____

_____

scheme

_____

_____

sob

_____

_____

stake

_____

_____

steep

substantial

suspended

tide

toil

tour

tread

vex

warrant

_____

_____

weigh

_____

_____

Lesson 7
Finding and Interpreting Details

Not every answer to an ACT question will be served to you on a silver platter in the passage.

With some questions, you'll be required to find exact details in the passage and then interpret their meaning in order to find your answer.

In other words, unlike the questions you just worked through where the answers were basically found word for word in the passage, in the next set of questions you'll need to take an additional step of applying logic to figure out what the words in the passage mean.

You'll practice skimming a new passage and answering the 10 questions that go with it. All of them will require you to interpret the details you identify. Then we'll go through some tips on how to quickly and accurately answer this question type.

Passage

Instructions: Skim the passage in 3 minutes, then answer the 10 practice questions that appear below. Use a timer to keep track of when you should start answering the questions. Just like on the ACT, you are allowed to refer to the passage in order to find the correct answers.

LITERARY NARRATIVE: This passage is adapted from the novel *The Napoleon of Notting Hill* by G.K. Chesterton, published in 1904 by Bodley Head. By "Cheat the Prophet," the author refers to the phenomenon where people attentively listen to wise predictions about the future, "then go out and do something else."

In the beginning of the twentieth century the game of Cheat the Prophet was made far more difficult than it had ever been before. The reason was, that there were so many prophets and so many prophecies, that it was
5 difficult to elude all their ingenuities. When a man did something free and frantic and entirely his own, a horrible thought struck him afterwards; it might have been predicted. Whenever a duke climbed a lamp-post, when a dean got drunk, he could not be really happy,
10 he could not be certain that he was not fulfilling some prophecy. In the beginning of the twentieth century you could not see the ground for clever men. They were so common that a stupid man was quite exceptional, and when they found him, they followed him in crowds
15 down the street and treasured him up and gave him some high post in the State. And all these clever men were at work giving accounts of what would happen in the next age, all quite clear, all quite keen-sighted and ruthless, and all quite different. And it seemed that the
20 good old game of hoodwinking your ancestors could not really be managed this time, because the ancestors neglected meat and sleep and practical politics, so that they might meditate day and night on what their descendants would be likely to do.

25 But the way the prophets of the twentieth century went to work was this. They took something or other that was certainly going on in their time, and then said that it would go on more and more until something extraordinary happened. And very often they added
30 that in some odd place that extraordinary thing had happened, and that it showed the signs of the times.

Thus, for instance, there were Mr. H. G. Wells and others, who thought that science would take charge of the future; and just as the motor-car was quicker than
35 the coach, so some lovely thing would be quicker than the motor-car; and so on forever. And there arose from their ashes Dr. Quilp, who said that a man could be sent on his machine so fast round the world that he could keep up a long, chatty conversation in some old-world
40 village by saying a word of a sentence each time he came round. And it was said that the experiment had been tried on an apoplectic old major, who was sent round the world so fast that there seemed to be (to the inhabitants of some other star) a continuous band
45 round the earth of white whiskers, red complexion and tweeds—a thing like the ring of Saturn.

Then there was the opposite school. There was Mr. Edward Carpenter, who thought we should in a very short time return to Nature, and live simply and slowly
50 as the animals do. And Edward Carpenter was followed by James Pickie, D.D. (of Pocohontas College), who said that men were immensely improved by grazing, or taking their food slowly and continuously, after the manner of cows. And he said that he had, with the most
55 encouraging results, turned city men out on all fours in a field covered with veal cutlets. Then Tolstoy and the Humanitarians said that the world was growing more merciful, and therefore no one would ever desire to kill. And Mr. Mick not only became a vegetarian, but
60 at length declared vegetarianism doomed ("shedding," as he called it finely, "the green blood of the silent animals"), and predicted that men in a better age would live on nothing but salt.

There was Mr. Sidney Webb, also, who said that
65 the future would see a continuously increasing order and neatness in the life of the people, and his poor friend Fipps, who went mad and ran about the country with an axe, hacking branches off the trees whenever there were not the same number on both sides.

70 All these clever men were prophesying with every variety of ingenuity what would happen soon, and they all did it in the same way, by taking something they saw "going strong," as the saying is, and carrying it as far as ever their imagination could stretch. This, they said,
75 was the true and simple way of anticipating the future. "Just as," said Dr. Pellkins, in a fine passage,—"just as when we see a pig in a litter larger than the other pigs, we know that by an unalterable law of the Inscrutable it will some day be larger than an elephant,—just as
80 we know, when we see weeds and dandelions growing more and more thickly in a garden, that they must, in spite of all our efforts, grow taller than the chimney-pots and swallow the house from sight, so we know and reverently acknowledge, that when any power in
85 human politics has shown for any period of time any considerable activity, it will go on until it reaches to the sky."

And it did certainly appear that the prophets had put the people (engaged in the old game of Cheat the
90 Prophet) in a quite unprecedented difficulty. It seemed really hard to do anything without fulfilling some of their prophecies.

But there was, nevertheless, in the eyes of laborers in the streets, of peasants in the fields, of sailors and
95 children, and especially women, a strange look that kept the wise men in a perfect fever of doubt. They could not fathom the motionless mirth in their eyes. They still had some-thing up their sleeve; they were still playing the game of Cheat the Prophet.

Lesson 7 - Finding and Interpreting Details

1. The approach of the various people described in this passage towards predicting the future can best be described as:

   A. copying the ideas of one another.
   B. identifying a growing trend and stretching it with their imagination.
   C. prophesying by seeing the future in their dreams.
   D. reading books about the future.

2. In the third paragraph (lines 32-46), the predictions of H. G. Wells and Dr. Quilp could be best characterized as anticipating that:

   F. scientific advances would dramatically improve transportation.
   G. man would return to a more natural state.
   H. plant life would eventually grow out of control.
   J. Earth would eventually become a planet more like Saturn.

3. According to the narrator, which of the following statements was true about the beginning of the 20th century?

   A. Mankind was becoming increasingly orderly and neat.
   B. Vehicles were moving faster than the speed of sound.
   C. Mankind wanted to move simply and slowly, like animals.
   D. Many people were making predictions about the future.

4. The narrator claims that in the 20th century it was difficult to play "Cheat the Prophet" because:

   F. people were becoming far too cynical.
   G. people were becoming more merciful, which meant they would do what the prophet says.
   H. so many people were making predictions that it was hard to not accidentally fulfill one of them.
   J. so many people were making accurate predictions.

5. According to the narrator, which of the following best describes Edward Carpenter's views of the future?

   A. He believed that the animal population of the Earth will greatly increase.
   B. He thought that mankind would move to living in a simpler, more natural way.
   C. He felt that men would improve by eating food continuously, like a grazing animal.
   D. He felt that people of the 20th century would tend toward pacifism.

6. Which of the following statements about early 20th century predictions is best supported by the passage?

   F. Only a few people made truly accurate predictions.
   G. Most of the predictions people made were concerning how science would dominate the world.
   H. None of the predictions that people in the early 20th century made actually came true.
   J. The predictions were voluminous and tended to follow a pattern in how they were formulated.

7. Throughout the passage, the phrase "Cheat the Prophet" is mentioned primarily to:

   A. point out how the large number of predictions might defy people who tried to avoid them.
   B. introduce a new game to the reader.
   C. introduce the concepts of prophets and prophecies as they were seen in the early 20th century.
   D. classify the authors and luminaries who made predictions in the 1900s.

8. In the passage, the narrator most nearly describes Mr. Sidney Webb's friend Fipps as:

   F. an orderly, neat person.
   G. an owner of an orchard.
   H. a crazy person.
   J. a clever man.

9. The passage contains recurring references to all of the following, EXCEPT:

   A. prophecy.
   B. the future.
   C. the past.
   D. imagination.

10. The first two paragraphs (lines 1-31) of the passage establish all of the following, EXCEPT that:

    F. the passage is discussing the beginning of the 20th century.
    G. various people were engaged in hoodwinking their ancestors.
    H. many of the predictions made in the 1900s were regarding extraordinary occurrences.
    J. many people who thought themselves clever were predicting the future.

1. The approach of the various people described in this passage towards predicting the future can best be described as:

   A. copying the ideas of one another.
   B. identifying a growing trend and stretching it with their imagination.
   C. prophesying by seeing the future in their dreams.
   D. reading books about the future.

Lines 70-74 states that "All these clever men were prophesying with every variety of ingenuity what would happen soon, and they all did it in the same way, by taking something they saw 'going strong,' as the saying is, and carrying it as far as ever their imagination could stretch." This is supported by the following statement in lines 26-29: "They took something or other that was certainly going on in their time, and then said that it would go on more and more until something extraordinary happened." Choice B is therefore the best answer. Choices A, C and D are not supported by the passage.

2. In the third paragraph (lines 32-46), the predictions of H. G. Wells and Dr. Quilp could be best characterized as anticipating that:

   F. scientific advances would dramatically improve transportation.
   G. man would return to a more natural state.
   H. plant life would eventually grow out of control.
   J. Earth would eventually become a planet more like Saturn.

Paragraph 3, in lines 32-36, states "Mr. H. G. Wells and others, who thought that science would take charge of the future; and just as the motor-car was quicker than the coach, so some lovely thing would be quicker than the motor-car; and so on forever," which supports choice F. Paragraph 4 (lines 47-63) describes an "opposite school" of thought: that man would "return to nature." Since this paragraph describes the "opposite" of the perspectives of Wells and Quilp, we can eliminate choice G. Plants are mentioned in a metaphor in paragraph 6 (lines 70-87), but this has no bearing on Wells and Quilp, so scratch out H. Saturn is mentioned at the end of paragraph 3, on line 46, but only to describe what it would look like if a vehicle whizzed around the Earth continuously at great speed, so we eliminate choice J. Choice F is the best answer.

3. According to the narrator, which of the following statements was true about the beginning of the 20th century?

   A. Mankind was becoming increasingly orderly and neat.
   B. Vehicles were moving faster than the speed of sound.
   C. Mankind wanted to move simply and slowly, like animals.
   D. Many people were making predictions about the future.

Choices A, B and C all describe the predictions about the future that are mentioned in the passage. Since the entire passage discusses the wide variety of people making predictions about the future in the 20th century, the best option is choice D.

Lesson 7 - Finding and Interpreting Details

4. The narrator claims that in the 20th century it was difficult to play "Cheat the Prophet" because:

   F. people were becoming far too cynical.
   G. people were becoming more merciful, which meant they would do what the prophet says.
   H. so many people were making predictions that it was hard to not accidentally fulfill one of them.
   J. so many people were making accurate predictions.

The intro tells us that to "Cheat the Prophet" means to "attentively listen to wise predictions about the future, 'then go out and do something else.'" Lines 3-8 state: "The reason was, that there were so many prophets and so many prophecies, that it was difficult to elude all their ingenuities. When a man did something free and frantic and entirely his own, a horrible thought struck him afterwards; it might have been predicted." This directly supports choice H. Choice F is not supported anywhere in the passage. Paragraph 4 (lines 47-63) mentions a prediction that man might become more merciful, but this is only a prediction and has nothing to do with the ability to play "Cheat the Profit," so we can eliminate choice G. Nowhere in the passage does the narrator say that he feels that the people described were making particularly accurate predictions, and in fact seems to poke fun at their apparent lack of accuracy in paragraph 6 (lines 70-87), so choice H is a better answer than choice J.

5. According to the narrator, which of the following best describes Edward Carpenter's views of the future?

   A. He believed that the animal population of the Earth will greatly increase.
   B. He thought that mankind would move to living in a simpler, more natural way.
   C. He felt that men would improve by eating food continuously, like a grazing animal.
   D. He felt that people of the 20th century would tend toward pacifism.

Choices C and D refer to descriptions of the predictions of Pickie and Tolstoy from paragraph 4 (lines 47-63), so we are left with choices A and B as possibilities. Since the sentence about Carpenter in lines 48-50 states that he "thought we should in a very short time return to Nature, and live simply and slowly as the animals do," choice B is a better answer than choice A. While it's possible that in such a state the animal population would increase, this is not supported directly by the passage.

6. Which of the following statements about early 20th century predictions is best supported by the passage?

F. Only a few people made truly accurate predictions.
G. Most of the predictions people made were concerning how science would dominate the world.
H. None of the predictions that people in the early 20th century made actually came true.
J. The predictions were voluminous and tended to follow a pattern in how they were formulated.

Choice F is not supported by the passage. While this may be a true statement, nowhere does the passage concern itself with the accuracy of the predictions. Lines 32-34 mention "Mr. H. G. Wells and others, who thought that science would take charge of the future," but the next paragraph discusses predictions regarding nature, so choice G does not work. Lines 90-92 say, "It seemed really hard to do anything without fulfilling some of their prophecies," which seems to contradict choice H. Furthermore, nowhere does it indicate in the passage that none of the predictions come true. Watch out for absolute statements on ACT answers like none or all. Unless they are supported by the passage, they're usually wrong. Choice J is the best answer. "Voluminous" in this sense means "in a high quantity" or "a lot of them." Lines 3-5 of paragraph 1 support choice J by saying that "there were so many prophets and so many prophecies... it was difficult to elude all their ingenuities," and paragraph 2 (lines 25-31) describes a pattern that the "prophets" followed.

7. Throughout the passage, the phrase "Cheat the Prophet" is mentioned primarily to:

A. point out how the large number of predictions might defy people who tried to avoid them.
B. introduce a new game to the reader.
C. introduce the concepts of prophets and prophecies as they were seen in the early 20th century.
D. classify the authors and luminaries who made predictions in the 1900s.

In the introduction to the passage, we find out that "Cheat the Prophet" is "where people attentively listen to wise predictions about the future, 'then go out and do something else.'" In paragraphs 1 (lines 1-24), 7 (lines 88-92) and 8 (lines 93-99), the phrase is used in reference to people who might try to avoid fulfilling the many predictions that experts were making about the coming age. Therefore choice A is the best answer. The author does not describe any sort of game in the passage, so we can eliminate choice B. Choice C doesn't work because the phrase "Cheat the Prophet" is used to introduce the people mentioned in the passage, but it is not used in a sincere manner in this text. Nowhere does the passage indicate that the phrase "Cheat the Prophet" is being used as a classification or label, so choice D can be eliminated.

8. In the passage, the narrator most nearly describes Mr. Sidney Webb's friend Fipps as:

F. an orderly, neat person.
G. an owner of an orchard.
H. a crazy person.
J. a clever man.

We look for mention of Sidney Webb and Fipps, which we find in paragraph 5 (lines 64-69). In this paragraph, the author describes Fipps as someone "who went mad and ran about the country with an axe, hacking branches off the trees whenever there were not the same number on both sides." This best supports choice H.

Lesson 7 - Finding and Interpreting Details

9. The passage contains recurring references to all of the following, EXCEPT:
   A. prophecy.
   B. the future.
   C. the past.
   D. imagination.

Prophecy is continually mentioned, starting in paragraph 1, in lines 3-5: "there were so many prophets and so many prophecies, that it was difficult to elude all their ingenuities." Lines 33 and 34 discuss the idea that "science would take charge of the future," so we can eliminate choice B. The concept of imagination recurs throughout the passage and is mentioned specifically in lines 70-74: "All these clever men were prophesying with every variety of ingenuity what would happen soon, and they all did it in the same way, by taking something they saw 'going strong,' as the saying is, and carrying it as far as ever their imagination could stretch." Choice C, the past, is the only option not supported by the passage, so this is the correct answer. "Recurring" in this sense means "occurring or happening again."

10. The first two paragraphs of the passage establish all of the following, EXCEPT that:
    F. the passage is discussing the beginning of the 20th century.
    G. various people were engaged in hoodwinking their ancestors.
    H. many of the predictions made in the 1900s were regarding extraordinary occurrences.
    J. many people who thought themselves clever were predicting the future.

Choice F is supported by the first sentence of the passage, which begins "in the beginning of the twentieth century." Choice H is supported by lines 26-29: "They took something or other that was certainly going on in their time, and then said that it would go on more and more until something extraordinary happened." Choice J is established by the line "all these clever men were at work giving accounts of what would happen in the next age," which appears in paragraph 1, lines 16-18. Only choice G is not supported by paragraphs 1 (lines 1-24) and 2 (lines 25-31). The line "and it seemed that the good old game of hoodwinking your ancestors could not really be managed this time," which appears in paragraph 1, lines 19-21, does not have the meaning that "various people were engaged in hoodwinking their ancestors," so choice G is the best answer. "Hoodwinking," in this sense, means "tricking." "Establish," in this sense, means "show to be true."

FINDING SUPPORTING DETAILS

A fact is a fact. With the easiest type of ACT question, you only have to hunt for the fact. When you find it, it's spelled out as clear as day. There is nothing else you have to do. You just match what you find in the passage to the answer choice.

In the passage you just completed, you may have noticed that it wasn't quite that simple. You were required to find the facts and then interpret them. It was a two-step process.

These questions can be a time trap. They seem identical to the FINDING EXACT DETAILS question types, so you go hunting for the facts. But if you don't recognize that they are asking for your interpretation, you can waste valuable time seeking an exact match where one doesn't exist.

A clue that you'll need to interpret comes from the way the question is asked. It will include words like *nearly*, *best* or *most*. These words tell you that your answer is relative. Your answer will be a better fit than the other answer choices, but it won't be exactly what the author said in the passage.

You have to find the details that support one of the answer choices and interpret what they mean. The detail won't be the answer choice all by itself.

Let's look at question 6 from the passage as an example:

> 6. Which of the following statements about early 20th century predictions is best supported by the passage?
>
>   F. Only a few people made truly accurate predictions.
>   G. Most of the predictions people made were concerning how science would dominate the world.
>   H. None of the predictions that people in the early 20th century made actually came true.
>   J. The predictions were voluminous and tended to follow a pattern in how they were formulated.

The question asks us "what prediction is best supported by the passage?" This is a clue that we probably won't find an exact match. Instead, we'll find supporting details that we interpret to find the answer.

The details will be close to the answer, but not an exact match.

The word *supported* in this sense means "backed up" or "confirmed." The question is asking us to find which answer choice is backed up by details in the passage.

We can eliminate choice F because there are no details in the passage that back up the idea that only a few people made truly accurate predictions. This is probably a true statement, but it doesn't matter whether the statement is true. The question didn't ask us what statement

Lesson 7 - Finding and Interpreting Details

is true; it asked us what statement is backed up by details in the passage.

We can also knock out choice H for the same reason. There are no details that back this up. The answer says that none of the predictions came true. Absolutes like *all* and *none* are usually easy to eliminate on the ACT.

There is mention of how "science would take charge of the future" in paragraph 3, but it doesn't mention that most of the predictions people made were concerned with how science would dominate the world. It's the little words in the answer choices that can make the biggest difference. If you were tempted by this answer choice, ask yourself this: "Well, it does mention science, but are there any details that make me think most of the predictions were about science taking over the world?"

Choice J is the only one that is supported by the passage. In paragraph 1, we see that "there are so many prophets and so many prophecies… it was difficult to elude all their ingenuities," and paragraph 2 describes a pattern that the prophets followed.

To answer this sort of question, we have to find supporting details, but we often can't find an exact match.

When you see a question like this, look over your answer choices. Find the one that looks most correct to you. Then go find the details to support your choice so you can be sure you've answered correctly. If an answer choice doesn't jump out at you, work on eliminating answer choices that don't fit. The *least worst* choice will be the right answer.

Many questions of this type won't give you a clue that they require your interpretation. If you start searching for details and can't find an exact match to your answer choices, shift gears and look for the answer that is best supported by the details you can find in the passage. The question's wording will usually give you a hint about where to look.

In the next passage, you'll need to answer both types of questions we've covered thus far: questions that point to exact details and questions that require you to interpret meaning.

Passage

Instructions: Skim the passage in 3 minutes, then answer the 10 practice questions that appear below. Use a timer to keep track of when you should start answering the questions. Just like on the ACT, you are allowed to refer to the passage in order to find the correct answers.

HUMANITIES: This passage is adapted from *Architecture and Democracy* by Claude Bragdon, published by A.A. Knopff.

Broadly speaking, there are not five orders of architecture—nor fifty—but only two: Arranged and Organic. These correspond to the two terms of that "inevitable duality" which bisects life. Talent and
5 genius, reason and intuition, bromide and sulfite are some of the names we know them by.

Arranged architecture is reasoned and artificial; produced by talent, governed by taste. Organic architecture, on the other hand, is the product of some
10 obscure inner necessity for self-expression which is sub-conscious. It is as though Nature herself, through some human organ of her activity, had addressed herself to the service of the sons and daughters of men.

Arranged architecture in its finest manifestations
15 is the product of a pride, a knowledge, a competence, a confidence staggering to behold. It seems to say of the works of Nature, "I'll show you a trick worth two of that." For the subtlety of Nature's geometry, and for her infinite variety and unexpectedness, Arranged
20 architecture substitutes a Euclidian system of straight lines and (for the most part) circular curves, assembled and arranged according to a definite logic of its own. It is created but not creative; it is imagined but not imaginative. Organic architecture is both creative and
25 imaginative. It is non-Euclidian in the sense that it is higher-dimensional—that is, it suggests extension in directions and into regions where the spirit finds itself at home, but of which the senses give no report to the brain.

30 To make the whole thing clearer it may be said that Arranged and Organic architecture bear much the same relation to one another that a piano bears to a violin. A piano is an instrument that does not give forth discords if one follows the rules. A violin requires absolutely an
35 ear—an inner rectitude. It has a way of betraying the man of talent and glorifying the genius, becoming one with his body and his soul.

Of course it stands to reason that there is not always a hard and fast differentiation between these
40 two orders of architecture, but there is one sure way by which each may be recognized and known. If the function appears to have created the form, and if everywhere the form follows the function, changing as that changes, the building is Organic; if on the contrary,
45 "the house confines the spirit," if the building presents not a face but however beautiful a mask, it is an example of Arranged architecture.

But in so far as it is anything at all, aesthetically, our architecture is Arranged, so if only by the operation
50 of the law of opposites, or alternation, we might reasonably expect the next manifestation to be Organic. There are other and better reasons, however, for such expectancy.

Organic architecture is ever a flower of the
55 religious spirit. When the soul draws near to the surface of life, as it did in the two mystic centuries of the Middle Ages, it organizes life; and architecture, along, with the other arts becomes truly creative. The informing force comes not so much from man as through him.
60 After the war that spirit of brotherhood, born in the camps and bred on the battlefields and in the trenches of Europe, is likely to take on all the attributes of a new religion of humanity, prompting men to such heroisms and renunciations, exciting in them such psychic
65 sublimations, as have characterized the great religious renewals of time past.

If this happens it is bound to write itself on space in an architecture beautiful and new; one which "takes its shape and sun-color" from the opulent heart. This
70 architecture will of necessity be organic, the product not of self-assertive personalities, but the work of the "Patient Demon" organizing the nation into a spiritual democracy.

The author is aware that in this point of view
75 there is little of the "scientific spirit"; but science fails to reckon with the soul. Science advances facing backward, so what prevision can it have of a miraculous and divinely inspired future—or for the matter of that, of any future at all? The old methods and categories
80 will no longer answer; the orderly course of evolution has been violently interrupted by the earthquake of the war; igneous action has superseded aqueous action. The casements of the human mind look out no longer upon familiar hills and valleys, but on a stark, strange,
85 devastated landscape, the ploughed land of some future harvest of the years. It is the end of the Age, the Kali Yuga—the completion of a major cycle; but all cycles follow the same sequence: after winter, Spring; and after the Iron Age, the Golden.

90 The specific features of this organic, divinely inspired architecture of the Golden Age cannot of course be discerned by any one, any more than the manner in which the Great Mystery will present itself anew to consciousness. The most imaginative artist
95 can imagine only in terms of the already-existent; he can speak only the language he has learned. And yet some germs of the future must be enfolded even in the present moment. The course of wisdom is to seek them neither in the old romance nor in the new rationalism,
100 but in the subtle and ever-changing spirit of the times.

Lesson 7 - Finding and Interpreting Details

1. Which of the following questions is NOT answered in the passage?

    A. What are the two main orders of architecture?
    B. What are the qualities of Arranged architecture?
    C. What was the name of the period before the Middle Ages?
    D. What are the qualities of Organic architecture?

2. All of the following descriptions are used in the passage to characterize Arranged architecture, EXCEPT that it is:

    F. based on a Euclidian system of straight lines and circular curves.
    G. creative and imaginative.
    H. assembled and arranged.
    J. reasoned and artificial.

3. Paragraphs 1 through 4 (lines 1-37) establish all of the following about Organic architecture, EXCEPT its:

    A. origins.
    B. differences from Arranged architecture.
    C. association with religion and spirituality.
    D. inevitable dual nature.

4. According to the passage, which of the following best describes the author's predictions about the architecture of the new "Golden Age"?

    F. The architecture of the future will likely be Organic.
    G. The architecture of the future will likely be Arranged.
    H. The architecture of the future will be for religious buildings.
    J. The architecture of the future will be the product of self-assertive personalities.

5. The author mentions the idea of how "the house confines the spirit" as part of his argument that:

    A. one can find clear signs to tell the difference between the two orders of architecture.
    B. the Arranged form of architecture follows the law of opposites.
    C. the Arranged form of architecture feels too closed in and claustrophobic.
    D. the Arranged form of architecture is based on an outgrowth of spirit.

6. In the context of the passage, paragraph 9 (lines 74-89) is best described as presenting images of all of the following, EXCEPT:

    F. disaster.
    G. devastation.
    H. war.
    J. mystery.

7. The author indicates that one reason he believed that the Organic order of architecture was on the rise was that:

    A. since the current trend was Arranged, it would alternate to being Organic because of the law of opposites.
    B. a spiritual democracy would have a law that all architecture must be Organic.
    C. Organic architecture is best and so it is the wave of the future.
    D. the Iron Age was populated mainly with Organic architecture.

8. Information in the passage suggests that the author believes the exact features of the future architectural style cannot be described primarily because:

    F. he is not sufficiently romantic or rational.
    G. we can only know what will come once the war is over.
    H. one can only imagine based on what already exists.
    J. even though he knows what it will look like, he cannot express it in words.

9. Based on paragraphs 1 through 4 (lines 1-37), which of the following statements indicates the author's opinion of the relationship between Organic and Arranged architecture?

    A. Though they are both styles of architecture, the Arranged style is more structured, while the Organic style is more imaginative.
    B. Both the Organic and the Arranged styles of architecture will soon give way to a spiritual form of architecture.
    C. All architecture is both Organic and Arranged.
    D. For thousands of years, mankind has alternated between an Arranged and an Organic architectural style.

10. The passage indicates that the violin described in paragraph 4 (lines 30-37) represents:

    F. the human spirit.
    G. Arranged architecture.
    H. Organic architecture.
    J. a lack of discord.

159

1. Which of the following questions is NOT answered in the passage?

   A. What are the two main orders of architecture?
   B. What are the qualities of Arranged architecture?
   C. **What was the name of the period before the Middle Ages?**
   D. What are the qualities of Organic architecture?

Scan for the unique words used in the answer choices to find the details you need. The phrase "orders of architecture" first appears in paragraph 1 (lines 1-6). This paragraph describes two main orders of architecture, Arranged and Organic, so we can eliminate A. Both paragraphs 2 (lines 7-13) and 3 (lines 14-29) describe the qualities of Arranged and Organic architecture, so we can eliminate choices B and D. While paragraph 7 (lines 54-66) mentions the Middle Ages, it does not describe the name of the time period before the Middle Ages, so choice C is the best answer. Since the question asked for what is NOT answered in the passage, we are looking for the one answer that does not have the details in the passage needed to support answering it.

2. All of the following descriptions are used in the passage to characterize Arranged architecture, EXCEPT that it is:

   F. based on a Euclidian system of straight lines and circular curves.
   G. **creative and imaginative.**
   H. assembled and arranged.
   J. reasoned and artificial.

Line 7 states that "Arranged architecture is reasoned and artificial," so we can eliminate choice J. Lines 19-22 say that "Arranged architecture substitutes a Euclidian system of straight lines and (for the most part) circular curves, assembled and arranged according to a definite logic of its own," so this allows us to eliminate choices F and H. In paragraph 3, lines 23 and 24, the author states that Arranged architecture "is created but not creative; it is imagined but not imaginative. Organic architecture is both creative and imaginative," so choice G is the best answer.

Lesson 7 - Finding and Interpreting Details

3. Paragraphs 1 through 4 (lines 1-37) establish all of the following about Organic architecture, EXCEPT its:

    A. origins.
    B. differences from Arranged architecture.
    C. association with religion and spirituality.
    D. inevitable dual nature.

When we look over the answer choices, we see that they are broad concepts that are probably not repeated word for word in the passage. We know we have to look for supporting details that will help us eliminate a few options. If a couple of the answer choices trigger your memory of the passage, pursue eliminating them first. Paragraph 7 (lines 54-66) begins "Organic architecture is ever a flower of the religious spirit," and goes on to further describe the relationship between Organic architecture, religion, and spirituality, so we can eliminate choice C. Paragraph 2 through 4 (lines 7-37) are dedicated to describing the differences between Organic and Arranged architecture, so we can eliminate choice B. Choice A is a little more difficult to eliminate, but since lines 9-11 state that it "is the product of some obscure inner necessity for self-expression which is sub-conscious," this at least in part addresses where it comes from. The word "origins" means in this sense "the point where something begins." The "inevitable duality" is mentioned in lines 1-6, but it is describing with this phrase the difference between Organic and Arranged architecture. The phrase is not being used to describe Organic architecture on its own, so choice D is the best answer. "Inevitable," in this sense, means "certain to happen."

4. According to the passage, which of the following best describes the author's predictions about the architecture of the new "Golden Age"?

    F. The architecture of the future will likely be Organic.
    G. The architecture of the future will likely be Arranged.
    H. The architecture of the future will be for religious buildings.
    J. The architecture of the future will be the product of self-assertive personalities.

The phrase "best describes" is a clue that we will likely not find an exact match between our answer choice and the passage. Lines 90-94, however, say that "the specific features of this organic, divinely inspired architecture of the Golden Age cannot of course be discerned by any one, any more than the manner in which the Great Mystery will present itself anew to consciousness," which supports choice F. Lines 48-53 further support this concept and helps us to eliminate choice G: "But in so far as it is anything at all, aesthetically, our architecture is Arranged, so if only by the operation of the law of opposites, or alternation, we might reasonably expect the next manifestation to be Organic. There are other and better reasons, however, for such expectancy." Choice H can be eliminated because paragraph 7 (lines 54-66) discusses the religious influence on Organic architecture, but does not go so far as to say that Organic architecture is mainly for religious buildings. Choice J is incorrect because lines 70 and 71 say that organic architecture is "the product not of self-assertive personalities," so since the author thinks future architecture will be Organic, it doesn't fit that it would be the product of self-assertive personalities.

5. The author mentions the idea of how "the house confines the spirit" as part of his argument that:

   A. **one can find clear signs to tell the difference between the two orders of architecture.**
   B. the Arranged form of architecture follows the law of opposites.
   C. the Arranged form of architecture feels too closed in and claustrophobic.
   D. the Arranged form of architecture is based on an outgrowth of spirit.

We find the unique phrase "the house confines the spirit" on line 45. In the first sentence of this paragraph, on lines 40 and 41, it says that "there is one sure way by which each may be recognized and known." It then goes on to talk about how to tell the difference between the two forms of architecture. For that reason, choice A is the best answer. Choice B can be eliminated because "the law of opposites" mentioned in paragraph 6, on line 50, is not referring to the "house that confines the spirit." While "confines" means "keep or restrict within limits," the phrase is not used to criticize the Arranged form or talk about its size or arrangement, so choice C is incorrect. Choice D is also incorrect because it is Organic architecture that is described as "ever a flower of the religious spirit," not the Arranged form.

6. In the context of the passage, paragraph 9 is best described as presenting images of all of the following, EXCEPT:

   F. disaster.
   G. devastation.
   H. war.
   J. **mystery.**

Paragraph 9 (lines 74-89) includes mention of "the earthquake of war," and "a stark, strange, devastated landscape," so we can eliminate choices F, G and H. Paragraph 10 mentions a "Great Mystery," on line 93, but this does not appear in paragraph 9 (lines 74-89), so choice J is the best answer.

7. The author indicates that one reason he believed that the Organic order of architecture was on the rise was that:

   A. **since the current trend was Arranged, it would alternate to being Organic because of the law of opposites.**
   B. a spiritual democracy would have a law that all architecture must be Organic.
   C. Organic architecture is best and so is the wave of the future.
   D. the Iron Age was populated mainly with Organic architecture.

Lines 48-51, located in paragraph 6, provide supporting details for choice A: "But in so far as it is anything at all, aesthetically, our architecture is Arranged, so if only by the operation of the law of opposites, or alternation, we might reasonably expect the next manifestation to be Organic." A "manifestation," in this sense, is "an appearance." The end of paragraph 8, in lines 72 and 73, mentions a "spiritual democracy," but does not clearly support the claims of choice B. Choices C and D are not supported by the details in the passage.

Lesson 7 - Finding and Interpreting Details

8. Information in the passage suggests that the author believes the exact features of the future architectural style cannot be described primarily because:

   F. he is not sufficiently romantic or rational.
   G. we can only know what will come once the war is over.
   H. one can only imagine based on what already exists.
   J. even though he knows what it will look like, he cannot express it in words.

Line 94 and 95 in the last paragraph state that "the most imaginative artist can imagine only in terms of the already-existent," which supports choice H and makes it our best answer. Choices F and G have words that are mentioned in the passage but that do not support the answer choices. Choice J is contradicted by lines 90-92 in the last paragraph: "The specific features of this organic, divinely inspired architecture of the Golden Age cannot of course be discerned by any one..." which means that the author doesn't know what the future architectural style will look like. "Discerned," in this sense, means "perceive or recognize."

9. Based on paragraphs 1 through 4 (lines 1-37), which of the following statements indicates the author's opinion of the relationship between Organic and Arranged architecture?

   A. Though they are both styles of architecture, the Arranged style is more structured, while the Organic style is more imaginative.
   B. Both the Organic and the Arranged styles of architecture will soon give way to a spiritual form of architecture.
   C. All architecture is both Organic and Arranged.
   D. For thousands of years, mankind has alternated between an Arranged and an Organic architectural style.

Paragraph 3 (lines 14-29) best supports choice A. The phrases "assembled and arranged" describing Arranged architecture supports the concept of it being structured, while the phrase "Organic architecture is both creative and imaginative" supports the concept of Organic style being more imaginative. Choice B is incorrect because paragraphs 1 through 4 (lines 1-37) do not mention a spiritual style, and furthermore the passage later describes the Organic style as being spiritual, but doesn't list a spiritual form as its own style of architecture. Paragraph 1 (lines 1-6) states there are two orders of architecture, and the passage describes how to tell them apart, which contradicts choice C. While paragraph 6 (lines 48-53) describes an alternation, it doesn't say it goes back thousands of years. Furthermore, the question limits us only to paragraphs 1 through 4 (lines 1-37).

10. The passage indicates that the violin described in the paragraph 4 (lines 30-37) represents:

    F. the human spirit.
    G. Arranged architecture.
    H. Organic architecture.
    J. a lack of discord.

Choice F is not mentioned in paragraph 4 (lines 30-37) and so should be eliminated. "A lack of discord" is used to describe a piano, not a violin ("A piano is an instrument that does not give forth discords if one follows the rules"), so we can eliminate choice J. The description of Arranged architecture in lines 7 and 8, "Arranged architecture is reasoned and artificial; produced by talent, governed by taste," better fits a piano than a violin, which means that the violin represents Organic architecture. Choice H is best supported by the passage.

Lesson 8.1
Vocabulary

proceedings

noun a sequence of actions that occur, typically in a legal setting

example sentences

The lawyer informed his client that the **proceedings** would be carried out on Thursday.

In the course of the legal **proceeding** the judge ruled that some evidence could not be submitted.

During the **proceedings** the judge called for a recess.

also written in this form **proceeding**

words that are similar **action, happening, incident, occurrence, operation, procedure, process, step**

Look up the full definition of "proceedings" in the dictionary and use each definition in sentences of your own creation until you feel you fully understand the word and can use it in conversation.

Write five sentences using the noun "proceedings":

_____

_____

_____

_____

_____

_____

_____

_____

exalt

verb **to praise or honor; to raise up to a higher status or rank**

example sentences

He often **exalted** her as if she were a pop star or a princess.

The nobles would **exalt** their king in order to gain favor.

The writer had won numerous awards, and so every novel he wrote was **exalted** by the critics and public alike.

also written in this form **exalted, exalting**

words that are similar **promote, praise, bless, build up, commend, dignify, honor, idolize, raise, revere, set on a pedestal, upgrade, worship**

words that are opposite **condemn, criticize, denounce, humiliate**

Look up the full definition of "exalt" in the dictionary and use each definition in sentences of your own creation until you feel you fully understand the word and can use it in conversation.

Write five sentences using the verb "exalt":

_____

_____

_____

_____

_____

_____

_____

consider

verb to think about, look at, or judge; to think about carefully

example sentences

Joe would never **consider** going back to the class after what happened.

She carefully **considered** her options before choosing the theater club.

He took the teacher's advice under **consideration**, but eventually decided to go with his gut instinct.

also written in this form considered, considering, consideration

words that are similar study, chew over, think over, contemplate, reflect, meditate, ponder

Look up the full definition of "consider" in the dictionary and use each definition in sentences of your own creation until you feel you fully understand the word and can use it in conversation.

Write five sentences using the verb "consider":

_____

_____

_____

_____

_____

_____

_____

_____

minute

adjective **tiny, very small or minuscule**

example sentences

The artist created a **minute** drawing on the grain of rice.

With his **minute** amount of money, he was unable to buy a ticket at the movies.

Ellen argued with her teacher that such a **minute** error shouldn't cost her so many points on her exam.

words that are similar **tiny, infinitesimal, small**

words that are opposite **large, big, gigantic**

Look up the full definition of "minute" in the dictionary and use each definition in sentences of your own creation until you feel you fully understand the word and can use it in conversation.

Write five sentences using the adjective "minute":

_____

_____

_____

_____

_____

_____

_____

_____

accord

noun **agreement or unity**

example sentences

The founding fathers signed the Declaration of Independence with one **accord**.

After an hour arguing, the brother and sister finally reached an **accord**.

The room of students was obviously in **accord** against the pop quiz.

also written in this form **humility**

words that are similar **harmony, sympathy, concord, conformity, deal, pact, sympathy, unanimity**

words that are opposite **antagonism, disagreement, opposition, refusal**

Look up the full definition of "accord" in the dictionary and use each definition in sentences of your own creation until you feel you fully understand the word and can use it in conversation.

Write five sentences using the noun "accord":

_____

_____

_____

_____

_____

_____

_____

Lesson 8.1 - Vocabulary

evident

adjective **obviously visible**

example sentences

When the girl walked in, it was **evident** that he had a crush on her.

It was plainly **evident** that someone had tried to break into his locker because the lock had been tampered with.

The difficulties in lighting a match in the rain are **evident** from the start.

also written in this form **evidently**

words that are similar **apparent, plain, unmistakable, obvious, observable, distinct, indisputable, noticeable, perceptible, visible**

words that are opposite **hidden, mistakable, obscure, secret, uncertain, unclear, unknown, unsure, vague**

Look up the full definition of "evident" in the dictionary and use each definition in sentences of your own creation until you feel you fully understand the word and can use it in conversation.

Write five sentences using the adjective "evident":

_____

_____

_____

_____

_____

_____

_____

practice

verb to carry out or do (a job or profession) on a regular basis; to do things a customary way; to learn by repetition

noun a profession that is practiced; the act of practicing

example sentences

When the doctor started his **practice**, he only had a few patients.

They say that **practice** makes perfect, and that saying is definitely true in sports.

The club has a **practice** of donating Christmas gifts to deserving, underprivileged youth.

also written in this form **practicing**

words that are similar **custom, habit, manner, method, tradition**

Look up the full definition of "practice" in the dictionary and use each definition in sentences of your own creation until you feel you fully understand the word and can use it in conversation.

Write five sentences using the noun and verb "practice":

_____

_____

_____

_____

_____

_____

_____

_____

Lesson 8.1 - Vocabulary

intend

verb to mean to do something, to have an action as your goal

example sentences

Please let me know if you **intend** to attend the party so I can save your seat.

Her mother punished her not because she hurt her sister but because she **intended** to do so.

I doubt that what he **intends** is in Paul's best interests.

also written in this form intending, intentions

words that are similar try, mean, plan, purpose, have in mind, hope to, expect, be resolved, be determined, attempt, aspire, aim

Look up the full definition of "intend" in the dictionary and use each definition in sentences of your own creation until you feel you fully understand the word and can use it in conversation.

Write five sentences using the verb "intend":

_____

_____

_____

_____

_____

_____

_____

_____

concern

noun something that interests you because it's important or affects you; an anxious feeling; a feeling of sympathy for someone or something

example sentences

His main **concern** during the summer was to make enough money to buy a car.

She had too little **concern** over her math test results. She should have studied more.

After she heard that Joe had received some bad news, she expressed her **concern** to him.

words that are similar **interest, involvement, worry, matter**

words that are opposite **unconcern**

Look up the full definition of "concern" in the dictionary and use each definition in sentences of your own creation until you feel you fully understand the word and can use it in conversation.

Write five sentences using the noun "concern":

_____

_____

_____

_____

_____

_____

_____

_____

commit

<small>verb</small> **to completely dedicate yourself to something; ALSO to perform an act**

<small>example sentences</small>

The robber **committed** a crime.

The young college student **committed** himself to a study of the arts.

It takes **commitment** to get a black belt in karate.

<small>also written in this form</small> commitment, committing, committed

<small>words that are similar</small> go for broke, go in for, carry out, complete, do, dedicate, devote, give all one's got

<small>words that are opposite</small> idle, loaf, rest, stop, wait

Look up the full definition of "commit" in the dictionary and use each definition in sentences of your own creation until you feel you fully understand the word and can use it in conversation.

Write five sentences using the verb "commit":

_____

_____

_____

_____

_____

_____

_____

_____

Lesson 8.2
Vocabulary

issue

noun a topic of concern; ALSO one publication of a series published periodically

verb to put out an issue (as in a magazine, etc.)

example sentences

He and his mother always discussed the political **issues** of the day.

Nobody worried about safety until one concerned parent raised the **issue**.

The next **issue** of the school newspaper has a humor section.

also written in this form **issued, issuing**

words that are similar **argument, concern, contention, controversy, matter, point, problem, subject, topic**

Look up the full definition of "issue" in the dictionary and use each definition in sentences of your own creation until you feel you fully understand the word and can use it in conversation.

Write five sentences using the noun and verb "issue":

_____

_____

_____

_____

_____

_____

_____

approach

verb **to get near to something**

example sentences

As his birthday **approached**, he got more and more excited.

I will **approach** the subject carefully so that I don't offend anyone.

As she **approached**, he noticed that she had dyed her hair since the last time he saw her.

also written in this form **approached, approaching**

words that are similar **advance, draw near, nearing, reaching, access, coming**

words that are opposite **departure, leaving, distancing**

Look up the full definition of "approach" in the dictionary and use each definition in sentences of your own creation until you feel you fully understand the word and can use it in conversation.

Write five sentences using the verb "approach":

_____

_____

_____

_____

_____

_____

_____

establish

verb to set up or found; to bring something about; to prove that something is true or valid

example sentences

The couple **established** the doughnut shop in 1966.

He wrote the book so that he could **establish** himself as an authority.

We **established** in the court room that the evidence was the key to the case.

also written in this form establishes, establishment

words that are similar build, create, enact, erect, form, found, lay foundation, originate, provide, set down, stabilize

words that are opposite destroy, disestablish, invalidate, disprove, ruin, unsettle

Look up the full definition of "establish" in the dictionary and use each definition in sentences of your own creation until you feel you fully understand the word and can use it in conversation.

Write five sentences using the verb "establish":

_____

_____

_____

_____

_____

_____

_____

_____

utter

adjective **total or complete**

verb **to make a sound**

example sentences

The young man felt like he was an **utter** failure after he missed the shot with only seconds left.

He felt like the politician's speech was **utter** pandering.

When grandmother **utters** her complaints, I can barely hear what she says.

also written in this form **uttered, uttering, utterly**

words that are similar **complete, downright, entire, flat-out, pure, straight-out, thorough, stark, total**

words that are opposite **incomplete, uncertain**

Look up the full definition of "utter" in the dictionary and use each definition in sentences of your own creation until you feel you fully understand the word and can use it in conversation.

Write five sentences using the adjective and verb "utter":

_____

_____

_____

_____

_____

_____

_____

conduct

noun the way you behave; the way you do something

verb to lead or direct; to behave or act in a certain way

example sentences

The girl's **conduct** earned her two demerits.

The way he **conducts** himself in choir will get him kicked out.

The manager **conducted** the company's day to day operations.

also written in this form **conducted, conducting**

words that are similar **control, direction, leadership, management, treatment, carrying on, behavior, behave, act**

Look up the full definition of "conduct" in the dictionary and use each definition in sentences of your own creation until you feel you fully understand the word and can use it in conversation.

Write five sentences using the noun "conduct":

_____

_____

_____

_____

_____

_____

_____

engage

verb to involve or catch

example sentences

Joe **engaged** the plumber to fix his sink.

The fireworks fully **engaged** the three-year-old's attention.

The salesman was so **engaging** over the phone that he got the meeting with the company.

also written in this form engaging, engaged, engagement

words that are similar concern, captivate, engross, get going, join, lock, appoint, book, take on, enlist, employ, contract

words that are opposite disengage, break off, break up, banish, discharge, dismiss, eject, expel, fire, let go, release

Look up the full definition of "engage" in the dictionary and use each definition in sentences of your own creation until you feel you fully understand the word and can use it in conversation.

Write five sentences using the verb "engage":

_____

_____

_____

_____

_____

_____

_____

obtain

verb to get (something that isn't easy to get)

example sentences

Ellen **obtained** permission from her parents to go to the party after asking twenty times.

It cost a considerable sum, but John finally **obtained** the last baseball card he needed to complete his collection.

The museum **obtained** a painting by Raphael.

also written in this form **obtained, obtaining**

words that are similar **accomplish, achieve, capture, collect, get, get hold of, gather, secure, seize, procure, purchase, receive, snag, take, win**

words that are opposite **forfeit, lose, sacrifice, forsake**

Look up the full definition of "obtain" in the dictionary and use each definition in sentences of your own creation until you feel you fully understand the word and can use it in conversation.

Write five sentences using the verb "obtain":

_____

_____

_____

_____

_____

_____

_____

_____

scarce

adjective **not enough, insufficient, hard to come by**

example sentences

The pilgrims suffered because food was **scarce** and hard to come by in the winter.

After a hurricane, gasoline is **scarce** in some towns.

As water becomes increasingly **scarce**, scientists are challenged to identify new methods of water purification.

also written in this form **scarcity**

words that are similar **few, few and far between, in short supply, limited, rare, sparse, uncommon, inadequate, incomplete, skimpy**

words that are opposite **adequate, ample, sufficient, enough, excessive, abundant, plentiful**

Look up the full definition of "scarce" in the dictionary and use each definition in sentences of your own creation until you feel you fully understand the word and can use it in conversation.

Write five sentences using the adjective "scarce":

_____

_____

_____

_____

_____

_____

_____

_____

policy

noun a plan of action adopted by an individual or group

example sentences

The company has a **policy** to not permit people to show up for work late.

I have a strict **policy** of fairness in my classroom.

The nation adopted a firm **policy** of expansion and industrialism.

also written in this form **policies**

words that are similar **plan, arrangement, protocol, rule, strategy, management, procedure, tactics**

Look up the full definition of "policy" in the dictionary and use each definition in sentences of your own creation until you feel you fully understand the word and can use it in conversation.

Write five sentences using the noun "policy":

_____
_____
_____
_____
_____
_____
_____
_____

straight

adjective not having any curves or interruptions; ALSO honest, conventional or old-fashioned

example sentences

After P.E. we went **straight** to the water cooler.

I'm not going to stop your grounding until you come **straight** with me about what happened at the party.

Let's cut out the small talk and go **straight** to what we need to learn in this class.

words that are similar continuous, direct, even, in a line, in a row, level, uninterrupted, correct, exact, organized, neat, pure, conventional, square, conservative, traditional

words that are opposite curved, indirect, twisted, different, unconventional, untraditional, diluted, mixed

Look up the full definition of "straight" in the dictionary and use each definition in sentences of your own creation until you feel you fully understand the word and can use it in conversation.

Write five sentences using the adjective "straight":

_____

_____

_____

_____

_____

_____

_____

Lesson 8.3
Vocabulary

stock

noun what a store has to sell; what is present and available for use or sale

example sentences

The library has a huge **stock** of books and is unlikely to ever run out.

The safety marshal said that we should build up a **stock** of foodstuffs in case of a hurricane.

Relations were tense with the country because they had built up a large **stock** of weapons, which they threatened to use at any moment.

words that are similar **accumulation, massing, aggregation, store, investment, inventory**

Look up the full definition of "stock" in the dictionary and use each definition in sentences of your own creation until you feel you fully understand the word and can use it in conversation.

Write five sentences using the noun "stock":

_____

_____

_____

_____

_____

_____

_____

_____

apparent

^{adjective} obvious; what's plain to see; ALSO something that seems to be true but isn't completely definite

example sentences

It was **apparent** that I missed my ride.

He is **apparently** the best actor for the job because he got the role.

It is completely **apparent** to me that she has a crush on him.

also written in this form **apparently**

words that are similar **obvious, clear-cut, definite, detectable, perceivable, plain, pronounced**

words that are opposite **imperceptible, negligible, unnoticed, doubtful, improbable, unclear**

Look up the full definition of "apparent" in the dictionary and use each definition in sentences of your own creation until you feel you fully understand the word and can use it in conversation.

Write five sentences using the adjective "apparent":

_____

_____

_____

_____

_____

_____

_____

_____

property

noun **anything someone owns; ALSO something's qualities**

example sentences

The lotion's soothing **properties** were great for her sunburn.

The man asked us to get off his **property** immediately.

I wish she would respect my **property** and ask me before she borrows my car!

also written in this form **properties**

words that are similar **possessions, real estate, assets, belongings, resources, wealth, feature, character, characteristic, quality**

Look up the full definition of "property" in the dictionary and use each definition in sentences of your own creation until you feel you fully understand the word and can use it in conversation.

Write five sentences using the noun "property":

_____

_____

_____

_____

_____

_____

_____

_____

fancy

_{adjective} decorated or ornamented, the opposite of plain; ALSO an imaginary thing

_{verb} to desire, want or like something

_{example sentences}
He should become a fiction author because he's always going on these flights of **fancy**.

That is a **fancy** dress if I've ever seen one.

I **fancy** a cup of coffee.

_{words that are similar} extravagant, complicated, ornate, resplendent, rich, frilly, fantasy, fondness, illusion, dream up, desire, love, want

_{words that are opposite} certainty, fact, reality, truth, plain, unfancy, unornamented, dislike, hate

Look up the full definition of "fancy" in the dictionary and use each definition in sentences of your own creation until you feel you fully understand the word and can use it in conversation.

Write five sentences using the adjective and verb "fancy":

_____

_____

_____

_____

_____

_____

_____

concept

noun **a thought or idea**

example sentences

The designer had a **concept** of what he wanted the room to look like, but he had to set it to paper before the construction workers understood.

That man does not have the slightest **concept** of how much work goes into putting on a play like this.

I was introduced to the **concept** of computerized billing in school, but now on my job I'm actually using it.

also written in this form **conceive**

words that are similar **conceptualization, consideration, idea, hypothesis, notion, perception, theory, thought**

Look up the full definition of "concept" in the dictionary and use each definition in sentences of your own creation until you feel you fully understand the word and can use it in conversation.

Write five sentences using the noun "concept":

_____

_____

_____

_____

_____

_____

_____

_____

court

noun a place where justice is administered, or where a judge presides

verb to try to win affection or favor

example sentences
He took the thief to **court** and won the case.

I will **court** Elizabeth until she lets me take her to the prom.

After I told my neighbor that he needed to stop parking in my yard, he told me that he would see me in **court**.

words that are similar judicial system, judge, justice, law court, love, fawn over, pay attention to, propose, ask in marriage, charm

words that are opposite disregard, ignore

Look up the full definition of "court" in the dictionary and use each definition in sentences of your own creation until you feel you fully understand the word and can use it in conversation.

Write five sentences using the noun and verb "court":

_____

_____

_____

_____

_____

_____

_____

_____

appoint

verb **to assign someone to a job**

example sentences

The governor **appointed** four judges this year.

I hope someone will **appoint** me to be hall monitor because it will look good on my resume.

The U.S. president has the power to **appoint** many different people to positions of power.

also written in this form **appointment, appointing**

words that are similar **choose, assign, command, commission, delegate, designate, nominate, ordain, select, set**

words that are opposite **dismiss, fire, refuse, reject, deny, disapprove**

Look up the full definition of "appoint" in the dictionary and use each definition in sentences of your own creation until you feel you fully understand the word and can use it in conversation.

Write five sentences using the verb "appoint":

_____

_____

_____

_____

_____

_____

_____

Lesson 8.3 - Vocabulary

passage

noun the act of passing or moving from one place to another place; ALSO a section of text

example sentences

Read the **passage** from beginning to end and let me know what you think once you're done.

His **passage** into adulthood was not an easy transition for him.

Thomas guided the boat through the **passage** deftly.

words that are similar channel, corridor, opening, pathway, route, way

words that are opposite blockage, stop

*Look up the full definition of "**passage**" in the dictionary and use each definition in sentences of your own creation until you feel you fully understand the word and can use it in conversation.*

Write five sentences using the noun "passage":

_____

_____

_____

_____

_____

_____

_____

vain

adjective **too proud of oneself; ALSO useless or not productive**

example sentences

The thing about Hillary is that she is too **vain** for me to be interested in her.

I think that searching for a lost needle in a haystack is a **vain** endeavor.

The young man was so **vain** that he spent the whole day looking at his reflection in the pond.

also written in this form **vanity**

words that are similar **arrogant, boastful, bigheaded, conceited, egocentric, haughty, pleased with oneself, self-important, stuck-up**

words that are opposite **modest, shy**

Look up the full definition of "vain" in the dictionary and use each definition in sentences of your own creation until you feel you fully understand the word and can use it in conversation.

Write five sentences using the adjective "vain":

_____

_____

_____

_____

_____

_____

_____

_____

instance

noun **an occurrence or example**

example sentences

In such an **instance** as her birthday, she prefers a small gathering as opposed to a large party.

You give me one **instance** where you haven't come in to work late, and I won't fire you.

There are too many **instances** of misbehavior for the principal to not recommend suspension.

words that are similar **case in point, example, occasion, occurrence, particular, sample, sampling**

Look up the full definition of "instance" in the dictionary and use each definition in sentences of your own creation until you feel you fully understand the word and can use it in conversation.

Write five sentences using the noun "instance":

_____

_____

_____

_____

_____

_____

_____

_____

Lesson 8.4
Vocabulary

coast

noun the place where the land meets the sea

verb to effortlessly move; to accomplish without difficulty

example sentences

The young man liked going to the **coast** with his family during the summer.

Her dream house is a mansion on the **coast**.

He was able to **coast** through that geometry class because he'd already studied it at his old school in the previous year.

also written in this form **coasting, coasted**

words that are similar **coast, coastline, shore, shoreline, drift, travel**

Look up the full definition of "coast" in the dictionary and use each definition in sentences of your own creation until you feel you fully understand the word and can use it in conversation.

Write five sentences using the noun and verb "coast":

_____

_____

_____

_____

_____

_____

_____

Lesson 8.4 - Vocabulary

project

noun **work that is planned for or intended**

verb **to jut out**

example sentences

He needed to get started on his merit badge **project,** or he was never going to finish.

It was quite a **project** putting a new roof on the house.

The rock **projected** from the road in such a way as to make it dangerous.

also written in this form **projection, projecting, projected**

words that are similar **work, undertaking, activity, job, occupation, task, extend, overhang, stand out, stick out, stretch out, thrust**

words that are opposite **cave in**

Look up the full definition of "project" in the dictionary and use each definition in sentences of your own creation until you feel you fully understand the word and can use it in conversation.

Write five sentences using the noun and verb "project":

_____

_____

_____

_____

_____

_____

_____

_____

commission

noun the passing of responsibility to someone else; ALSO money received by an employee when he or she sells something

verb to pass or assign responsibility

example sentences

The government gave him a **commission** to research the effects of various vitamins on plant life.

The salesman received a **commission** for every car he sold, so he might not have been the most reliable source of information about cars on that lot.

Julie **commissioned** her brother to guard the lemonade stand while she took a break.

also written in this form commissioned, commissioning

words that are similar task, duty, appointment, function, instruction, work, charge, appoint, assign, entrust, empower, enable, send

words that are opposite retract, unauthorize

Look up the full definition of "commission" in the dictionary and use each definition in sentences of your own creation until you feel you fully understand the word and can use it in conversation.

Write five sentences using the noun and verb "commission":

_____

_____

_____

_____

_____

_____

_____

_____

constant

adjective **unchanging, continual**

noun **something that is continual or unchanging**

example sentences

Jim feels that a dog is a more **constant** companion than a cat.

The child's **constant** jumping up and down was an annoyance to the doctor.

Exercise was a **constant** in her life until she got injured.

also written in this form **constantly**

words that are similar **fixed, consistent, continual, even, firm, habitual, permanent, perpetual, steadfast, steady, unchanging, uninterrupted, unvarying**

words that are opposite **changeable, fickle, fluctuating, inconstant, irregular, unstable, unsteady**

Look up the full definition of "constant" in the dictionary and use each definition in sentences of your own creation until you feel you fully understand the word and can use it in conversation.

Write five sentences using the adjective and noun "constant":

_____

_____

_____

_____

_____

_____

_____

_____

circumstances

noun the conditions and factors that are part of determining a result or that are part of a situation or event; the overall condition of a person or thing

example sentences

His **circumstances** improved after he got the new job.

Under the **circumstances**, I don't blame her for quitting.

Susan wanted to be the new secretary, and if **circumstances** allow, she'll get the job.

words that are similar situation, condition, happening, incident, occurrence, standing, status, occasion, status

Look up the full definition of "circumstances" in the dictionary and use each definition in sentences of your own creation until you feel you fully understand the word and can use it in conversation.

Write five sentences using the noun "circumstances":

_____

_____

_____

_____

_____

_____

_____

_____

Lesson 8.4 - Vocabulary

constitute

verb to make up a whole from smaller parts

example sentences

Four wheels do not **constitute** a car.

Five cheerleaders **constituted** the cheerleading team.

Please send me the info on what **constitutes** a fully completed registration so that I can be sure not to have my application disqualified.

also written in this form **constituted, constituting**

words that are similar **comprise, form, aggregate, complete, compose, compound, construct, cook up, frame, incorporate**

Look up the full definition of "constitute" in the dictionary and use each definition in sentences of your own creation until you feel you fully understand the word and can use it in conversation.

Write five sentences using the verb "constitute":

_____

_____

_____

_____

_____

_____

_____

_____

level

noun a position on a scale, typically from low to high

verb to flatten or destroy

example sentences

I achieved a whole new **level** of friendship with Susan after we went on that Senior Trip.

The wrecking crew **leveled** the old school building.

The business deal increased the **level** of cooperation between the two companies.

also written in this form **levels, leveling, leveled**

words that are similar **bring down, destroy, demolish, rank, position, degree, grade, stage, standard, standing, status, flat, even**

words that are opposite **build, construct, uneven**

Look up the full definition of "level" in the dictionary and use each definition in sentences of your own creation until you feel you fully understand the word and can use it in conversation.

Write five sentences using the noun and verb "level":

_____

_____

_____

_____

_____

_____

_____

affect

verb **to have an impact on; to have an effect on**

example sentences

The earthquake **affected** countless families in California.

The movie **affected** him greatly, moving him to tears.

Please send me a summary of how new students might be **affected** by this policy.

also written in this form **affected, affecting, affectation**

words that are similar **influence, alter, change, impress, modify, move, touch, upset**

Look up the full definition of "affect" in the dictionary and use each definition in sentences of your own creation until you feel you fully understand the word and can use it in conversation.

Write five sentences using the verb "affect":

_____

_____

_____

_____

_____

_____

_____

_____

institute

noun an organization that studies or promotes something

verb to establish or advance

example sentences
John started a learning **institute** to help improve literacy amongst children.

After Ellen graduated in chemistry, she went to work at the **Institute** for Scientific Research & Application.

The assistant principal **instituted** a strict dress code policy.

also written in this form institution, instituted, instituting

words that are similar educational organization, academy, association, clinic, college, company, establishment, foundation, guild, hospital, orphanage, school, seminary, society, university, think tank, establish, produce, actualize, cause, embark on, enter on, initiate, found

Look up the full definition of "institute" in the dictionary and use each definition in sentences of your own creation until you feel you fully understand the word and can use it in conversation.

Write five sentences using the noun and verb "institute":

_____

_____

_____

_____

_____

_____

_____

_____

render

verb to cause to become; to make

example sentences

The cage **rendered** the bird powerless to fly away.

The illness **rendered** him unable to go to school that day.

Frank was **rendered** speechless when he heard the news.

also written in this form rendered, rendering

words that are similar deliver, distribute, exchange, minister, present, make

Look up the full definition of "render" in the dictionary and use each definition in sentences of your own creation until you feel you fully understand the word and can use it in conversation.

Write five sentences using the verb "render":

_____

_____

_____

_____

_____

_____

_____

_____

Lesson 8.5
Vocabulary Review

Draw a line matching each word to its definition. If you miss one, go back to the lesson that you missed and review by going through the steps of learning the definition of the word again.

accord •

• a sequence of actions that occur, typically in a legal setting

commit •

• agreement or unity

concern •

• obviously visible

consider •

• something that interests you because it's important or affects you

evident •

• tiny, very small or minuscule

exalt •

• to carry out or do (a job or profession) on a regular basis

intend •

• to completely dedicate yourself to something; ALSO to perform an act

minute •

• to mean to do something, to have an action as your goal

practice •

• to praise or honor; to raise up to a higher status or rank

proceedings •

• to think about, look at, or judge. To think about carefully

Reading Mastery - Level 1

accord — agreement or unity

commit — to completely dedicate yourself to something; ALSO to perform an act

concern — something that interests you because it's important or affects you

consider — to think about, look at, or judge. To think about carefully

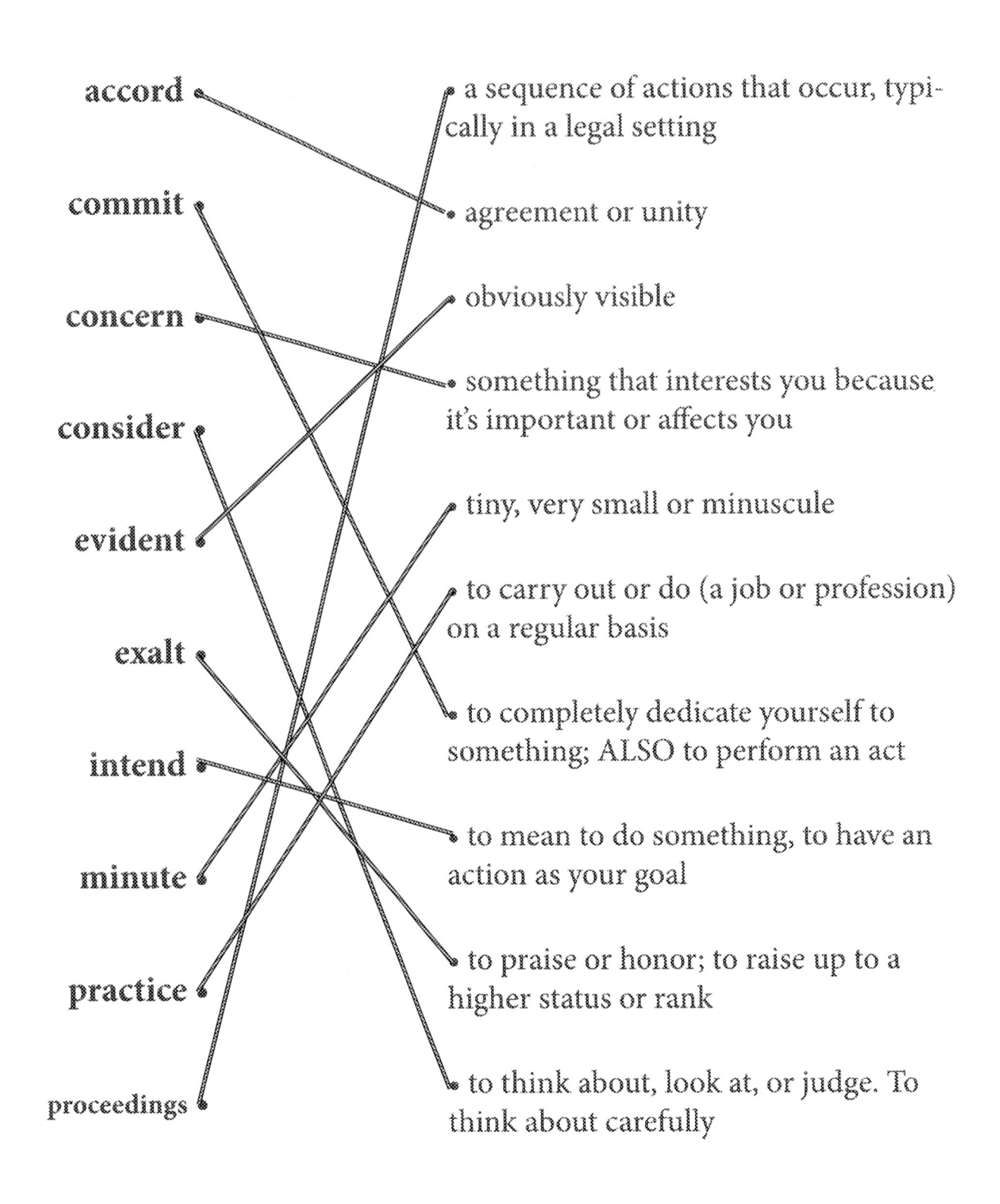

evident — obviously visible

exalt — to praise or honor; to raise up to a higher status or rank

intend — to mean to do something, to have an action as your goal

minute — tiny, very small or minuscule

practice — to carry out or do (a job or profession) on a regular basis

proceedings — a sequence of actions that occur, typically in a legal setting

Missed one? Review Lesson 8.1.

Draw a line matching each word to its definition. If you miss one, go back to the lesson that you missed and review by going through the steps of learning the definition of the word again.

approach •   • a plan of action adopted by an individual or group

conduct •
                           • a topic of concern

engage •   • not enough, insufficient, hard to come by

establish •
                           • not having any curves or interruptions

issue •
                           • the way one behaves

obtain •
                           • to get (something that isn't easy to get)

policy •   • to get near to something

scarce •   • to involve or catch

straight •   • to set up or found

utter •   • total or complete

Reading Mastery - Level 1

approach	a plan of action adopted by an individual or group
conduct	a topic of concern
engage	not enough, insufficient, hard to come by
establish	not having any curves or interruptions
issue	the way one behaves
obtain	to get (something that isn't easy to get)
policy	to get near to something
scarce	to involve or catch
straight	to set up or found
utter	total or complete

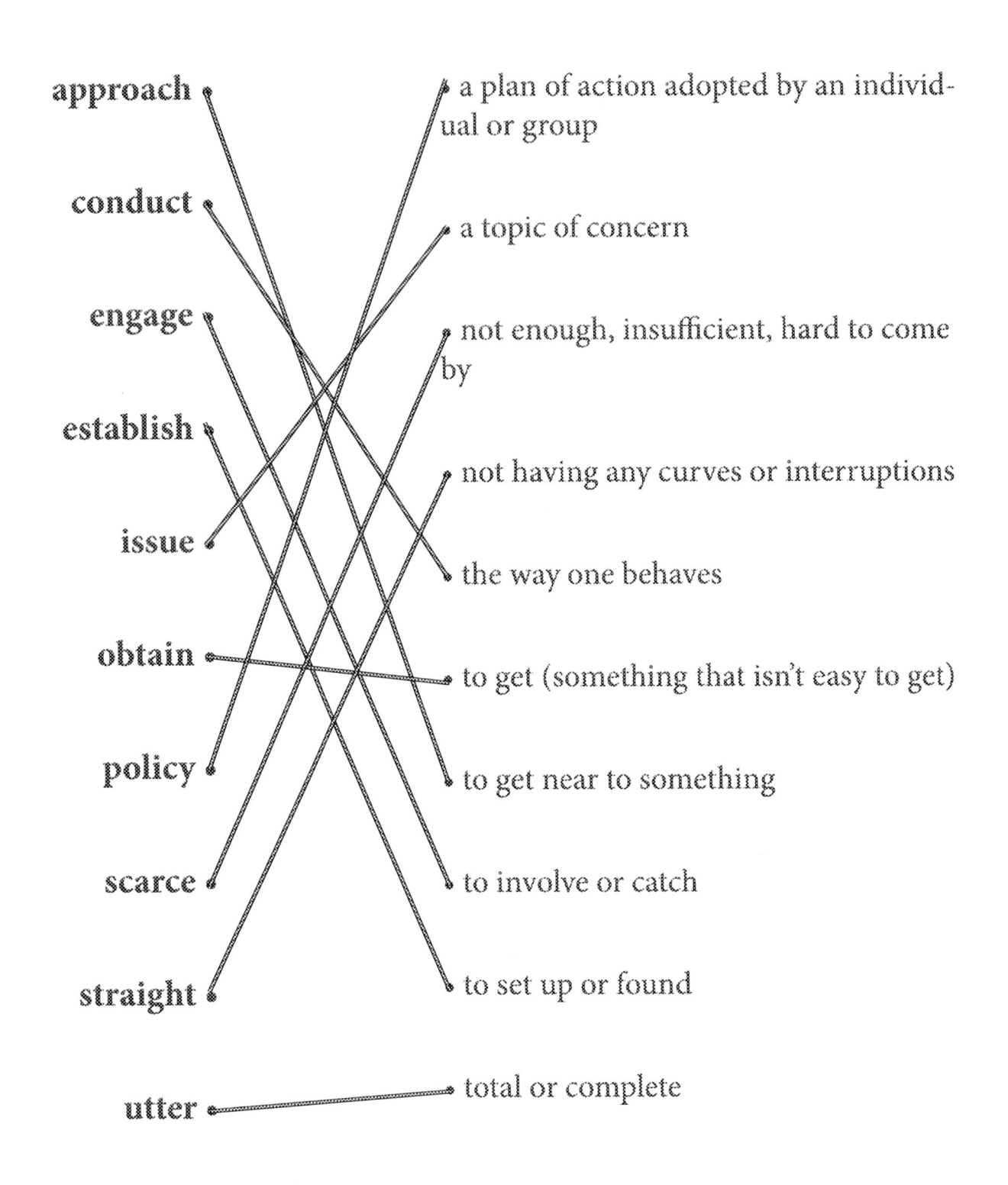

Missed one? Review Lesson 8.2.

Lesson 8.5 - Vocabulary Review

Draw a line matching each word to its definition. If you miss one, go back to the lesson that you missed and review by going through the steps of learning the definition of the word again.

apparent •   • a section of text

appoint •   • a thought or idea

concept •   • an occurrence or example

court •   • anything someone owns

fancy •   • decorated or ornamented, the opposite of plain

instance •   • obvious; what's plain to see

passage •   • to assign someone to a job

property •   • to try to win affection or favor

stock •   • too proud of oneself

vain •   • what a store has to sell; what is present and available for use or sale

219

Reading Mastery - Level 1

apparent — obvious; what's plain to see
appoint — to assign someone to a job
concept — a thought or idea
court — to try to win affection or favor
fancy — decorated or ornamented, the opposite of plain
instance — an occurrence or example
passage — a section of text
property — anything someone owns
stock — what a store has to sell; what is present and available for use or sale
vain — too proud of oneself

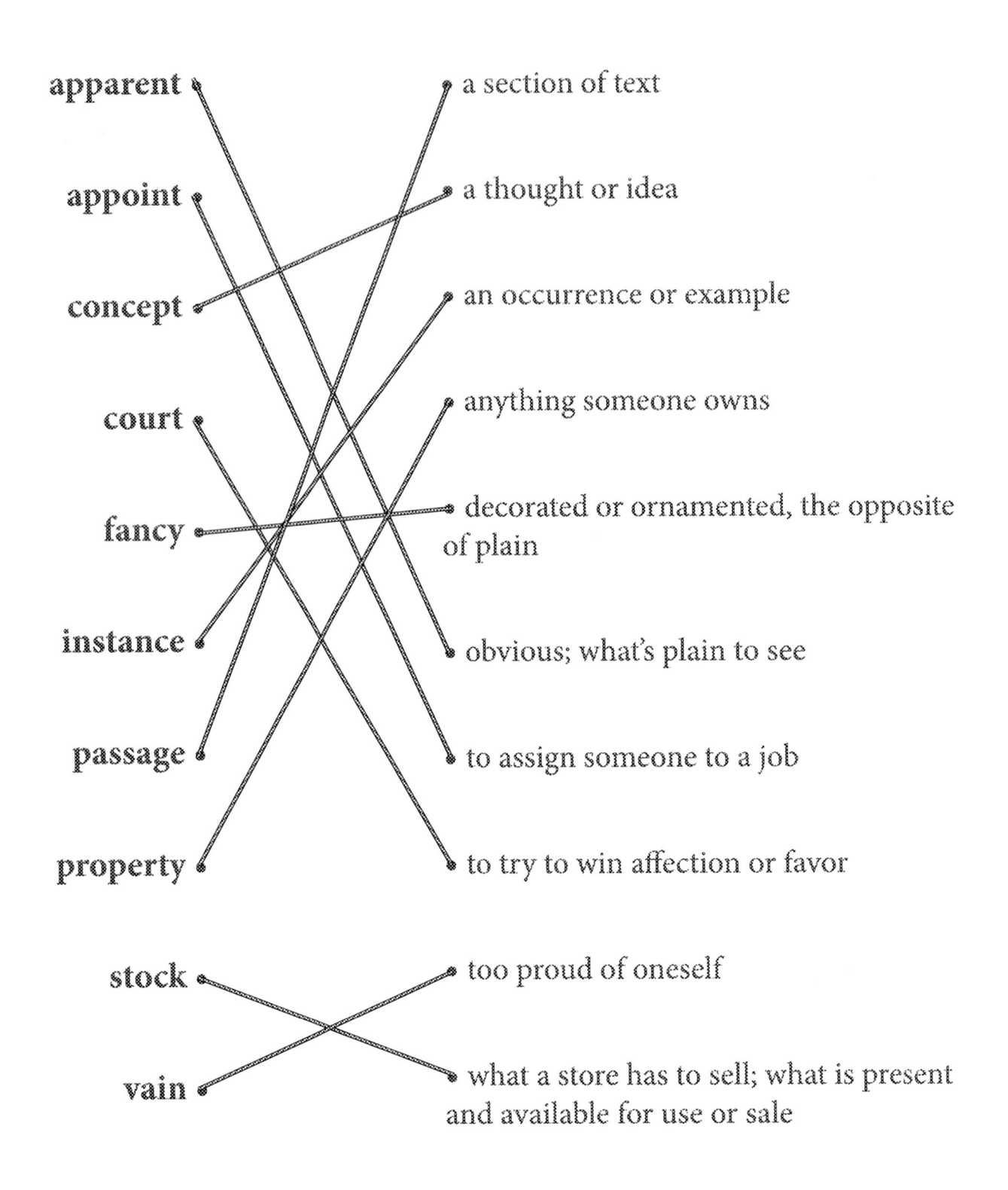

Missed one? Review Lesson 8.3.

Draw a line matching each word to its definition. If you miss one, go back to the lesson that you missed and review by going through the steps of learning the definition of the word again.

affect •

circumstances •

coast •

commission •

constant •

constitute •

institute •

level •

project •

render •

• something that is continual or unchanging

• the overall condition of a person or thing

• to cause to become

• to effortlessly move

• to establish or advance

• to flatten or destroy

• to have an impact on; to have an effect on

• to make up a whole from smaller parts

• to pass or assign responsibility

• work that is planned for or intended

Reading Mastery - Level 1

affect	something that is continual or unchanging
circumstances	the overall condition of a person or thing
coast	to cause to become
commission	to effortlessly move
constant	to establish or advance
constitute	to flatten or destroy
institute	to have an impact on; to have an effect on
level	to make up a whole from smaller parts
project	to pass or assign responsibility
render	work that is planned for or intended

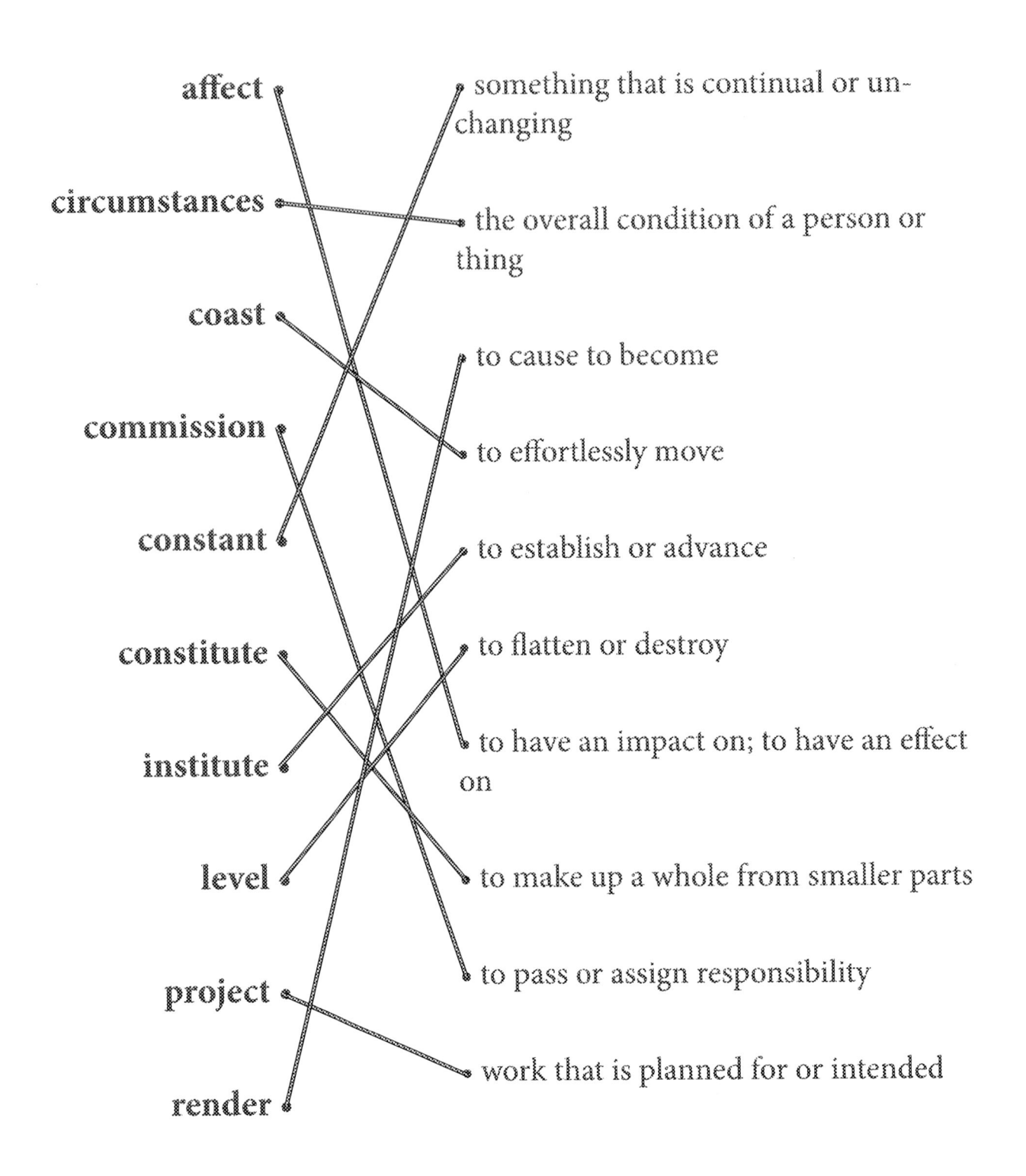

Missed one? Review Lesson 8.4.

Lesson 9
Reading Comprehension

We've covered quickly finding specific details and using them to support your answer choices. The next type of question measures your ability to understand what you are reading. In other words, these questions see if you know what's going on in the passage.

Usually these questions refer to a specific line number or paragraph, so when you see a reference to line numbers, read over what the question is talking about so you can clearly see what is being discussed and have your best shot at answering the question correctly.

If you get stuck and are unable to understand what the excerpt is talking about, use the process of elimination to arrive at the correct answer. Even if you aren't sure what the right answer is, you can usually determine which ones are wrong.

In the next mini-test, you'll skim the passage in 3 minutes (as always), and then try your hand at a number of ACT-level questions that challenge your ability to get meaning from a certain paragraph or from the passage as a whole.

After you review the answer explanations, we'll dive into some tips that can help you decipher this type of question.

Passage

Instructions: Skim the passage in 3 minutes, then answer the 10 practice questions that appear below. Use a timer to keep track of when you should start answering the questions. Just like on the ACT, you are allowed to refer to the passage in order to find the correct answers.

HUMANITIES: This passage is adapted from the essay "On Lying Awake at Night" by Stewart Edward White, which appeared in Christopher Morley's *Modern Essays* in 1921.

About once in so often you are due to lie awake at night. Why this is so I have never been able to discover. It apparently comes from no predisposing uneasiness of indigestion, no rashness in the matter of too much
5 tea or tobacco, no excitation of unusual incident or stimulating conversation. In fact, you turn in with the expectation of rather a good night's rest. Almost at once the little noises of the forest grow larger, blend in the hollow bigness of the first drowse; your thoughts drift
10 idly back and forth between reality and dream; when—snap!—you are broad awake!

Perhaps the reservoir of your vital forces is full to the overflow of a little waste; or perhaps, more subtly, the great Mother insists thus that you enter the temple
15 of her larger mysteries.

For, unlike mere insomnia, lying awake at night in the woods is pleasant. The eager, nervous straining for sleep gives way to a delicious indifference. You do not care. Your mind is cradled in an exquisite poppy-
20 suspension of judgment and of thought. Impressions slip vaguely into your consciousness and as vaguely out again. Sometimes they stand stark and naked for your inspection; sometimes they lose themselves in the mist of half-sleep. Always they lay soft velvet fingers
25 on the drowsy imagination, so that in their caressing you feel the vaster spaces from which they have come. Peaceful-brooding your faculties receive. Hearing, sight, smell—all are preternaturally keen to whatever of sound and sight and woods perfume is abroad through
30 the night; and yet at the same time active appreciation dozes, so these things lie on it sweet and cloying like fallen rose-leaves.

In such circumstance you will hear what the voyageurs call the voices of the rapids. Many people
35 never hear them at all. They speak very soft and low and distinct beneath the steady roar and dashing, beneath even the lesser tinklings and gurglings whose quality superimposes them over the louder sounds. They are like the tear-forms swimming across the field of vision,
40 which disappear so quickly when you concentrate your sight to look at them, and which reappear so magically when again your gaze turns vacant. In the stillness of your hazy half-consciousness they speak; when you bend your attention to listen, they are gone, and only
45 the tumults and the tinklings remain.

Nothing is more fantastically unreal to tell about, nothing more concretely real to experience, than this undernote of the quick water. And when you do lie awake at night, it is always making its unobtrusive appeal.
50 Gradually its hypnotic spell works. The distant chimes ring louder and nearer as you cross the borderland of sleep. And then outside the tent some little woods noise snaps the thread. An owl hoots, a whippoorwill cries, a twig cracks beneath the cautious prowl of some night
55 creature—at once the yellow sunlit French meadows puff away—you are staring at the blurred image of the moon spraying through the texture of your tent.

No beverage is more grateful than the cup of spring water you drink at such a time; no moment more
60 refreshing than that in which you look about you at the darkened forest. You have cast from you with the warm blanket the drowsiness of dreams. A coolness, physical and spiritual, bathes you from head to foot. All your senses are keyed to the last vibrations. You
65 hear the littler night prowlers; you glimpse the greater. A faint, searching woods perfume of dampness greets your nostrils. And somehow, mysteriously, in a manner not to be understood, the forces of the world seem in suspense, as though a touch might crystallize infinite
70 possibilities into infinite power and motion. But the touch lacks. The forces hover on the edge of action, unheeding the little noises. In all humbleness and awe, you are a dweller of the Silent Places.

At such a time you will meet with adventures.
75 One night we put fourteen inquisitive porcupines out of camp. Near McGregor's Bay I discovered in the large grass park of my campsite nine deer, cropping the herbage like so many beautiful ghosts. A friend tells me of a fawn that every night used to sleep outside
80 his tent and within a foot of his head, probably by way of protection against wolves. Its mother had in all likelihood been killed. The instant my friend moved toward the tent opening the little creature would disappear, and it was always gone by earliest daylight.
85 Nocturnal bears in search of pork are not uncommon. But even though your interest meets nothing but the bats and the woods shadows and the stars, that few moments of the sleeping world forces is a psychical experience to be gained in no other way. You cannot know the night
90 by sitting up; she will sit up with you. Only by coming into her presence from the borders of sleep can you meet her face to face in her intimate mood.

The night wind from the river, or from the open spaces of the wilds, chills you after a time. You begin
95 to think of your blankets. In a few moments you roll yourself in their soft wool. Instantly it is morning.

And, strange to say, you have not to pay by going through the day unrefreshed. You may feel like turning in at eight instead of nine, and you may fall asleep with
100 unusual promptitude, but your journey will begin clear-headedly, proceed springily, and end with much in reserve. No languor, no dull headache, no exhaustion, follows your experience. For this once your two hours of sleep have been as effective as nine.

224

Lesson 9 - Reading Comprehension

1. In the paragraph 2 (lines 12-15), the narrator indicates that one reason someone might lie awake at night because he or she is:

   A. in unfamiliar territory.
   B. like a water reservoir.
   C. too full of energy.
   D. afraid of ghosts.

2. The author develops paragraph 6 (lines 58-73) mainly through:

   F. an abstract allegory for the cycle of life.
   G. a vivid description of a moment standing alone in the woods in the middle of the night.
   H. an allusion to hunting and mythology.
   J. a detailed description of a dream sequence.

3. The narrator uses the sounds described in paragraph 5 (lines 46-57) primarily to depict the transition from:

   A. sleep to awake.
   B. calm to frightened.
   C. city to country.
   D. clear to blurry.

4. By his statements in paragraph 9 (lines 97-104), the narrator is most nearly asserting that:

   F. staying awake at night might leave you exhausted.
   G. you should stay awake in the woods in order to be able to go to sleep more quickly.
   H. two hours of sleep can always be as effective as nine.
   J. a night awake in the woods can be nearly as restful as a night sleeping.

5. The primary focus of paragraph 7 (lines 74-92) is to:

   A. discuss old ghost stories told with the narrator's friends.
   B. depict experiences had while camping at night.
   C. describe the ambiance of a campsite.
   D. warn the reader about bears at a campsite.

6. Which of the following statements best expresses the main idea of the passage?

   F. Many people never know the power of Mother Nature because they live in the city.
   G. People often don't know why they can't go to sleep at night.
   H. Staying awake in the woods in the middle of the night is a unique and powerful experience.
   J. Camping experiences are memorable and energizing.

7. One of the main ideas established by the first paragraph (lines 1-11) is that:

   A. many reasons explain not being able to fall asleep at night.
   B. occasionally, for reasons unexplained, you can't fall asleep.
   C. people shouldn't expect to have a good night's rest.
   D. when you wake up at night, it happens suddenly, like a snap.

8. By his statements in the second sentence (lines 17-18) in paragraph 3 (lines 16-32), the author most nearly means that:

   F. if you can't sleep, you shouldn't be nervous.
   G. lying awake at night tends to induce insomnia.
   H. failing to go to sleep makes one indifferent about life.
   J. after some time, one stops worrying about going to sleep.

9. As it is revealed in the passage, the forest at night is best described as:

   A. frightening and horrible.
   B. dull and mellow.
   C. mysterious and fantastical.
   D. dark and damp.

10. The author presents the qualities of the woods at night as exceptional because at night he:

    F. perceives the woods in a different, more wonderful way than during the day.
    G. is not in a rush like he is during the day.
    H. feels that only in the woods can you come in contact with the spirit of Mother Nature.
    J. has delightful dreams about the woods and nature.

Reading Mastery - Level 1

1. In paragraph 2 (lines 12-15), the narrator indicates that one reason someone might lie awake at night because he or she is:

   A. in unfamiliar territory.
   B. like a water reservoir.
   C. too full of energy.
   D. afraid of ghosts.

The question tells us to look in paragraph 2 (lines 12-15). Scan over the answers and find the one that matches the meaning of the paragraph. If you are unsure of the meaning in this paragraph, use the process of elimination. We can eliminate choice B, since the reservoir mentioned in this paragraph, on line 12, is a "reservoir of vital forces," not of water. "Reservoir" in this sense means "a supply or source of something." Choice D can also be eliminated, since nothing in the passage indicates that the "great Mother" is a ghost. We are left making a decision between choices A and C. Of these two, choice C is the better option. Even if we're not sure of the meaning of "the reservoir of your vital forces is full to the overflow," it definitely sounds more like "too full of energy" than "in unfamiliar territory." In this sense, "vital" means "necessary for life" and "force" means "strength or energy." The word "indicates" in the sense of the question means "points out."

2. The author develops paragraph 6 (lines 58-73) mainly through:

   F. an abstract allegory for the cycle of life.
   G. a vivid description of a moment standing alone in the woods in the middle of the night.
   H. an allusion to hunting and mythology.
   J. a detailed description of a dream sequence.

This question tests our comprehension of paragraph 6 (lines 58-73). If the answer doesn't immediately jump out at you, begin eliminating answer choices that don't work. We can knock out choice H because, although there is mention of "night prowlers," there is no discussion of hunting or mythology or even a hint of them. "Allusion" in this sense means "an expression designed to call something to mind without exactly mentioning it." We can also eliminate choice J, since the second sentence (lines 61 and 62) says "You have cast from you with the warm blanket the drowsiness of dreams." Even if we aren't sure about the meaning of choice F, choice G seems to be the better option because this paragraph is basically describing a moment in the woods at night. An "allegory," in this sense, is "a story that can be interpreted to reveal a hidden meaning." This paragraph is not a story so much as a description, so choice F doesn't work. Choice G is the best answer.

Lesson 9 - Reading Comprehension

3. The narrator uses the sounds described in paragraph 5 (46-57) primarily to depict the transition from:

    A. sleep to awake.
    B. calm to frightened.
    C. city to country.
    D. clear to blurry.

The first half of paragraph 5 (lines 46-57) describes listening to quick water as you gradually "cross the borderland of sleep." The second half of the paragraph indicates a transition: "And then outside the tent some little woods noise snaps the thread. An owl hoots, a whippoorwill cries, a twig cracks beneath the cautious prowl of some night creature—at once the yellow sunlit French meadows puff away—you are staring at the blurred image of the moon spraying through the texture of your tent." These noises being described bring the narrator back to reality. Therefore, choice A is the best answer. We can eliminate choice B because there is no mention of fear or fright in this paragraph. We can also eliminate choice C since there is no description of the city in this paragraph. Choice D doesn't work because, while a "blurred image of the moon" is mentioned at the end of the paragraph, the sounds don't contribute to this transition. In this sense, "depict" means "show using words, describe" and "transition" means "a period of changing from one condition to another."

4. By his statements in paragraph 9 (97-104), the narrator is most nearly asserting that:

    F. staying awake at night might leave you exhausted.
    G. you should stay awake in the woods in order to be able to go to sleep more quickly.
    H. two hours of sleep can always be as effective as nine.
    J. a night awake in the woods can be nearly as restful as a night sleeping.

This question is checking our understanding of the main idea of paragraph 9 (97-104). If the answer doesn't immediately jump out at us, we can use the process of elimination to make our job easier. In the sense it is used in the question, "asserting" means "stating a fact or belief confidently and forcefully." We can eliminate choice F because, while it is certainly true that staying awake at night might leave you exhausted, this isn't the narrator's entire point in this paragraph. Likewise, while the paragraph does say that "you may fall asleep with unusual promptitude," this is not the overall concept asserted by the paragraph. Keep in mind that if the question asks you for the meaning of a certain paragraph or set of lines, you want to choose the answer that applies to all of the lines referred to. The phrase, "For this once" contradicts the phrase, "two hours of sleep are as effective as nine." Therefore choice H is incorrect. The entire paragraph discusses how you can feel refreshed after a night awake in the woods, so choice J is the best answer.

227

5. The primary focus of paragraph 7 (lines 74-92) is to:

   A. discuss old ghost stories told with the narrator's friends.
   B. depict experiences had while camping at night.
   C. describe the ambiance of a campsite.
   D. warn the reader about bears at a campsite.

In the sense it is used in this question, "focus" means "the center of interest." We are being asked for the overall center of interest in this paragraph. For that reason, we can eliminate choice D, since only one sentence (line 85) mentions bears ("Nocturnal bears in search of pork are not uncommon") and this isn't even a warning. We can also eliminate choice A, since there is no mention of ghost stories. Choice B is better than choice C because, while the end of the paragraph does establish a sort of "ambiance" (which in this sense means "the character or atmosphere of a place"), the paragraph mainly discusses experiences while camping. In this sense, "experiences" mean "events or occurrences." "Primary," as it is used here, means "most important, main."

6. Which of the following statements best expresses the main idea of the passage?

   F. Many people never know the power of Mother Nature because they live in the city.
   G. People often don't know why they can't go to sleep at night.
   H. Staying awake in the woods in the middle of the night is a unique and powerful experience.
   J. Camping experiences are memorable and energizing.

We are looking for the answer choice that best describes the idea put forward by the entire passage. "Expresses," as it is used in this sense, means "says." While Mother Nature is mentioned in paragraph 2 (lines 12-15), the concept that people don't know her because they live in the city is never really discussed in the passage. We are looking for the main idea of the entire passage, not just one segment. Likewise, paragraph 1 (lines 1-11) discusses reasons why people can't sleep at night, but the entire passage is about experiences in the woods, not about difficulties sleeping, so we can eliminate choice G. Choice J is somewhat right, but choice H is a better answer. Almost all of the paragraphs fit into the concept that "staying awake in the woods in the middle of the night is a unique and powerful experience." Choice H is a more precise statement of the passage than choice J.

Lesson 9 - Reading Comprehension

7. One of the main ideas established by the first paragraph (lines 1-11) is that:
   A. many reasons explain not being able to fall asleep at night.
   B. **occasionally, for reasons unexplained, you can't fall asleep.**
   C. people shouldn't expect to have a good night's rest.
   D. when you wake up at night, it happens suddenly, like a snap.

Since the question mentions the first paragraph (lines 1-11), we look that over to find the main idea of the paragraph. Choice B jumps out at us as the correct answer, especially because it matches the first sentences of the paragraph, which seem to be an introduction to what comes next in the paragraph: "About once in so often you are due to lie awake at night. Why this is so I have never been able to discover." Let's eliminate the other choices to be sure. Choice A is contradicted by the line, "It apparently comes from no predisposing uneasiness of indigestion, no rashness in the matter of too much tea or tobacco, no excitation of unusual incident or stimulating conversation." These are reasons presented that don't explain being unable to sleep. Choice C is not supported by the paragraph. It says that "once in so often" not falling asleep happens, not regularly. While the last sentence of the paragraph describes snapping awake, this is not the subject of the entire paragraph. Therefore, choice B is best answer.

8. By his statements in the second sentence (lines 17 and 18) in paragraph 3 (lines 16-32), the author most nearly means that:
   F. if you can't sleep, you shouldn't be nervous.
   G. lying awake at night tends to induce insomnia.
   H. failing to go to sleep makes one indifferent about life.
   J. **after some time, one stops worrying about going to sleep.**

The question is asking for us to find the meaning of this sentence: "The eager, nervous straining for sleep gives way to a delicious indifference." If the answer doesn't immediately jump out at you, start eliminating the worst choices. Choice F is not supported by the passage. The sentence mentions "nervous straining," but doesn't tell us that we shouldn't be nervous about lying awake. Although the sentence that comes before mentions "insomnia," which in this sense means "inability," the sentence we are considering does not, so we can eliminate choice G. Choice H uses the word "indifferent," which means in this sense "unconcerned," and which appears in the sentence, but the answer choice has a different meaning than the question. The sentence is saying that one becomes indifferent about falling to sleep, not about life, so choice H is incorrect. Choice J is the closest fit. Going from "eager, nervous straining for sleep" to "delicious indifference" could also be described as stopping worrying.

9. As it is revealed in the passage, the forest at night is best described as:

   A. frightening and horrible.
   B. dull and mellow.
   C. mysterious and fantastical.
   D. dark and damp.

Since the entire passage concerns the forest, we know we might not be able to focus in on a specific detail to prove our answer is correct. Let's look over our choices and eliminate the ones that don't work. Choice A is incorrect because nothing in the passage indicates fright or horror. The narrator is intensely interested in these experiences in the woods, so "dull and mellow" does not work either, and therefore, we can eliminate choice B. While the woods are obviously dark at night, and some of the passage does talk about water, choice C is a better fit than choice D, "dark and damp." The author describes how "the great Mother insists thus that you enter the temple of her larger mysteries," and he creates vivid images which border on fantasy. Choice C is the best answer. "Fantastical," in this sense, means "imaginative or fanciful, not realistic."

10. The author presents the qualities of the woods at night as exceptional because at night he:

    F. perceives the woods in a different, more wonderful way than during the day.
    G. is not in a rush like he is during the day.
    H. feels that only in the woods can you come in contact with the spirit of Mother Nature.
    J. has delightful dreams about the woods and nature.

While it may be true that the author is in a rush during the day, it does not say this in the passage, so we can eliminate choice G. Choice H is also not supported by the passage. While it does mention "the Mother," it does not say that this happens only in the woods, and it also does not explain why being in the woods at night is exceptional. Choice J doesn't work because the author describes being awake in the woods, not asleep dreaming. Choice F is supported by paragraph 3 (lines 16-32), which describes the unique way the author experiences the woods while lying awake at night.

READING COMPREHENSION

There are two types of reading comprehension questions. There is the kind where you understand what is going on. These are the questions you don't have to worry about. The answer just jumps out at you, or there are only two likely answers and you're able to weigh them out and make the best choice.

The sort of reading comprehension question you have to prep for, however, is the one that asks you about a part of a passage that you didn't understand, or one which asks you a question or provides you an answer choice that is incomprehensible.

Words that you're not sure about can make it impossible to grasp what's going on with this sort of question. Let's take a look at an example:

> 5. The primary focus of paragraph 7 (lines 74-92) is to:
>   A. discuss old ghost stories told with the narrator's friends.
>   B. depict experiences had while camping at night.
>   C. describe the ambiance of a campsite.
>   D. warn the reader about bears at a campsite.

Let's say that you have eliminated choices A and D. You're not sure what *ambiance* means. Because you're not sure what it means, you're at a standstill. Sure, choice B fits somewhat, but choice C might be even better. If only you knew what that word meant!

An easy guideline to follow here is that if you have two possible answer choices, and one fits (even if it doesn't seem great) and you don't know what the other answer choice means, go with the one that fits. Resist the urge to choose the one with the big, more confusing word.

Of course, if none of the choices fit except the one that has the word you don't understand, go with the one you don't understand. That's the process of elimination at work!

Another way you can overcome not understanding a paragraph or answer choice is to focus on the emotion related to the words. Every phrase is either positive, negative, or neutral. Before you know how to use a word, you get a vague idea of what it means or what it feels like. There will be some context in your brain of how the word is used. Chances are you've been exposed to every ACT word at least once.

The key is to pay attention to the *feel* of the words and answer choices. Look at this example:

> 9. As it is revealed in the passage, the forest at night is best described as:
>   A. frightening and horrible.
>   B. dull and mellow.
>   C. mysterious and fantastical.
>   D. dark and damp.

If we don't know what the word *fantastical* means, and if we were thrown off by the passage as a whole, we can still answer this question correctly. We know that the author is pretty excited and happy about the forest. He is positive. *Frightening, horrible, dull, dark,* and *damp* are all negative words. *Mellow* is a neutral word in terms of emotion, but it is the opposite of excitement. We can eliminate these choices solely on the basis of the feeling of the words. *Fantastical* is based on the word fantastic, which is a positive word. *Mysterious* can be either positive or negative. Choice C is definitely the most positive of the bunch, so we go with that.

If you find yourself stumped by a question because you're not sure of the meaning of the passage, the question, or the answer choices, use the process of elimination, and consider the emotions of the words involved.

Another thing to keep in mind is that when a question asks you for the main idea or the primary focus, you need to choose an answer which fits the entire passage or paragraph being asked about. Just because an answer choice is mentioned in the paragraph does not mean that it's a sure bet for the answer. A good test for this is to ask yourself, "Are almost all of the sentences in the paragraph pretty much talking about this answer choice?" or "Do almost all of the paragraphs fit with the answer choice?" If the answer to this question is "no," then eliminate the choice.

In the next passage, you'll answer questions of all of the types that we have covered thus far. Be sure to focus on what the question is asking for. If it is seeking a specific detail, go find it in the passage. If it's looking for an answer that isn't specifically mentioned in the passage, find supporting details to prove an answer right. And if it's asking for you to understand something that you don't understand, use logic to eliminate bad answers and go with what's left.

Passage

Instructions: Skim the passage in 3 minutes, then answer the 10 practice questions that appear below. Use a timer to keep track of when you should start answering the questions. Just like on the ACT, you are allowed to refer to the passage in order to find the correct answers.

NATURAL SCIENCE: This passage is adapted from *Birds of the Indian Hills* by Douglas Dewar, published by Bodley Head. (Note: An ornithologist is someone who studies birds.)

The avifauna of the Himalayas is a large one. It includes birds found throughout the range, birds confined to the eastern or western portions, birds resident all through the year, birds that are mere seasonal visitors, birds found only at high elevations, birds confined to the lower hills, birds abundant everywhere, birds nowhere common. Most ornithological books treat of all these sorts and conditions of birds impartially, with the result that the non-ornithological reader who dips into them finds himself completely out of his depth.

Himalayan birds inhabit what is perhaps the most wonderful tract of country in the world. The Himalayas are not so much a chain of mountains as a mountainous country, some eighty miles broad and several hundred long—a country composed entirely of mountains and valleys with no large plains or broad plateau.

The Himalayas are a kind of Dr. Jekyll and Mr. Hyde. They have two faces—the fair and the plain. In May they are at their worst. Those of the hillsides which are not forested are brown, arid, and desolate, and the valleys, in addition to being unpleasantly hot, are dry and dusty. The foliage of the trees lacks freshness, and everywhere there is a remarkable absence of water, save in the valleys through which the rivers flow. On the other hand, September is the month in which the Himalayas attain perfection or something approaching it. The eye is refreshed by the bright emerald garment which the hills have newly donned. The foliage is green and luxuriant. Waterfalls, cascades, mighty torrents and rivulets abound. Himachal has been converted into fairyland by the monsoon rains.

A remarkable feature of the Himalayas is the abruptness with which they rise from the plains in most places. In some parts there are low foothills; but speaking generally the mountains that rise from the plain attain a height of 4000 or 5000 feet.

It is difficult for any person who has not passed from the plains of India to the Himalayas to realize fully the vast difference between the two countries and the dramatic suddenness with which the change takes place.

Thus the birds of the Himalayas inhabit a country in every respect unlike the plains of India. They dwell in a different environment, are subjected to a different climate, and feed upon different food. It is therefore not surprising that the two avifaunas should exhibit great divergence. Nevertheless few people who have not actually been in both localities are able to realize the startlingly abrupt transformation of the bird-fauna seen by one who passes from the plains to the hills.

The 5-mile journey from Rajpur to Mussoorie transports the traveler from one bird-realm to another. The caw of the house-crow is replaced by the deeper note of the corby. Instead of the crescendo shriek of the koel, the pleasing double note of the European cuckoo meets the ear. For the eternal coo-coo-coo-coo of the little brown dove, the melodious kokla-kokla of the hill green-pigeon is substituted. The harsh cries of the rose-ringed paroquets give place to the softer call of the slaty-headed species. The monotonous tonk-tonk-tonk of the coppersmith and the kutur-kutur-kutur of the green barbet are no more heard; in their stead the curious calls of the great Himalayan barbet resound among the hills. The dissonant voices of the seven sisters no longer issue from the thicket; their place is taken by the weird but less unpleasant calls of the Himalayan streaked laughing-thrushes. Even the sounds of the night are different. The chuckles and cackles of the spotted owlets no longer fill the welkin; the silence of the darkness is broken in the mountains by the low monotonous whistle of the pigmy-collared owlet.

The eye equally with the ear testifies to the traveler that when he has reached an altitude of 5000 feet he has entered another avian realm. The golden-backed woodpecker, the green bee-eater, the "blue jay" or roller, the paddy bird, the Indian and the magpie-robin, most familiar birds of the plains, are no longer seen. Their places are taken by the blue-magpies, the beautiful verditer flycatcher, the Himalayan and the black-headed jays, the black bulbul, and tits of several species.

All the birds, it is true, are not new. Some of our familiar friends of the plains are still with us. There are the kite, the scavenger vulture, the common myna, and a number of others, but these are the exceptions which prove the rule.

Scientific ornithologists recognize this great difference between the two faunas, and include the Himalayas in the Palaearctic region, while the plains form part of the Oriental region.

The chief things which affect the distribution of birds appear to be food-supply and temperature. Hence it is evident that in the Himalayas the avifauna along the snow-line differs greatly from that of the low, warm valleys. The range of temperature in all parts of the hills varies greatly with the season. At the ordinary hill stations the minimum temperature in the summer is sometimes as high as 70°, while in the winter it may drop to 23° F. Thus in midwinter many of the birds which normally live near the snow-line at 12,000 feet descend to 7000 or 6000 feet, and not a few hill birds leave the Himalayas for a time and tarry in the plains until the severity of the winter has passed away.

Lesson 9 - Reading Comprehension

1. The transition mentioned in paragraph 7 (lines 51-72) is best described by which of the following statements?

   A. The hill green-pigeon makes a more melodious sound near Mussoorie.
   B. Bird sounds are dramatically different when you travel from Rajpur to Mussoorie.
   C. The two bird-realms feature similar sounds and animals.
   D. Rajpur only has birds in zoos, while Mussoorie is populated by birds in the wild.

2. The passage most strongly emphasizes that which of the following causes a divergence in traits between the birds of the Himalayas and the birds of the plains of India?

   F. Their habitat, its climate, and the available food
   G. The sounds that the birds make
   H. Their migration from the plains to the mountains
   J. The difference in language between the areas' inhabitants

3. According to the passage, which of the following phrases most accurately characterizes the Himalayas in May?

   A. Evil and menacing
   B. Bright and green
   C. Dry and hot
   D. Fresh and remarkable

4. The passage notes that all of the following birds are found in the Himalayas, EXCEPT the:

   F. Corby
   G. Golden-backed woodpecker
   H. Hill green-pigeon
   J. Himalayan barbet

5. One of the main ideas established by the passage is that:

   A. September is much more pleasant than May in the Himalayas.
   B. the Himalayas have a higher altitude than the Indian plains.
   C. Rajpur and Mussoorie are two cities within 5 miles of the Himalayas.
   D. the birds of the Himalayas are very different from the birds in the plains of India.

6. According to the passage, having which of the following experiences would have the largest impact on an observer's understanding of the difference between birds in the Indian plains and those in the Himalayas?

   F. Studying the food-supply and temperatures of the region
   G. Reading about both areas thoroughly
   H. Actually visiting both places
   J. Going on an expedition in the Himalayas

7. When the author says that the Himalayas are "a kind of Dr. Jekyll and Mr. Hyde," he most nearly means that:

   A. the Himalayas can be deadly in the wrong conditions.
   B. the birds of the Himalayas are very different from the birds of the Indian plains.
   C. depending on the season, the area can be inhospitable or welcoming.
   D. the Himalayas always look refreshing and luxuriant, even if the truth isn't what meets the eye.

8. The details described in the first paragraph (lines 1-10) can best explain:

   F. why the author only writes about the Himalayas.
   G. the fact that so many ornithologists visit the Himalayas.
   H. the extinction of many bird species in the areas surrounding the Himalayas.
   J. the diversity of birds found in the Himalayas.

9. Information contained in the last paragraph (lines 92-104) indicates that research into the distribution of birds in the Himalayas has found that it varies mainly as a result of changes in:

   A. available food and in the climate.
   B. altitude.
   C. bird population numbers.
   D. location.

10. The passage states that birds that normally live near the snow-line might descend several thousand feet during:

    F. midwinter.
    G. midsummer.
    H. autumn.
    J. spring.

1. The transition mentioned in paragraph 7 (lines 51-72) is best described by which of the following statements?
   A. The hill green-pigeon makes a more melodious sound near Mussoorie.
   B. Bird sounds are dramatically different when you travel from Rajpur to Mussoorie.
   C. The two bird-realms feature similar sounds and animals.
   D. Rajpur only has birds in zoos, while Mussoorie is populated by birds in the wild.

The transition being referred to in this question is traveling from one bird-realm to another. A "transition," in this sense, means "changing from one state or condition to another." While the author describes hearing the green-pigeon instead of the brown dove as one approaches Mussoorie, this doesn't mean that the green-pigeon is less melodious near Rajpur. We can eliminate choice A. Choice C doesn't work because the entire paragraph describes the differences between birds near Mussoorie and those near Rajpur, not their similarities. Choice D is not supported at all by the passage: there is no mention of zoos. Choice B is the best answer. The paragraph describes how, as one travels to Mussoorie from Rajpur, the bird-sounds become completely different. The word "dramatically," in this sense, means "in a way that impresses." When the answer choice says that the bird sounds are dramatically different, it means that they are different in a way that you clearly notice.

2. The passage most strongly emphasizes that which of the following causes a divergence in traits between the birds of the Himalayas and the birds of the plains of India?
   F. Their habitat, its climate, and the available food
   G. The sounds that the birds make
   H. Their migration from the plains to the mountains
   J. The difference in language between the areas' inhabitants

Look for the unique word "divergence." We find it in paragraph 6, in lines 43-47, which states, "They dwell in a different environment, are subjected to a different climate, and feed upon different food. It is therefore not surprising that the two avifaunas should exhibit great divergence." This statement best supports choice F. While these supporting statements do not completely spell out the connection, it makes choice F more attractive than the rest of the choices. The word "avifaunas" means "birds of a particular region." It isn't logical to suppose that the sounds a bird makes could fundamentally change the traits of birds, and this idea isn't supported by the passage in any event, so we can eliminate G. While the first paragraph (lines 1-10) mentions birds that are "seasonal visitors," there is no mention of a migration in the passage, so choice H can be knocked out. Choice J is incorrect because nowhere does it mention differences in language or even the inhabitants of the areas at all. This is a passage totally centered around birds.

Lesson 9 - Reading Comprehension

3. According to the passage, which of the following phrases most accurately characterizes the Himalayas in May?

    A. Evil and menacing
    B. Bright and green
    C. Dry and hot
    D. Fresh and remarkable

We look for the unique word "May" and find it in paragraph 3 (lines 17-31). This sentence describes the Himalayas in May: "Those of the hillsides which are not forested are brown, arid, and desolate, and the valleys, in addition to being unpleasantly hot, are dry and dusty. The foliage of the trees lacks freshness, and everywhere there is a remarkable absence of water, save in the valleys through which the rivers flow." This description fits most closely with choice C.

4. The passage notes that all of the following birds are found in the Himalayas, EXCEPT the:

    F. Corby
    G. Golden-backed woodpecker
    H. Hill green-pigeon
    J. Himalayan barbet

Paragraph 7 (lines 51-72) mentions several of the birds that can be found in the Himalayas. This paragraph describes a journey from Rajpur to Mussoorie. We can conclude that Mussoorie, and not Rajpur, is in the Himalayas because one sentence says, "The dissonant voices of the seven sisters no longer issue from the thicket; their place is taken by the weird but less unpleasant calls of the Himalayan streaked laughing-thrushes," so we know that the transition to Mussoorie is into the Himalayas. In this paragraph are mentioned the hill green-pigeon, the corby, and the Himalayan barbet, so we can eliminate these choices. In paragraph 8 (lines 73-82), it says that, as part of this transition, "the golden-backed woodpecker, the green bee-eater, the 'blue jay' or roller, the paddy bird, the Indian and the magpie-robin, most familiar birds of the plains, are no longer seen," so choice G is the best answer.

5. One of the main ideas established by the passage is that:

    A. September is much more pleasant than May in the Himalayas.
    B. the Himalayas have a higher altitude than the Indian plains.
    C. Rajpur and Mussoorie are two cities within 5 miles of the Himalayas.
    D. the birds of the Himalayas are very different from the birds in the plains of India.

Choices A, B, and C are all facts that are established by the passage, but they are not main ideas. One paragraph might support these facts, but they are not central points of the passage. Choice D is a much better statement of one of the passage's main ideas, since the concept of the difference between the Himalayas and the plains are covered again and again by the passage's paragraphs.

6. According to the passage, having which of the following experiences would have the largest impact on an observer's understanding of the difference between birds in the Indian plains and those in the Himalayas?

F. Studying the food-supply and temperatures of the region
G. Reading about both areas thoroughly
H. **Actually visiting both places**
J. Going on an expedition in the Himalayas

We scan for a paragraph that will help support our conclusion about understanding the difference between the birds in these two regions. Paragraph 6 (lines 42-50) discusses this topic exclusively, and ends with the sentence, "Nevertheless few people who have not actually been in both localities are able to realize the startlingly abrupt transformation of the bird-fauna seen by one who passes from the plains to the hills." This best supports choice H. "Fauna," in this sense, means "the animals of a particular region." We can eliminate choices F, G, and J. They are all plausible answers, but they are not directly supported by details in the passage. Paragraph 11 states in lines 92-93 that "The chief things which affect the distribution of birds appear to be food-supply and temperature," but this does not indicate that this would have a large impact on an observer's understanding of the difference, so we eliminate choice F. Choice G is not recommended directly in the passage, so eliminate that choice as well. Likewise, choice J is not supported by the passage, so we eliminate that.

7. When the author says that the Himalayas are "a kind of Dr. Jekyll and Mr. Hyde," he most nearly means that:

A. the Himalayas can be deadly in the wrong conditions.
B. the birds of the Himalayas are very different from the birds of the Indian plains.
C. **depending on the season, the area can be inhospitable or welcoming.**
D. the Himalayas always look refreshing and luxuriant, even if the truth isn't what meets the eye.

First, find where the unique phrase "a kind of Dr. Jekyll and Mr. Hyde" appears: paragraph 3, in lines 17-18. Let's eliminate answers before we settle on our final choice. While the paragraph does describe an "absence of water," a "desolate" area, it doesn't go so far as to say that they Himalayas are deadly, so we can't immediately choose choice A as the correct answer. While the main idea of the whole passage centers around choice B, paragraph 3 (lines 17-31) does not mention birds at all, so choice B is incorrect. We can eliminate choice D because the paragraph says that "in May they are at their worst..." and goes on to describe a landscape that is anything but "refreshing and luxuriant." Choice C is supported by the fact that May is described as "inhospitable" (which in this sense means "harsh and difficult to live in") with such words as "desolate" and "unpleasantly hot," while in September it says the Himalayas "attain perfection or something approaching it." "Desolate" in this sense means "depressingly empty or bare."

Lesson 9 - Reading Comprehension

8. The details described in the first paragraph (lines 1-10) can best explain:

   F. why the author only writes about the Himalayas.
   G. the fact that so many ornithologists visit the Himalayas.
   H. the extinction of many bird species in the areas surrounding the Himalayas.
   J. the diversity of birds found in the Himalayas.

The details provided in the first paragraph (lines 1-10) best support the idea that there is a broad diversity of birds to be found in the Himalayas, so choice J is the best answer. "Diversity" in this sense means "variety; a range of different things." Extinction is never mentioned in this paragraph, so we can eliminate choice H. While a diversity of birds might cause a number of ornithologists to visit a particular area, we don't have enough supporting details to draw this conclusion. Choice G is a weak choice. Choice F is not supported by the passage at all: We don't know if the author writes only about the Himalayas or not, but there being a wide variety of bird species there does not allow us to draw the conclusion that this is the only thing the author writes about. An ornithologist is "a scientist who studies birds."

9. Information contained in the last paragraph (lines 92-104) indicates that research into the distribution of birds in the Himalayas has found that it varies mainly as a result of changes in:

   A. available food and in the climate.
   B. altitude.
   C. bird population numbers.
   D. location.

The first sentence (lines 92-93) of this paragraph states the main idea: "The chief things which affect the distribution of birds appear to be food-supply and temperature." Since "available food and climate" is another way of saying "food-supply and temperature," choice A is best supported by the passage. We can eliminate choice D since we are talking about only one location in this paragraph: the Himalayas. Nowhere in the paragraph does it mention bird population numbers or overcrowding, so we eliminate choice C. While altitude is mentioned several times, it is not described as something which causes birds to be distributed in certain ways. Therefore, choice B is an incorrect answer. In this sense, "altitude" means "height above sea level or ground level."

10. The passage states that birds that normally live near the snow-line might descend several thousand feet during:

    F. midwinter.
    G. midsummer.
    H. autumn.
    J. spring.

We scan for where the passage uses the words "snow-line" and "descend." These words are found in the last paragraph, in lines 100-102: "Thus in midwinter many of the birds which normally live near the snow-line at 12,000 feet descend to 7000 or 6000 feet." Therefore, choice F is the best answer. In this sense, "descend" means "move downward."

Lesson 10.1
Vocabulary

appeal

noun to ask

verb the act of asking

example sentences

Susan **appealed** to her teacher's better nature and got an opportunity to re-test.

The principal is considering our club's **appeal** today.

One can't deny that the job offering he received has a certain **appeal**.

also written in this form **appealing, appealed**

words that are similar **address, application, petition, prayer, proposal, question, recourse, submission**

words that are opposite **denial, disavowal, disclaimer, refusal, retraction, revocation**

Look up the full definition of "appeal" in the dictionary and use each definition in sentences of your own creation until you feel you fully understand the word and can use it in conversation.

Write five sentences using the verb and noun "appeal":

_____

_____

_____

_____

_____

_____

_____

_____

generate

verb **to produce or create**

example sentences

He **generated** a lot of interest in the play by handing out flyers to his friends.

His mother told him that once he's an adult he'll need to **generate** his own revenue.

I wish I could **generate** more enthusiasm for my math lesson.

also written in this form **generating, generated, generation**

words that are similar **breed, bring about, cause, develop, found, make, originate, parent, set up, whip up**

words that are opposite **break, destroy, halt, kill, stop**

Look up the full definition of "generate" in the dictionary and use each definition in sentences of your own creation until you feel you fully understand the word and can use it in conversation.

Write five sentences using the verb "generate":

_____

_____

_____

_____

_____

_____

_____

_____

theory

noun a set of beliefs or principles that may or may not be proven yet

example sentences

The scientist advanced his newest **theory** of physics at the conference.

Joe had a **theory** that Rebecca secretly had a crush on Damian.

For all her study of musical **theory**, you would think that she knew how to play an instrument.

also written in this form theories, theorize

words that are similar hypothesis, belief, concept, conjecture, guesswork, premise, thesis, suspicion, supposition

words that are opposite certainty, fact, proof, law

Look up the full definition of "theory" in the dictionary and use each definition in sentences of your own creation until you feel you fully understand the word and can use it in conversation.

Write five sentences using the noun "theory":

_____

_____

_____

_____

_____

_____

_____

range

noun a variety of things or activities

example sentences

There is a broad **range** of clubs and activities from which you may choose.

The baseball scout was impressed with the wide **range** of skills that Jim demonstrated he could exercise.

In the review class, we took up a **range** of subjects from basic math to advanced calculus.

also written in this form **ranged, ranging**

words that are similar **sphere, distance, extent, area, bounds, gamut, panorama, span, spectrum, spread, stretch**

Look up the full definition of "range" in the dictionary and use each definition in sentences of your own creation until you feel you fully understand the word and can use it in conversation.

Write five sentences using the noun "range":

_____

_____

_____

_____

_____

_____

_____

_____

campaign

noun a series of actions or occurrences designed to achieve a specific result

example sentences

The church began a letter writing **campaign** to raise awareness about the need to adequately fund homeless shelters.

John Smith's political **campaign** has been gaining momentum since day one.

Suzy has been on a tireless **campaign** to get her sister to keep their room cleaner.

also written in this form campaigned, campaigning

words that are similar crusade, drive, operation, attempt to win

Look up the full definition of "campaign" in the dictionary and use each definition in sentences of your own creation until you feel you fully understand the word and can use it in conversation.

Write five sentences using the noun "campaign":

_____

_____

_____

_____

_____

_____

_____

_____

league

noun a group or federation with a common purpose or goal

example sentences

The **League** of Nations was an organization created to help forward the aims of its member nations and promote peace.

Darius was in **league** with his brother to throw his mother a surprise party.

That kid is in my baseball **league**.

words that are similar association, federation, alliance, band, confederacy, group, guild, organization, partnership, union

Look up the full definition of "league" in the dictionary and use each definition in sentences of your own creation until you feel you fully understand the word and can use it in conversation.

Write five sentences using the noun "league":

_____

_____

_____

_____

_____

_____

_____

_____

labor

noun **any piece of work undertaken or attempted**

verb **to do work**

example sentences

I **labored** all night to finish my term paper.

He only worked because he would be compensated for his **labor**.

The contractor would like to know what the cost of **labor** would be for digging that ditch.

also written in this form **labored, labors, laboring**

words that are similar **work, undertaking, activity, chore, endeavor, toil, travail, strain, stress, industry, exertion**

words that are opposite **entertainment, fun**

Look up the full definition of "labor" in the dictionary and use each definition in sentences of your own creation until you feel you fully understand the word and can use it in conversation.

Write five sentences using the noun and verb "labor":

_____

_____

_____

_____

_____

_____

_____

_____

confer

verb **to talk with and consult; ALSO to bestow, assign or grant**

example sentences

Before I can sign that deal, I must **confer** with my associates.

John thought we should **confer** about buying a new family car.

His teachers **conferred** upon him the status of Student of the Year.

also written in this form **conferred, conferring**

words that are similar **discuss, deliberate, bargain, debate, discourse, negotiate, speak, talk, treat**

Look up the full definition of "confer" in the dictionary and use each definition in sentences of your own creation until you feel you fully understand the word and can use it in conversation.

Write five sentences using the verb "confer":

_____

_____

_____

_____

_____

_____

_____

grant

verb to let someone have something or fulfill a request

example sentences

The judge **granted** his request for a hearing.

I doubt the governor will **grant** any pardons until the election has passed.

If you will please **grant** him a loan, he will pay you back within a month.

also written in this form **granting, granted**

words that are similar **allowance, gift, admission, allocation, appropriation, contributation, handout, present, privilege, accept, admit, allow, give the go-ahead**

words that are opposite **forfeit, loss, refuse**

Look up the full definition of "grant" in the dictionary and use each definition in sentences of your own creation until you feel you fully understand the word and can use it in conversation.

Write five sentences using the verb "grant":

_____

_____

_____

_____

_____

_____

_____

_____

dwell

verb **to live in; ALSO to think moodily or anxiously about something**

example sentences

Jerry **dwelled** in his parents' house until the age of 21, when he transferred to a college in another state.

His counselor told him that he shouldn't **dwell** too much on the past.

If we move to Oregon, where will we **dwell**?

also written in this form **dwelling, dwelled**

words that are similar **live in, lodge, occupy, remain, reside, ponder, think, worry**

Look up the full definition of "dwell" in the dictionary and use each definition in sentences of your own creation until you feel you fully understand the word and can use it in conversation.

Write five sentences using the verb "dwell":

_____
_____
_____
_____
_____
_____
_____
_____
_____

Lesson 10.2
Vocabulary

entertain

verb to provide interesting amusement to others; ALSO to take into consideration

example sentences

He **entertained** his guests with the new movie.

I don't want to **entertain** that notion until you tell me the bottom line of how much it will cost.

Jim was fully **entertained** by the Shakespearean play.

also written in this form **entertained, entertaining, entertainment**

words that are similar **absorb, interest, please, recreate, captivate, charm cheer, delight, enliven, humor, pique, stimulates**

words that are opposite **bore, tire**

Look up the full definition of "entertain" in the dictionary and use each definition in sentences of your own creation until you feel you fully understand the word and can use it in conversation.

Write five sentences using the verb "entertain":

_____

_____

_____

_____

_____

_____

_____

contract

noun an agreement that is both binding and enforceable by law

verb to hire; ALSO to shrink

example sentences

He had to sign a **contract** before he moved into his new apartment.

She didn't want to enter into a **contract** with the company, but they left her no choice.

Their business kept **contracting** until only one person was working there.

also written in this form contracted, contracting, contraction

words that are similar agreement, deal, commitment, compact, understanding, shrink

words that are opposite disagreement, discord, grow, enlarge, expand

Look up the full definition of "contract" in the dictionary and use each definition in sentences of your own creation until you feel you fully understand the word and can use it in conversation.

Write five sentences using the verb and noun "contract":

_____

_____

_____

_____

_____

_____

_____

earnest

adjective being serious about something

example sentences

Tim was **earnest** about his new job, unlike Gary who had been working there for a long time.

If you would be more **earnest** about your studies, you might get better grades.

I think she's too **earnest** about winning those carnival games.

also written in this form earnestly, earnestness

words that are similar enthusiastic, ardent, devoted, eager, purposeful, sincere, wholehearted

words that are opposite flippant, unconcerned, unenthusiastic

Look up the full definition of "earnest" in the dictionary and use each definition in sentences of your own creation until you feel you fully understand the word and can use it in conversation.

Write five sentences using the adjective "earnest":

_____

_____

_____

_____

_____

_____

_____

_____

yield

verb produce or provide; ALSO to give way to arguments, demands or pressure

example sentences

The investment **yielded** her an extra $1.00 for every $10.00 she put in.

You must **yield** to oncoming traffic or you'll end up in a wreck.

James **yielded** to his sense of caution and decided not to dive off the twenty-foot diving board.

also written in this form yielded, yielding

words that are similar crop, earnings, harvest, income, output, outturn, revenue, assent, go with the flow, concede, cede, defer

words that are opposite deny, oppose, prevent

Look up the full definition of "yield" in the dictionary and use each definition in sentences of your own creation until you feel you fully understand the word and can use it in conversation.

Write five sentences using the verb "yield":

_____

_____

_____

_____

_____

_____

_____

_____

wander

verb to move without direction; to drift aimlessly

example sentences

His mind **wandered** from one problem to the next until he fell asleep.

The poet liked to **wander** through the woods to clear his head.

There is no time for **wandering** because we have somewhere to go.

also written in this form **wandered, wandering**

words that are similar **deviate, float, drift, ramble**

words that are opposite **stay**

Look up the full definition of "wander" in the dictionary and use each definition in sentences of your own creation until you feel you fully understand the word and can use it in conversation.

Write five sentences using the verb "wander":

_____

_____

_____

_____

_____

_____

_____

_____

insist

verb to demand; ALSO to swear that something is true

example sentences

If you **insist** on being so picky about your food, you might starve.

Danny always **insisted** that we buckle our safety belts before he put the car in drive.

She **insisted** that she wasn't the one that cheated on the test.

also written in this form insisting, insisted, insistance

words that are similar assert, persist, require, swear, vow, demand, contend

words that are opposite forget, tolerate

Look up the full definition of "insist" in the dictionary and use each definition in sentences of your own creation until you feel you fully understand the word and can use it in conversation.

Write five sentences using the verb "insist":

_____

_____

_____

_____

_____

_____

_____

_____

knight

noun a noble warrior, usually in heavy armor, from the Middle Ages; informally, someone who is brave or chivalrous

example sentences

I read about the **Knights** of the Round Table in English class.

Knights were trained in fighting on horseback.

Brianna's boyfriend was a **knight** of old in her eyes.

words that are similar cavalier, champion, gallant, chevalier, gentleman, horseman, paladin

Look up the full definition of "knight" in the dictionary and use each definition in sentences of your own creation until you feel you fully understand the word and can use it in conversation.

Write five sentences using the noun "knight":

_____

_____

_____

_____

_____

_____

_____

_____

convince

verb to talk someone into something or get someone to change his or her mind to your point of view

example sentences

Darryl worked at **convincing** his parents to allow him to go to his friend's party for ages.

You'll need to be more **convincing** if you want me to reconsider the score on your essay.

She didn't look **convinced**, even after I completed my presentation.

also written in this form convincing, convinced

words that are similar argue into, bring to reason, induce, make a believer, prove, talk into, turn

Look up the full definition of "convince" in the dictionary and use each definition in sentences of your own creation until you feel you fully understand the word and can use it in conversation.

Write five sentences using the verb "convince":

_____
_____
_____
_____
_____
_____
_____
_____

inspire

verb **to excite or encourage; to cause to take action**

example sentences

The book I read **inspired** me to try a diet one more time.

Louise enjoys hearing the lectures because they **inspire** her to do great things.

He always loved sports movies that were **inspired** by a true story.

also written in this form **inspiring, inspired, inspiration, inspirational**

words that are similar **encourage, stimulate, enliven, excite, galvanize, impress, infuse, instill, invigorate, motivate, stir**

words that are opposite **discourage, dissuade**

Look up the full definition of "inspire" in the dictionary and use each definition in sentences of your own creation until you feel you fully understand the word and can use it in conversation.

Write five sentences using the verb "inspire":

_____

_____

_____

_____

_____

_____

_____

convention

noun a meeting, typically of a particular group; ALSO the normal or accepted way of doing things

example sentences

Paul did not know that he had received the most votes until the last day of the Youth Legislature **convention**.

It is a **convention** to not speak with your mouth full of food.

The city is expecting more visitors than ever before because of the unusually high number of **conventions** being held this year in its convention center.

also written in this form **conventional**

words that are similar **conference, assembly, congress, get together, meeting, rally**

Look up the full definition of "convention" in the dictionary and use each definition in sentences of your own creation until you feel you fully understand the word and can use it in conversation.

Write five sentences using the noun "convention":

_____

_____

_____

_____

_____

_____

_____

Lesson 10.3
Vocabulary

skill

noun **an ability gained from practice or training**

example sentences

The young man went to swimming lessons so that he could improve his aquatic **skills**.

The robber was infamous for his **skills** of stealth and deception.

George took a class on improving test taking **skills**.

also written in this form **skills, skilled**

words that are similar **ability, talent, aptitude, deftness, expertise, prowess, technique**

words that are opposite **inability, incapability, inexperience**

Look up the full definition of "skill" in the dictionary and use each definition in sentences of your own creation until you feel you fully understand the word and can use it in conversation.

Write five sentences using the noun "skill":

_____

_____

_____

_____

_____

_____

_____

harried

adjective having the feeling of being asked for or attacked from all sides

example sentences

Joan gets **harried** when it's her day to do payroll for the company.

The mother was always **harried** after she had her fourth child.

Elizabeth told her **harried** friend to sit down, take a deep breath, and relax.

also written in this form **harried, harrying**

words that are similar **pester, annoy, bedevil, disturb, perturb, pillage, tease, torment, upset**

words that are opposite **aid, assist, help, support**

Look up the full definition of "harried" in the dictionary and use each definition in sentences of your own creation until you feel you fully understand the word and can use it in conversation.

Write five sentences using the adjective "harried":

_____

_____

_____

_____

_____

_____

_____

_____

financial

adjective having to do with money

example sentences

He eventually had to close his business because he failed to meet his **financial** obligations.

The book claimed that it would help you improve your **financial** health.

The committee asked for a **financial** statement from the company it was examining.

also written in this form **finance**

words that are similar **banking, economic, fiscal, monetary, money**

Look up the full definition of "financial" in the dictionary and use each definition in sentences of your own creation until you feel you fully understand the word and can use it in conversation.

Write five sentences using the adjective "financial":

_____

_____

_____

_____

_____

_____

_____

_____

reflect

verb to throw or bend back from a surface or show an image of; ALSO to show or give evidence of

example sentences

Yolanda checked her hair in the view **reflected** from the mirror to make sure it was perfect.

His misbehavior **reflects** the poor job his parents did in teaching him manners.

Please don't do anything that **reflects** poorly on the firm.

also written in this form reflection, reflecting, reflected

words that are similar mirror, rebound, cast, catch, copy, echo, emulate, reproduce, resonate, demonstrate, indicate, express, display, manifest, reveal, show

Look up the full definition of "reflect" in the dictionary and use each definition in sentences of your own creation until you feel you fully understand the word and can use it in conversation.

Write five sentences using the verb "reflect":

novel

adjective **something new, original, not seen before**

noun **a long fictional work of prose**

example sentences

When we went to the technology fair we saw several **novel** inventions.

When he repeated all of the same advice I had given her, it irritated me that she acted as though what he was saying was completely **novel**.

Ricky liked reading **novels** because they transported him into different world of imagination.

words that are similar **new, original, breaking new ground, innovative, uncommon, unique, unusual, singular, rare**

words that are opposite **common, familiar, old, ordinary, overused, used, usual, worn**

Look up the full definition of "novel" in the dictionary and use each definition in sentences of your own creation until you feel you fully understand the word and can use it in conversation.

Write five sentences using the noun and adjective "novel":

_____

_____

_____

_____

_____

_____

_____

_____

furnish

verb to provide something that is needed

example sentences

The apartment was **furnished** with everything they needed to move in.

The test administrator **furnished** each student with scratch paper and two pencils.

Jerry's new job should **furnish** him with the income he needs to provide for his family.

also written in this form furnished, furnishing

words that are similar afford, aid, assist, serve, submit, support, supply, decorate, outfit, provide, provision

Look up the full definition of "furnish" in the dictionary and use each definition in sentences of your own creation until you feel you fully understand the word and can use it in conversation.

Write five sentences using the verb "furnish":

_____

_____

_____

_____

_____

_____

_____

_____

compel

verb to force someone to do something

example sentences

The police officers **compelled** the criminal to go to prison.

I felt **compelled** to open the door, although I did not know what awaited me behind it.

Jimmy's mom was always **compelling** him to obey by grabbing his ear.

also written in this form **compelled, compelling**

words that are similar **force to act, coerce, drive, enforce, oblige, necessitate, enforce, urge**

words that are opposite **block, delay, impede, obstruct, stop**

Look up the full definition of "compel" in the dictionary and use each definition in sentences of your own creation until you feel you fully understand the word and can use it in conversation.

Write five sentences using the verb "compel":

_____

_____

_____

_____

_____

_____

_____

venture

noun an action or pursuit that is risky but could be rewarding

verb to go somewhere despite possible dangers

example sentences

Starting the candy shop at the school was a **venture** the club hoped would pay for Senior Prom.

He **ventured** into the wilderness without even shoes to protect his feet.

William had a possible business **venture** to discuss with his father.

also written in this form **ventured, venturing**

words that are similar **gamble, attempt, chance, deal, enterprise, experiment, investment, project, pursuit, risk, speculation, undertaking**

Look up the full definition of "venture" in the dictionary and use each definition in sentences of your own creation until you feel you fully understand the word and can use it in conversation.

Write five sentences using the verb and noun "venture":

_____

_____

_____

_____

_____

_____

_____

_____

territory

noun the area under the control of someone else; any region

example sentences

The salesman's **territory** stretched all the way to the Mississippi River.

World War I's beginnings had a lot to do with squabbling about **territory**.

The guard said that it wasn't really his **territory** to decide whether or not he could let us in without a pass.

also written in this form **territories**

words that are similar **domain, region, area, boundary, dominion, expanse, extent, field, section, sector, sphere, state, zone**

Look up the full definition of "territory" in the dictionary and use each definition in sentences of your own creation until you feel you fully understand the word and can use it in conversation.

Write five sentences using the noun "territory":

_____

_____

_____

_____

_____

_____

_____

_____

temper

noun **tending to display uncontrolled anger; a sudden outburst of anger**

verb **to restrain**

example sentences

He had to take an anger management class because he had such a **temper**.

In social settings, it's best to control your **temper** and hear what the other side has to say before jumping to any conclusions.

Mary was a good drama teacher because she would **temper** any criticism by pointing out what she liked about the performance as well.

also written in this form **tempered, tempering**

words that are similar **mad, blow up, annoyance, antagonism, hatred, irritation, infuriation**

words that are opposite **calmness, contentment, enjoyment, good nature, happiness**

Look up the full definition of "temper" in the dictionary and use each definition in sentences of your own creation until you feel you fully understand the word and can use it in conversation.

Write five sentences using the noun and verb "temper":

_____

_____

_____

_____

_____

_____

_____

Lesson 10.4
Vocabulary

bent

noun a natural skill or ability for doing something; ALSO a strong tendency to react to certain things in a specific manner

example sentences

Jeremy has a **bent** for track and field that has taken him all the way to the state championship.

The carpenter had a **bent** for making cabinets.

Leah has a conservative **bent** and will tend to tune you out if you start talking about gun control.

words that are similar **ability, aptitude, disposition, skill, knack**

Look up the full definition of "bent" in the dictionary and use each definition in sentences of your own creation until you feel you fully understand the word and can use it in conversation.

Write five sentences using the noun "bent":

_____

_____

_____

_____

_____

_____

_____

intimate

adjective to be close or familiar with something or particularly someone

verb to suggest

example sentences

I only wanted to invite my most **intimate** friends to my birthday party.

Joe didn't think that they were as **intimate** as Susan thought they were.

Before you **intimate** that he's committed a crime, please have some evidence.

also written in this form **intimately**

words that are similar friendly, devoted, affectionate, close, confidential, faithful, near, dear

words that are opposite cool, formal, incompatible, unfriendly

Look up the full definition of "intimate" in the dictionary and use each definition in sentences of your own creation until you feel you fully understand the word and can use it in conversation.

Write five sentences using the adjective and verb "intimate":

_____

_____

_____

_____

_____

_____

_____

_____

undertake

verb to attempt to accomplish something

example sentences

Before we **undertake** starting this test, the teacher has a few instructions.

He would never forget the day he **undertook** the task of breaking the world record in swimming.

John will **undertake** this job with the utmost sincerity.

also written in this form **undertook, undertaking**

words that are similar **attempt, engage in, devote, embark, endeavor, initiate, launch, make a run at, set out, tackle, take on, try**

words that are opposite **abstain, forego, forget**

Look up the full definition of "undertake" in the dictionary and use each definition in sentences of your own creation until you feel you fully understand the word and can use it in conversation.

Write five sentences using the verb "undertake":

_____

_____

_____

_____

_____

_____

_____

majority

noun the most of something, the biggest part

example sentences

Isabel was excited because after years of campaigning, her political party was finally in the **majority** in her state.

Over the course of thirty years, the chef worked for the **majority** of famous restaurants in New Orleans.

The **majority** of people who subscribe to the newspaper don't read it all the way through.

words that are similar bulk, greater number, greater part, larger part, most, mass, more, more than half

words that are opposite minority

Look up the full definition of "majority" in the dictionary and use each definition in sentences of your own creation until you feel you fully understand the word and can use it in conversation.

Write five sentences using the noun "majority":

_____

_____

_____

_____

_____

_____

_____

assert

verb to declare that something is true (formally); ALSO to insist on having your opinions and rights recognized

example sentences

The small country **asserted** itself at the meeting by reminding the other nations that they controlled a key trade route.

Hale Smith **asserted** that he was innocent and had an alibi.

The teacher **asserted** that she graded each test fairly.

also written in this form **asserted, asserting**

words that are similar **insist, declare, maintain, affirm, argue, claim, contend, justify, proclaim, profess, protest, swear**

words that are opposite **deny, reject**

Look up the full definition of "assert" in the dictionary and use each definition in sentences of your own creation until you feel you fully understand the word and can use it in conversation.

Write five sentences using the verb "assert":

_____

_____

_____

_____

_____

_____

_____

_____

crew

noun an organized group of workers; ALSO an informal group of friends

example sentences

The airplane's **crew** was happy to have a break after the flights were cancelled.

You'll need a larger **crew** if you expect to get all of the work done before the deadline.

Jim's mother felt that he was running with the wrong **crew** and might end up in trouble.

words that are similar **aggregation, assemblage, band, bunch, company, faction, gang, mob, organization, team, troop, workers**

Look up the full definition of "crew" in the dictionary and use each definition in sentences of your own creation until you feel you fully understand the word and can use it in conversation.

Write five sentences using the noun "crew":

_____

_____

_____

_____

_____

_____

_____

_____

chamber

noun **any enclosed space**

example sentences

The final exhibit of the museum was the sleeping **chamber** of the former emperor.

The judge asked the lawyers to meet her in her **chambers**.

The housemaid's job was to keep all **chambers** free of dust and dirt.

words that are similar **room, bedchamber, cell, enclosure, lodging, alcove**

Look up the full definition of "chamber" in the dictionary and use each definition in sentences of your own creation until you feel you fully understand the word and can use it in conversation.

Write five sentences using the noun "chamber":

_____

_____

_____

_____

_____

_____

_____

siege

noun the action of a military force surrounding a fort or other location to isolate it and continue assaulting it; ALSO, figuratively, harassment or bother

example sentences

The army laid **siege** to the castle with catapults.

Tim felt like he was under **siege** when he found that he had a thousand new emails.

The kids had built a snow fort, and their friends soon **sieged** them with a barrage of snowballs.

words that are similar **harass, besiege, annoy, badger, enclose, corral, surround**

Look up the full definition of "siege" in the dictionary and use each definition in sentences of your own creation until you feel you fully understand the word and can use it in conversation.

Write five sentences using the noun "siege":

_____

_____

_____

_____

_____

_____

_____

_____

malice

noun the intention to cause harm

example sentences

After the cruel prank, Jacob had nothing but **malice** for his friends.

The villain's vile plans were fueled by his **malice** for the superhero.

After firing half their employees without notice, the company received a great deal of **malice** from former employees as well as from the public.

also written in this form **malicious**

words that are similar **hate, vengefulness, animosity, dislike, resentment, spite, venom**

words that are opposite **benevolence, friendliness, like, sympathy**

Look up the full definition of "malice" in the dictionary and use each definition in sentences of your own creation until you feel you fully understand the word and can use it in conversation.

Write five sentences using the noun "malice":

_____

_____

_____

_____

_____

_____

_____

_____

extravagant

adjective **excessive, expensive, recklessly wasteful**

example sentences

Her painting collection was **extravagant,** with every inch of every wall covered by a framed work of art.

Her dress was an **extravagant** affair with complex embroidery.

Everything in his room was made of gold; it was **extravagant** to say the least.

also written in this form **extravagance, extravagancy**

words that are similar **indulgent, wasteful, costly, excessive, exorbitant, gaudy, grandiose, nonsensical, reckless, unrestrained**

words that are opposite **close, economical, moderate, provident, thrifty, unpretentious**

Look up the full definition of "extravagant" in the dictionary and use each definition in sentences of your own creation until you feel you fully understand the word and can use it in conversation.

Write five sentences using the adjective "extravagant":

_____

_____

_____

_____

_____

_____

_____

_____

Lesson 10.5
Vocabulary Review

As a review, **you will write one sentence using each of the words from the second group of vocabulary lessons in this workbook.** Write a sentence that demonstrates your understanding of the word, not just its part of speech. For example, "It is substantial," is not a good demonstration of the word "substantial!" Create a sentence that you would provide if you were helping someone else to understand the word. This will deepen your understanding of the vocabulary and help you remember it more easily.

If you don't remember the meaning of the word, have no fear! Look it up in your dictionary. This is an OPEN BOOK REVIEW! Look up what you need to help you make the sentences. It takes a lot of repetition to get this information down—nobody can remember it all just by looking at the vocabulary once.

accord

_____

_____

affect

_____

_____

apparent

_____

_____

appeal

_____

_____

appoint

_____

_____

Lesson 10.5 - Vocabulary Review

approach

_____

_____

assert

_____

_____

bent

_____

_____

campaign

_____

_____

chamber

_____

_____

circumstances

_____

_____

coast

_____

_____

commission

_____

_____

commit

_____

_____

compel

_____

_____

concept

_____

_____

concern

_____

_____

conduct

_____

_____

confer

_____

_____

consider

_____

_____

constant

_____

_____

Lesson 10.5 - Vocabulary Review

constitute

_____

_____

contract

_____

_____

convention

_____

_____

convince

_____

_____

court

_____

_____

crew

_____

_____

dwell

_____

_____

earnest

_____

_____

engage

entertain

evident

exalt

extravagant

fancy

financial

furnish

Lesson 10.5 - Vocabulary Review

generate

_____

_____

grant

_____

_____

harried

_____

_____

insist

_____

_____

inspire

_____

_____

instance

_____

_____

institute

_____

_____

intend

_____

_____

intimate

knight

labor

league

level

majority

malice

minute

Lesson 10.5 - Vocabulary Review

novel

---

obtain

---

passage

---

policy

---

practice

---

proceedings

---

project

---

property

---

range

___

___

reflect

___

___

render

___

___

scarce

___

___

siege

___

___

skill

___

___

stock

___

___

straight

___

___

Lesson 10.5 - Vocabulary Review

temper

territory

theory

undertake

utter

vain

venture

wander

yield

Lesson 11
Making Inference

The type of ACT Reading question that asks you to make an inference or "read between the lines" can be the most challenging you'll encounter on the test. The trick is to "back into the answer." If the correct choice doesn't immediately pop out at you, get to work eliminating answers that don't work, that contradict the passage, that aren't supported by the passage, or that don't actually answer the question.

It can help to keep in mind that every single answer choice that isn't the correct answer has a hole in it. It has some reason why it doesn't work.

Here are the top reasons why an answer choice is wrong:

1. It's not supported by the passage.

In other words, there are no details that fit with what the answer choice is talking about. Sure, you might need to figure out something that isn't said in the passage, but there should be details or evidence that support your conclusion. If the answer choice is totally "out of the blue" with nothing that supports it, it's incorrect.

2. It's contradicted by the passage.

If the passage says that the trees are green, but the answer choice says they're brown, you can cross it out. This is the case even if only a tiny part of the answer contradicts the passage. It's like the person who tells a crazy story that has one little fact in it wrong: Once you know they're lying about one thing, it's hard to believe a single thing they say. The correct answer choice never contradicts the passage.

3. It doesn't answer the question.

If it doesn't suitably answer the question, then it's incorrect, even if it's supported by the passage. This could mean that the question asks you for the main idea, and the answer choice is just a detail, or it could mean that the reason provided in the answer choice doesn't adequately answer what you're looking for.

4. It doesn't work as well as another choice.

Once you have eliminated at least two of the choices by identifying reasons 1-3 above, you will need to compare the two choices left. One will be worse or weaker than the other. Knock it out and you're left with the best answer choice.

Imagine that you're sifting for gold on the ACT and you have the correct idea. You knock out one bad answer, and then another, and then another, until all you have left is that golden, correct answer.

With the earlier question types that we have covered in this course, it was quite possible that the answer choice would pop out at you, and you would be able to pick the correct choice without having to walk through the process of elimination. With the tougher ACT Reading questions, you'll need to rely more heavily on this technique.

The wording of the question can give you a clue that you'll need to "read between the lines," and so you will probably need to start out with the process of elimination as you try to decide on your answer. These words and phrases can indicate to you that you're being asked to make an educated guess about the answer choice.

"Suggests," in the sense it is often used in ACT questions, means "states indirectly; causes you to think that something is the case." Here is an example of how this word might be used:

Details in the passage most strongly suggest that...

In this sense, you are being asked to choose the answer that is most supported by the passage. What do the details in the passage make you think is right?

"Refers," as it is used in ACT questions, means "mentions, talks about, or speaks of." Since a reading passage is only a small part of a longer essay or book, there might be some things that are mentioned but not really explained. The ACT asks you to figure out what is being talked about. Here is an example of how a question might use "refers":

When the narrator refers to _____, he is most likely making a statement about:

There will be a specific detail mentioned in the blank. Your task is to go find that detail in the passage, then work out what is being talked about.

"Infer," in one sense, means "make a conclusion based on reasoning and evidence, rather than from direct statements." On the ACT, this word often appears in the phrase "it can reasonably be inferred," which means that "it would be supported by the passage to conclude the following based on the evidence."

Here is an example of how the ACT might ask a question using the word "infer":

It can reasonably be inferred from the passage that the main character most strongly desires to:

You're asked to fill in the blank, using the details provided in the passage.

Look out for words like "nearly" and "likely," which clue you in that the answer won't be found directly in the passage. Instead, you need to draw conclusions based on the supporting details.

Passage

Instructions: Skim the passage in 3 minutes, then answer the 10 practice questions that appear below. Use a timer to keep track of when you should start answering the questions. Just like on the ACT, you are allowed to refer to the passage in order to find the correct answers.

LITERARY NARRATIVE: This passage is adapted from the novella *The Metamorphosis* by Franz Kafka, published in 1915.

One morning, when Gregor Samsa woke from troubled dreams, he found himself transformed in his bed into a horrible vermin. He lay on his armor-like back, and if he lifted his head a little he could see his
[5] brown belly, slightly domed and divided by arches into stiff sections. The bedding was hardly able to cover it and seemed ready to slide off any moment. His many legs, pitifully thin compared with the size of the rest of him, waved about helplessly as he looked.

[10] "What's happened to me?" he thought. It wasn't a dream. His room, a proper human room although a little too small, lay peacefully between its four familiar walls. A collection of textile samples lay spread out on the table—Samsa was a traveling salesman—and above
[15] it there hung a picture that he had recently cut out of an illustrated magazine and housed in a nice, gilded frame. It showed a lady fitted out with a fur hat and fur boa who sat upright, raising a heavy fur muff that covered the whole of her lower arm towards the viewer.

[20] Gregor then turned to look out the window at the dull weather. Drops of rain could be heard hitting the pane, which made him feel quite sad. "How about if I sleep a little bit longer and forget all this nonsense,",he thought, but that was something he was unable to do
[25] because he was used to sleeping on his right, and in his present state couldn't get into that position. However hard he threw himself onto his right, he always rolled back to where he was. He must have tried it a hundred times, shut his eyes so that he wouldn't have to look at
[30] the floundering legs, and only stopped when he began to feel a mild, dull pain there that he had never felt before.

"Oh, God," he thought, "what a strenuous career it is that I've chosen! Traveling day in and day out.
[35] Doing business like this takes much more effort than doing your own business at home, and on top of that there's the curse of traveling, worries about making train connections, bad and irregular food, contact with different people all the time so that you can never get
[40] to know anyone or become friendly with them." He felt a slight itch up on his belly; pushed himself slowly up on his back towards the headboard so that he could lift his head better; found where the itch was, and saw that it was covered with lots of little white spots which he
[45] didn't know what to make of; and when he tried to feel the place with one of his legs he drew it quickly back because as soon as he touched it he was overcome by a cold shudder.

He slid back into his former position. "Getting up
[50] early all the time", he thought, "it makes you stupid. Other traveling salesmen live a life of luxury. For instance, whenever I go back to the guest house during the morning to copy out the contract, these gentlemen are always still sitting there eating their breakfasts. I
[55] ought to just try that with my boss; I'd get kicked out on the spot. If I didn't have my parents to think about I'd have given in my notice a long time ago, I'd have gone up to the boss and told him just what I think, tell him everything I would, let him know just what I feel. He'd
[60] fall right off his desk! Well, there's still some hope; once I've got the money together to pay off my parents' debt to him - another five or six years I suppose - that's definitely what I'll do. First of all though, I've got to get up, my train leaves at five."

[65] And he looked over at the alarm clock, ticking on the chest of drawers. "God in Heaven!" he thought. It was half past six and the hands were quietly moving forwards. Had the alarm clock not rung? He could see from the bed that it had been set for four o'clock as it
[70] should have been; it certainly must have rung. Yes, but was it possible to quietly sleep through that furniture-rattling noise? True, he had not slept peacefully, but probably all the more deeply because of that. What should he do now?

[75] The next train went at seven; if he were to catch that he would have to rush like mad and the collection of samples was still not packed, and he did not at all feel particularly fresh and lively. And even if he did catch the train he would not avoid his boss's anger as
[80] the office assistant would have been there to see the five o'clock train go, he would have put in his report about Gregor's not being there a long time ago. The office assistant was the boss's man, spineless, and with no understanding.

[85] What about if he reported sick? But that would be extremely strained and suspicious as in fifteen years of service Gregor had never once yet been ill. His boss would certainly come round with the doctor from the medical insurance company, accuse his parents of having
[90] a lazy son, and accept the doctor's recommendation not to make any claim as the doctor believed that no-one was ever ill but that many were workshy. And what's more, would he have been entirely wrong in this case? Gregor did in fact, apart from excessive sleepiness after
[95] sleeping for so long, feel completely well and even felt much hungrier than usual.

Lesson 11 - Making Inference

1. Details in the passage most strongly suggest that Gregor is having difficulty getting out of bed because:

    A. he is sick.
    B. he has experienced a transformation.
    C. he is always late for work.
    D. he is afraid of his boss's anger.

2. When the narrator refers to the office assistant as the "boss's man," he is most likely directly referring to:

    F. the office assistant being employed by the boss.
    G. the bone and joint problems possessed by the office assistant.
    H. the likelihood that the office assistant would not protect Gregor.
    J. the fact that the office assistant and the boss are related.

3. It can reasonably be inferred from the passage that with regards to his job, Gregor most strongly desires to attain which of the following?

    A. He wants to stop having to travel and make train connections.
    B. He wishes to be able to call in sick so that he doesn't have to come in that day.
    C. He wants to have the office assistant's job.
    D. He wishes to pay off his parents' debts and quit.

4. Details in the passage help establish that Gregor is:

    F. content with his life.
    G. always late for his work.
    H. unhappy about his job.
    J. a train conductor.

5. Gregor makes which of the following comparisons between himself and other people of his profession?

    A. He could one day have a life of luxury, just like the other traveling salesmen he knows.
    B. He has to eat bad or irregular food, while other traveling salesmen don't.
    C. All traveling salesmen have to do pretty much the same thing.
    D. Gregor has to work much harder than other people who have a similar job.

6. In the context of the passage, which of the following statements best describes Gregor Samsa's emotional state regarding his transformation?

    F. Gregor's friends are much more worried about it than he is.
    G. He has no idea how he'll be a traveling salesman and a vermin at the same time.
    H. It has not yet set in for Gregor that he has transformed, and he is more concerned with his day-to-day troubles.
    J. Gregor is extremely upset about his transformation into a horrible vermin.

7. In the context of the passage, the statement "he found himself transformed in his bed into a horrible vermin" most nearly suggests that Gregor Samsa had turned into:

    A. an insect-like creature.
    B. a turtle.
    C. an alcoholic.
    D. a soldier.

8. In the context of the passage, the author's statement that reporting sick "would be extremely strained and suspicious" most nearly means that:

    F. the doctor would make him take a medical leave.
    G. Gregor's transformation would create a difficult situation with his work.
    H. Gregor's illness would cause suspicion and a strained relationship with his boss.
    J. it was unlikely that Gregor's boss would believe him about being sick.

9. According to the passage, Gregor would not have been working for his boss if which of the following statements were true?

    A. Gregor was a hard worker and never stopped trying to make his own way.
    B. Gregor had another skill besides sales.
    C. Gregor's family never owed a debt to Gregor's boss.
    D. Gregor didn't suffer a transformation into vermin.

10. One of the main points in the last three paragraphs (lines 65-96) is that, with regard to his being late to work, Gregor is most nearly experiencing the emotion of:

    F. panic.
    G. anger.
    H. apathy.
    J. triumph.

1. Details in the passage most strongly suggest that Gregor is having difficulty getting out of bed because:

   A. he is sick.
   B. he has experienced a transformation.
   C. he is always late for work.
   D. he is afraid of his boss's anger.

Since this question is asking for us to "read between the lines" and figure out what the passage is suggesting, let's eliminate the choices that don't work. We can eliminate choice A because the last sentence (lines 94-96) of the passage says that he does not feel sick: "Gregor did in fact, apart from excessive sleepiness after sleeping for so long, feel completely well and even felt much hungrier than usual." We can also eliminate choice C, since details in the passage tell us that being late is not a regular occurrence. While Gregor is afraid of his boss's anger, it isn't the reason that he had difficulty getting out of bed, so we knock out choice D. Choice B is the correct answer because it is supported by lines 1-3 in the first paragraph: "One morning, when Gregor Samsa woke from troubled dreams, he found himself transformed in his bed into a horrible vermin." It then describes how he tries to go back to sleep.

2. When the narrator refers to the office assistant as the "boss's man," he is most likely directly referring to:

   F. the office assistant being employed by the boss.
   G. the bone and joint problems possessed by the office assistant.
   H. the likelihood that the office assistant would not protect Gregor.
   J. the fact that the office assistant and the boss are related.

First we scan for where the phrase "boss's man" appears. We find it in paragraph 7 (lines 78-84): "And even if he did catch the train he would not avoid his boss's anger as the office assistant would have been there to see the five o'clock train go, he would have put in his report about Gregor's not being there a long time ago. The office assistant was the boss's man, "spineless", and with no understanding." In this sense, spineless means "weak and without courage." It doesn't mean that he has no spine; he would not be an office assistant in that case. So we can eliminate choice G. We can also eliminate choice J as unsupported by the passage; nothing in the passage mentions the boss and office assistant being family. While the office assistant is obviously employed by the boss, this mention of him being the "boss's man" is in reference to the office assistant putting "in his report about Gregor's not being there," so choice H is the best answer. The office assistant would report on Gregor instead of trying to protect him from his boss's anger.

Lesson 11 - Making Inference

3. It can reasonably be inferred from the passage that with regard to his job, Gregor most strongly desires to attain which of the following?
   A. He wants to stop having to travel and make train connections.
   B. He wishes to be able to call in sick so that he doesn't have to come in that day.
   C. He wants to have the office assistant's job.
   D. He wishes to pay off his parents' debts and quit.

Toward the end of paragraph 5, in lines 56-63, it says, "If I didn't have my parents to think about I'd have given in my notice a long time ago, I'd have gone up to the boss and told him just what I think, tell him everything I would, let him know just what I feel. He'd fall right off his desk! Well, there's still some hope; once I've got the money together to pay off my parents' debt to him - another five or six years I suppose - that's definitely what I'll do." This best supports choice D. The fact that he fantasizes about quitting and telling his boss off supports the idea that he strongly desires this. "Giving in his notice" is another way of saying "quitting." Nothing in the passage supports Gregor having ambitions to be the office assistant, so choice C does not work. While Gregor does wish to call in sick, there is no indication that this is a strong desire of his, so choice B is incorrect. Likewise, in paragraph 4, in lines 37-40, Gregor complains that "there's the curse of traveling, worries about making train connections, bad and irregular food, contact with different people all the time so that you can never get to know anyone or become friendly with them." But the desire to quit is clearly stronger than the desire to not travel, which is just one aspect of his gripe with his job.

4. Details in the passage help establish that Gregor is:
   F. content with his life.
   G. always late for his work.
   H. unhappy about his job.
   J. a train conductor.

In paragraph 4 (lines 33-48), Gregor complains "what a strenuous career it is that I've chosen!" and he continues to complain in paragraph 5 (lines 49-64), so choice H is the best answer. Choice F can be eliminated because it is not supported by the passage; if anything, he's discontented with his life. We can eliminate choice G because his being late for work seems to be an unusual occurrence. The passage states that he is a "traveling salesman" in paragraph 2 (lines 10-19), so we can't conclude that he is a train conductor and therefore can cross out choice J.

5. Gregor makes which of the following comparisons between himself and other people of his profession?

   A. He could one day have a life of luxury, just like the other traveling salesmen he knows.
   B. He has to eat bad or irregular food, while other traveling salesmen don't.
   C. All traveling salesmen have to do pretty much the same thing.
   D. Gregor has to work much harder than other people who have a similar job.

Paragraph 5 (lines 49-64) contains details that compare Gregor's life to that of other traveling salesmen. While Gregor does mention that "other traveling salesmen live a life of luxury," he never says anything that would make us conclude that he thinks he, himself, will have a life of luxury, so we cross out choice A. Choice B also does not work: He describes having to eat bad or irregular food as a traveler in paragraph 4 (lines 33-48), but he does not give us any clue that other traveling salesman don't have the same problem. Since in paragraph 5 (lines 49-64) he is describing his situation as different from that of other traveling salesmen, we can eliminate choice C. Choice D is supported by the line "Other traveling salesmen live a life of luxury. For instance, whenever I go back to the guest house during the morning to copy out the contract, these gentlemen are always still sitting there eating their breakfasts," so this is our best answer choice. Context, in this sense, means "the set of circumstances or facts surrounding a particular event or question."

6. In the context of the passage, which of the following statements best describes Gregor Samsa's emotional state regarding his transformation?

   F. Gregor's friends are much more worried about it than he is.
   G. He has no idea how he'll be a traveling salesman and a vermin at the same time.
   H. It has not yet set in for Gregor that he has transformed, and he is more concerned with his day-to-day troubles.
   J. Gregor is extremely upset about his transformation into a horrible vermin.

There is no line from the passage that directly indicates what Gregor Samsa's emotional state is regarding his transformation. However, much of the passage is devoted to Gregor's day-to-day worries, not about his thoughts regarding his transformation, so choice H is the best answer. We can eliminate choices F (since Gregor's friends are never mentioned), G (because this thought of how he'll be a traveling salesman and a vermin at the same time does not occur to him in this passage), and J (because Gregor seems much more upset about his job than his transformation).

7. In the context of the passage, the statement "he found himself transformed in his bed into a horrible vermin" most nearly suggests that Gregor Samsa had turned into:

   A. an insect-like creature.
   B. a turtle.
   C. an alcoholic.
   D. a soldier.

In the context of the passage, choice A is the best fit. Paragraph 1 (lines 1-9) describes Gregor as having an "armor-like back," which could also fit with choice B, a turtle, but it also says that he has "many legs, pitifully thin compared with the size of the rest of him," which allows us to eliminate choices B, C, and D. His "brown belly, slightly domed and divided by arches into stiff sections," also supports choice A.

Lesson 11 - Making Inference

8. In the context of the passage, the author's statement that reporting sick "would be extremely strained and suspicious" most nearly means that:

   F. the doctor would make him take a medical leave.
   G. Gregor's transformation would create a difficult situation with his work.
   H. Gregor's illness would cause suspicion and a strained relationship with his boss.
   J. it was unlikely that Gregor's boss would believe him about being sick.

In this sense, the word "strained" means "forced or artificial." The idea of reporting sick is mentioned in the last paragraph (lines 85-96). Since the paragraph describes the boss coming around with the medical doctor to check up on him, and "accuse his parents of having a lazy son," we can conclude that the boss would doubt the truthfulness of Gregor's claim of being sick. Therefore, choice J is the best answer. There is no mention of a medical leave; indeed, the doctor mentioned here "believed no-one was ever ill," so we can eliminate choice F. Gregor is not thinking about the effects of his transformation on people who would see him in this paragraph, so choice G does not work. Since Gregor is not actually ill, as we see in the last sentence, in lines 94-96, "Gregor did in fact, apart from excessive sleepiness after sleeping for so long, feel completely well and even felt much hungrier than usual," we can knock out choice H.

9. According to the passage, Gregor would not have been working for his boss if which of the following statements were true?

   A. Gregor was a hard worker and never stopped trying to make his own way.
   B. Gregor had another skill besides sales.
   C. Gregor's family never owed a debt to Gregor's boss.
   D. Gregor didn't suffer a transformation into vermin.

In lines 56-63, Gregor states, "If I didn't have my parents to think about I'd have given in my notice a long time ago, I'd have gone up to the boss and told him just what I think, tell him everything I would, let him know just what I feel. He'd fall right off his desk! Well, there's still some hope; once I've got the money together to pay off my parents' debt to him - another five or six years I suppose - that's definitely what I'll do." We can therefore conclude that if Gregor's family did not owe the boss a debt, Gregor would no longer be working for him. Choice C is the best answer. The other choices are not supported by the passage. Gregor is not stuck working for his boss because he doesn't work hard enough (choice A), nor because he has no other skills (choice B). Since Gregor worked for his boss before his transformation, choice D doesn't work either.

10. One of the main points in the last three paragraphs (lines 65-96) is that, with regard to his being late to work, Gregor is most nearly experiencing the emotion of:

    F. panic.
    G. anger.
    H. apathy.
    J. triumph.

Since the last three paragraphs (lines 65-96) mainly concern Gregor frantically trying to figure out what to do and start with the exclamation "God in Heaven!" we can conclude that he is most likely experiencing panic. Choice F is the best answer. He does not express anger or "triumph," which in this sense means "joy or satisfaction from success or victory," so we can eliminate choices G and J. "Apathy" in this sense means "lack of interest, enthusiasm, or concern." Since Gregor is anything but unconcerned about being late, we can also eliminate choice H.

Let's take a look at a practice question and break down how we can back into the answer by using the process of elimination:

> 6. In the context of the passage, which of the following statements best describes Gregor Samsa's emotional state regarding his transformation?
>   - F. Gregor's friends are much more worried about it than he is.
>   - G. He has no idea how he'll be a traveling salesman and a vermin at the same time.
>   - H. It has not yet set in for Gregor that he has transformed, and he is more concerned with his day-to-day troubles.
>   - J. Gregor is extremely upset about his transformation into a horrible vermin.

The answer choice H might immediately jump out at us if we were able to read through the entire passage within the 3 minutes, but even if it does we might not feel very certain about it. Let's start knocking out incorrect answers. We know choice F is incorrect because there is no mention of Gregor's friends. This is the kind of answer choice that can stick with us because there's nothing in the passage that says his friends aren't worried about him. Be ruthless! If the passage doesn't even come close to mentioning an answer choice, get rid of it—no regrets!

Choice G can be eliminated because it does not answer the question. The question asks for Gregor's emotional state. "Having no idea" is not an emotion, it's at best a state of mind or a thought.

Choice J is contradicted by the passage. If anything, we might say he's a little irritated or bothered by not being able to get out of bed, but he's mainly concerned with being late for work. (In other words, he's worried about his day-to-day troubles.)

In this way, we've confirmed that choice H is our best answer.

Lesson 12.1
Vocabulary

wax

verb to grow larger or increase

example sentences

It was thought that the companies' stock prices would shrink, but they **waxed** instead.

High tide is when the water could be said to **wax,** and low tide is when the water seems to lower.

The speaker was known to **wax** enthusiastic when it came to the topic of history.

also written in this form **waxed, waxing**

words that are similar **grow, build, develop, become fuller, enlarge, expand, increase, magnify, multiply, swell, rise**

words that are opposite **wane, shrink**

Look up the full definition of "wax" in the dictionary and use each definition in sentences of your own creation until you feel you fully understand the word and can use it in conversation.

Write five sentences using the verb "wax":

_____

_____

_____

_____

_____

_____

_____

throng

noun a large gathering or crowd of people

verb to push or squeeze together in an area

example sentences

The **throng** of water buffalo migrated across the river every year.

A **throng** of people had gathered outside the theater for the midnight showing of the movie.

The fans **thronged** the lobby when it was revealed that the celebrity was in the building.

also written in this form thronged, thronging

words that are similar crowd, assembly, collection, mass, mob, pack, multitude, swarm

words that are opposite dispersal, scattering

Look up the full definition of "throng" in the dictionary and use each definition in sentences of your own creation until you feel you fully understand the word and can use it in conversation.

Write five sentences using the noun and verb "throng":

_____

_____

_____

_____

_____

_____

_____

venerate

verb to worship, adore, or revere

example sentences

Behind his back the employee talked poorly about his boss, but in his presence it seemed as though the employee **venerated** his employer.

He was **venerated** for his attempts to bring peace to the country.

Though people often exalt their kings, it could also be said they **venerate** them as well.

also written in this form **venerated, venerating**

words that are similar **admire, adore, appreciate, cherish, honor, idolize, respect, revere, treasure, value**

Look up the full definition of "venerate" in the dictionary and use each definition in sentences of your own creation until you feel you fully understand the word and can use it in conversation.

Write five sentences using the verb "venerate":

_____

_____

_____

_____

_____

_____

_____

_____

assail

verb to attack with words; ALSO to attack physically or emotionally

example sentences

In the movie the martial artist was **assailed** by ninjas with throwing stars.

The critic was unrelenting in his review of the work, **assailing** any seemingly positive aspect of the piece.

The boxer was **assailed** by a series of punches.

also written in this form **assailed**

words that are similar **abuse, assault, attack, bash, berate, criticize, vilify**

Look up the full definition of "assail" in the dictionary and use each definition in sentences of your own creation until you feel you fully understand the word and can use it in conversation.

Write five sentences using the verb "assail":

_____

_____

_____

_____

_____

_____

_____

_____

sublime

adjective **of high moral or intellectual value, great or magnificent**

example sentences

The cheesecake was so **sublime** that she recommended the dessert to everyone she knew.

The new song struck the audience as a work of truly **sublime** beauty.

The perfectly executed swing of the bat was a **sublime** action that won the team the game.

also written in this form **sublimely**

words that are similar **great, magnificent, divine, exalted, glorious, gorgeous, grand, resplendent, superb**

words that are opposite **poor, lowly, second-rate**

Look up the full definition of "sublime" in the dictionary and use each definition in sentences of your own creation until you feel you fully understand the word and can use it in conversation.

Write five sentences using the adjective "sublime":

_____

_____

_____

_____

_____

_____

_____

exploit

verb to manipulate or use for personal advantage

noun an accomplishment

example sentences

After the knight slayed the dragon it wasn't long before the entire countryside heard of her heroic **exploit**.

Heroes and villains alike are known for their **exploits**, either great deeds or manipulative schemes.

He **exploited** his friend by getting him to do all the work for the school project.

also written in this form **exploits, exploitation**

words that are similar **abuse, use, wrong, accomplishment, adventure, attainment, feat, job, venture**

words that are opposite **cherish, esteem, honor, respect, revere, treasure**

Look up the full definition of "exploit" in the dictionary and use each definition in sentences of your own creation until you feel you fully understand the word and can use it in conversation.

Write five sentences using the verb and noun "exploit":

_____

_____

_____

_____

_____

_____

_____

_____

exertion

noun effort, the use of physical energy; hard work

example sentences

It took a large measure of physical **exertion** for him to swim a hundred laps.

Moving the furniture required a great deal of **exertion** from the couple.

Great physical **exertion** was required from the construction crew in order to finish building the stadium on time.

words that are similar action, attempt, effort, industry, labor, strain, struggle, toil, travail, trouble, trial

words that are opposite idleness, laziness

Look up the full definition of "exertion" in the dictionary and use each definition in sentences of your own creation until you feel you fully understand the word and can use it in conversation.

Write five sentences using the noun "exertion":

_____

_____

_____

_____

_____

_____

_____

kindle

verb to arouse interest or passion

example sentences

In order to stay warm in the cold of the night, the campers had to **kindle** a fire.

Out of a long term friendship a romance was eventually **kindled** between the two.

After the woods caught fire it was only a matter of time before nearby houses **kindled** which spread the fire through the neighborhood.

also written in this form kindled, kindling

words that are similar bring to life, arouse, energize, burn, ignite, inflame, set fire, liven, make alive, spark, spur, urge

words that are opposite extinguish, put out, deaden, discourage, kill

Look up the full definition of "kindle" in the dictionary and use each definition in sentences of your own creation until you feel you fully understand the word and can use it in conversation.

Write five sentences using the verb "kindle":

_____

_____

_____

_____

_____

_____

_____

_____

_____

endow

verb **to give qualities or abilities to**

example sentences

Even from youth, it was clear that he was **endowed** with a talent for art.

At her birthday party her friends would **endow** her with many gifts.

The lottery **endowed** him with ten million dollars.

also written in this form **endowed, endowing, endowment**

words that are similar **give, award, bestow, enhance, empower, grant, leave, supply**

words that are opposite **receive, take**

Look up the full definition of "endow" in the dictionary and use each definition in sentences of your own creation until you feel you fully understand the word and can use it in conversation.

Write five sentences using the verb "endow":

_____

_____

_____

_____

_____

_____

_____

… Lesson 12.1 - Vocabulary

impose

verb **to put into effect from an authority as an obligation**

example sentences

They hadn't made dinner plans, but their friends **imposed** on them so they had to make additional food.

He had only wanted to teach a single class, but the administration **imposed** three additional classes on him.

Though not written down, there are many unspoken rules that are **imposed** on people by society.

words that are similar **set, dictated, commanded, decreed, required**

Look up the full definition of "impose" in the dictionary and use each definition in sentences of your own creation until you feel you fully understand the word and can use it in conversation.

Write five sentences using the verb "impose":

_____

_____

_____

_____

_____

_____

_____

_____

Lesson 12.2
Vocabulary

humiliate

verb **to cause shame**

example sentences

Peter was **humiliated** by the prank his friends had played on him at school.

The father unintentionally **humiliated** his son by telling childhood stories when his date came over.

Bullies will often **humiliate** the kids they pick on.

also written in this form **humiliated, humiliating, humiliation**

words that are similar **embarrass, put down, demean, disgrace, make a fool of, shame**

words that are opposite **build up, praise, elevate**

Look up the full definition of "humiliate" in the dictionary and use each definition in sentences of your own creation until you feel you fully understand the word and can use it in conversation.

Write five sentences using the verb "humiliate":

_____

_____

_____

_____

_____

_____

_____

_____

suffrage

noun **the right to vote**

example sentences

It took many years before universal **suffrage** came into practice in the United States, and all people were allowed to vote.

At the turn of the 18th century many women protested in support of women's **suffrage**; they too wanted the right to vote.

Suffrage is a right guaranteed by amendments of the U.S. Constitution.

Look up the full definition of "suffrage" in the dictionary and use each definition in sentences of your own creation until you feel you fully understand the word and can use it in conversation.

Write five sentences using the noun "suffrage":

_____

_____

_____

_____

_____

_____

_____

ensue

verb to follow afterwards or be the result

example sentences

They both disagreed about the topic and so a debate **ensued**.

If the soup had a fly in it, a long-winded complaint from the customer was sure to **ensue**.

When the son was caught sneaking out of the house at night, he knew a speech from his father would **ensue**.

also written in this form **ensued, ensuing**

words that are similar **come to pass, start to happen, develop, occur, proceed, result, stem, succeed, turn out**

words that are opposite **precede**

Look up the full definition of "ensue" in the dictionary and use each definition in sentences of your own creation until you feel you fully understand the word and can use it in conversation.

Write five sentences using the verb "ensue":

_____

_____

_____

_____

_____

_____

_____

brook

verb to put up with something or somebody unpleasant

example sentences

The police officer would **brook** no violation of the law.

The older brother would never **brook** his younger brother's annoying behavior, often yelling at him to stop.

If I have too **brook** his temper one more day, I might be the one making a scene.

also written in this form **brooked, brooking**

words that are similar **endure, consent, let, put up with, sit still for, suffer, take kindly to**

words that are opposite **deny, disallow, disapprove, refuse, reject, resist, withstand**

Look up the full definition of "brook" in the dictionary and use each definition in sentences of your own creation until you feel you fully understand the word and can use it in conversation.

Write five sentences using the verb "brook":

_____

_____

_____

_____

_____

_____

_____

_____

gale

noun a strong wind or violent storm

example sentences

A **gale** hit the small town before the hurricane arrived.

A **gale** swept through the old west town and brought dirt and tumbleweeds along with it.

Pedestrians held on tightly to their umbrellas as a **gale** nearly pulled them free from their hands.

words that are similar **storm, wind, tempest, cyclone, blow, monsoon, squall, windstorm**

Look up the full definition of "gale" in the dictionary and use each definition in sentences of your own creation until you feel you fully understand the word and can use it in conversation.

Write five sentences using the noun "gale":

_____

_____

_____

_____

_____

_____

_____

_____

Lesson 12.2 - Vocabulary

satire

noun **witty wording used to insult or scorn**

example sentences

Sketch comedy shows often use **satire** to poke fun at presidential candidates.

When the talk show host got in trouble because of his imitation of a celebrity, he quickly explained that it was only meant as **satire**, not as an insult.

Blockbuster films often have **satires** of them made in order to poke fun at their more absurd elements.

also written in this form **satirical**

words that are similar **comedy, irony, mockery, parody, sarcasm, wit**

Look up the full definition of "satire" in the dictionary and use each definition in sentences of your own creation until you feel you fully understand the word and can use it in conversation.

Write five sentences using the verb "satire":

_____

_____

_____

_____

_____

_____

_____

_____

muse

verb to think over deeply

example sentences

The philosophical question was one he had to **muse** over for a few days before he had an answer.

She was his **muse**, a neverending source of inspiration.

He told her that he would **muse** over the idea of a vacation.

also written in this form **mused, musing**

words that are similar **think about, dream, brood, consider, contemplate, ponder, puzzle over, reflect, speculate, think**

words that are opposite **ignore, neglect**

Look up the full definition of "muse" in the dictionary and use each definition in sentences of your own creation until you feel you fully understand the word and can use it in conversation.

Write five sentences using the verb "muse":

_____

_____

_____

_____

_____

_____

_____

_____

intrigue

noun a secret plot or plan

verb to cause interest or curiosity

example sentences

Readers are often **intrigued** by a complex story.

A ruler of a country has to be wary of any **intrigue** against him or her.

Interesting characters are often enough to **intrigue** an audience when watching a film.

words that are similar scheme, conspiracy, fraud, plan, plot, ruse, trickery, wile

Look up the full definition of "intrigue" in the dictionary and use each definition in sentences of your own creation until you feel you fully understand the word and can use it in conversation.

Write five sentences using the noun and verb "intrigue":

_____

_____

_____

_____

_____

_____

_____

_____

indication

noun **a sign, something that points out or suggests something**

example sentences

Despite having been glued back together, the vase's cracks were **indication** enough that it had broken in the past.

Not being able to sleep is a clear **indication** of insomnia.

The fact that the children all had fevers was an **indication** that they might be ill.

words that are similar **evidence, clue, cue, hint, implication, mark, note, proof, reminder, suggestion, trace, warning**

words that are opposite **misinformation**

Look up the full definition of "indication" in the dictionary and use each definition in sentences of your own creation until you feel you fully understand the word and can use it in conversation.

Write five sentences using the noun "indication":

_____

_____

_____

_____

_____

_____

_____

dispatch

verb **to send**

noun **the quality of being prompt or efficient**

example sentences

Within minutes of when the fire started, the firemen were **dispatched**.

He was told to **dispatch** the letter immediately so that it would arrive on time.

A call was made for a **dispatch** of police officers after it was discovered that the bank was being robbed.

also written in this form **dispatched, dispatching**

words that are similar **speed, hustle, hurry, haste, swiftness, send, forward, issue, remit, ship**

words that are opposite **hold, hold back, keep, retain**

Look up the full definition of "dispatch" in the dictionary and use each definition in sentences of your own creation until you feel you fully understand the word and can use it in conversation.

Write five sentences using the verb and noun "dispatch":

_____

_____

_____

_____

_____

_____

_____

_____

Lesson 12.3
Vocabulary

cower

verb to show submission or fear; to crouch or curl up

example sentences

The barking dog **cowered** as soon as the cat hissed at him.

To everyone's surprise Leon did not **cower** when the bully approached him.

When it came time to ask for a promotion, Susan did not **cower**.

also written in this form **cowered, cowering**

words that are similar **hide, recoil, shrink, tremble, skulk, grovel, flinch, cringe**

Look up the full definition of "cower" in the dictionary and use each definition in sentences of your own creation until you feel you fully understand the word and can use it in conversation.

Write five sentences using the verb "cower":

_____

_____

_____

_____

_____

_____

_____

_____

Lesson 12.3 - Vocabulary

wont

noun a custom or habit

example sentences

Kevin's **wont** is to drink two cups of coffee every morning.

Although to Adam it was simply his **wont** to wash his hands twenty times a day, his friends saw it as a compulsion.

The baby cried, as such young children are **wont** to do.

words that are similar accustomed, given, inclined, used, used to

Look up the full definition of "wont" in the dictionary and use each definition in sentences of your own creation until you feel you fully understand the word and can use it in conversation.

Write five sentences using the noun "wont":

tract

noun a large area of land; ALSO a system of body parts; ALSO a brief booklet written on a particular subject

example sentences

The property consisted of a **tract** of four acres.

He turned the pages of the **tract** every so often, and within an hour he had completed his reading.

The doctor was certain the health problem originated in his intestinal **tract**.

words that are similar land, estate, field, region, booklet, system

Look up the full definition of "tract" in the dictionary and use each definition in sentences of your own creation until you feel you fully understand the word and can use it in conversation.

Write five sentences using the noun "tract":

_____

_____

_____

_____

_____

_____

_____

Lesson 12.3 - Vocabulary

canon

noun a general law, rule, or principle by which something is judged; ALSO a list of works of an author accepted as authentic

example sentences

Stories written by fans are not considered part of the **canon** of an established fantasy franchise.

In some television shows the pilots are not considered part of the **canon** of the series and sometimes never air.

"Is it fun?" is the **canon** by which children's television programming is judged.

words that are similar rule, law, maxim, precept, standard, yardstick

Look up the full definition of "canon" in the dictionary and use each definition in sentences of your own creation until you feel you fully understand the word and can use it in conversation.

Write five sentences using the noun "canon":

_____

_____

_____

_____

_____

_____

_____

_____

impel

verb **to urge or force to move forward or to take an action**

example sentences

He didn't know why he was walking toward the door, only that he felt **impelled** to do so.

His loneliness seemed to **impel** the teenager to finally talk to another person.

Horror movies sometimes **impel** people to scream out in fear.

also written in this form impelling, impelled

words that are similar compel, boost, drive, excite, goad, induce, influence, inspire, instigate, motivate, move, poke, press, prod, push

words that are opposite dissuade, delay, repress, slow, suppress

Look up the full definition of "impel" in the dictionary and use each definition in sentences of your own creation until you feel you fully understand the word and can use it in conversation.

Write five sentences using the verb "impel":

_____

_____

_____

_____

_____

_____

_____

_____

_____

Lesson 12.3 - Vocabulary

latitude

noun **freedom from normal restraints in conduct**

example sentences

The child had little **latitude** when it came to bed time because he wasn't allowed to stay up even five minutes past nine.

Workers had five minutes for a break and there was zero **latitude** for them to take longer.

Because he didn't want to fight, Sean gave Jill some **latitude** when it came to picking which movie they would watch.

also written in this form **humility**

words that are similar **freedom, extent, independence, range, space, span, spread, unrestrictedness**

words that are opposite **limitation, restriction**

Look up the full definition of "latitude" in the dictionary and use each definition in sentences of your own creation until you feel you fully understand the word and can use it in conversation.

Write five sentences using the noun "latitude":

_____

_____

_____

_____

_____

_____

_____

_____

vacate

verb **to leave or abandon**

example sentences

The house was found to be infected with termites, and shortly thereafter the occupants **vacated** the building.

Once the fire got started, the people in the apartment were quick to **vacate** the vicinity.

Criminals often **vacate** the scene of the crime quickly but usually leave behind clues.

also written in this form **vacating, vacated**

words that are similar **abandon, depart, empty, give up, go away, leave, quit, relinquish, withdraw**

words that are opposite **fill, occupy, overflow**

Look up the full definition of "vacate" in the dictionary and use each definition in sentences of your own creation until you feel you fully understand the word and can use it in conversation.

Write five sentences using the verb "vacate":

_____

_____

_____

_____

_____

_____

_____

_____

undertaking

noun **any piece of work that is attempted**

example sentences

To build the entire house was a serious **undertaking** for a single man.

Building a Mars rover is no simple **undertaking**; it requires years of work.

The goal of getting a gold medal in the Olympics is a tremendous **undertaking** that only the most committed athletes will achieve.

words that are similar **attempt, work, try, setting in motion, embarking, endeavor**

words that are opposite **abstaining, forgoing, forgetting**

Look up the full definition of "undertaking" in the dictionary and use each definition in sentences of your own creation until you feel you fully understand the word and can use it in conversation.

Write five sentences using the noun "undertaking":

_____

_____

_____

_____

_____

_____

_____

slay

verb to kill intentionally

example sentences

It was a long fight, but the hero was finally able to **slay** the monster.

The knight often recounted the tale of when he **slew** the dragon with his sword.

In times of war men will **slay** one another.

also written in this form **slay, slew, slain, slayed**

words that are similar **kill, destroy, dispatch, erase, murder, massacre, slaughter**

words that are opposite **bear, create, give birth**

Look up the full definition of "slay" in the dictionary and use each definition in sentences of your own creation until you feel you fully understand the word and can use it in conversation.

Write five sentences using the verb "slay":

_____

_____

_____

_____

_____

_____

_____

Lesson 12.3 - Vocabulary

predecessor

noun **someone or something that came before in time**

example sentences

The VHS player is the **predecessor** to current recording technology such as DVDs.

Kenny's father was his **predecessor**.

The blacksmith would one day be the **predecessor** of his apprentice.

words that are similar **ancestor, forerunner, former, precursor, previous, prior**

words that are opposite **derivative, descendent, successor**

Look up the full definition of "predecessor" in the dictionary and use each definition in sentences of your own creation until you feel you fully understand the word and can use it in conversation.

Write five sentences using the noun "predecessor":

Lesson 12.4
Vocabulary

delicacy

noun the property of being beautiful, small or light; ALSO refined taste or tact

example sentences

He pulled the covers over her with the utmost **delicacy**, so as not to wake her.

Caviar is considered by many to be a fine **delicacy**.

Critics had described every dessert on the menu as a **delicacy** to be savored.

also written in this form **delicacies**

words that are similar **daintiness, fine, airiness, elegance, exquisiteness, fragility, frailty, lightness, transparency, weakness**

words that are opposite **coarseness, heaviness, indelicacy, inelegance, robustness, roughness**

Look up the full definition of "delicacy" in the dictionary and use each definition in sentences of your own creation until you feel you fully understand the word and can use it in conversation.

Write five sentences using the noun "delicacy":

_____

_____

_____

_____

_____

_____

_____

forsake

verb **to leave someone (who needs you or is counting on you)**

example sentences

It had been his idea to steal the car, but when his father found them in the driveway, he **forsook** his friend and blamed him for the wreck they'd been in.

The baron would **forsake** his country to lead the army of his family's enemies in order to take the throne for himself.

The hermit felt as though the world had forgotten and **forsaken** him.

also written in this form **forsook, forsaken, forsaking**

words that are similar **desert, disown, forgo, forswear, give up, leave, quit, renounce, resign, surrender, spurn**

words that are opposite **go back, rediscover, return, revert**

Look up the full definition of "forsake" in the dictionary and use each definition in sentences of your own creation until you feel you fully understand the word and can use it in conversation.

Write five sentences using the verb "forsake":

_____

_____

_____

_____

_____

_____

_____

_____

beseech

verb **to ask for or request seriously or eagerly**

example sentences

He **beseeched** his mom to make a chocolate cake for his birthday.

Math being his worst subject, the bully had to **beseech** a student he always picked on for help with his homework.

Some people might feel compelled to **beseech** world leaders for peaceful solutions to problems.

also written in this form **besought, beseeched, beseeching**

words that are similar **appeal, ask, entreat, implore, petition, plead, pray, solicit**

words that are opposite **give, offer**

Look up the full definition of "beseech" in the dictionary and use each definition in sentences of your own creation until you feel you fully understand the word and can use it in conversation.

Write five sentences using the verb "beseech":

_____

_____

_____

_____

_____

_____

_____

Lesson 12.4 - Vocabulary

philosophical

adjective characterized by the attitude of a philosopher: level-headed detachment about something

example sentences

Even though the relationship had lasted three years, he remained **philosophical** and told himself that it wasn't mean to be.

The senator remained **philosophical** about the budget cuts until it was his own wallet that would be affected.

She remained **philosophical** as her best friend recounted a story that was supposed to be entertaining.

words that are similar rational, logical, reflective, thoughtful, wise

words that are opposite irrational, thoughtless, unreasonable

Look up the full definition of "philosophical" in the dictionary and use each definition in sentences of your own creation until you feel you fully understand the word and can use it in conversation.

Write five sentences using the adjective "philosophical":

_____

_____

_____

_____

_____

_____

_____

_____

grove

noun a small growth of trees without any underbrush

example sentences

The family went out into the apple **grove** that morning to pick the fruit from the trees.

The peaceful **grove** was filled with the sounds of chirping birds.

The orange **grove** consisted of a few dozen trees.

words that are similar forest, orchard, plantation, thicket, wood, woodland

Look up the full definition of "grove" in the dictionary and use each definition in sentences of your own creation until you feel you fully understand the word and can use it in conversation.

Write five sentences using the noun "grove":

_____

_____

_____

_____

_____

_____

_____

_____

Lesson 12.4 - Vocabulary

frustrate

verb to get in the way of or hinder

example sentences

Changing the channel was enough for his little sister to **frustrate** him.

Connor was **frustrated** by the biology homework, which he couldn't understand.

He thought his mom always ruffled his hair after he brushed it just to **frustrate** him.

also written in this form frustrated, frustrating

words that are similar thwart, disappoint, hinder, block, cancel, counteract, defeat, discourage, halt, impede, inhibit, negate, prevent, prohibit

words that are opposite aid, assist, cooperate, encourage, facilitate, help, support

Look up the full definition of "frustrate" in the dictionary and use each definition in sentences of your own creation until you feel you fully understand the word and can use it in conversation.

Write five sentences using the verb "frustrate":

_____

_____

_____

_____

_____

_____

_____

illustrious

adjective **well known and considered esteemed or distinguished; famous**

example sentences

Many celebrities have **illustrious** careers that leave their mark on history.

The Noble Prize is an **illustrious** honor given only to the most deserving.

Acquiring a degree after years of study is an **illustrious** achievement.

words that are similar famous, prominent, celebrated, distinguished, glorious, noble, notable, noted, outstanding, remarkable, splendid, star, well-known

words that are opposite infamous, lowly, unimportant, unknown, unremarkable

Look up the full definition of "illustrious" in the dictionary and use each definition in sentences of your own creation until you feel you fully understand the word and can use it in conversation.

Write five sentences using the adjective "illustrious":

_____

_____

_____

_____

_____

_____

_____

_____

Lesson 12.4 - Vocabulary

device

noun an instrument invented for a particular purpose

example sentences

Jules hit the computer with his hand in the hopes that a jolt would fix the **device**.

He had to explain to his son that a blender is a **device** often used for making smoothies.

The film utilized many symbolic **devices** in order to get its message across.

words that are similar instrument, tool, apparatus, equipment, gadget, gear, mechanism, resource

Look up the full definition of "device" in the dictionary and use each definition in sentences of your own creation until you feel you fully understand the word and can use it in conversation.

Write five sentences using the noun "device":

_____

_____

_____

_____

_____

_____

_____

_____

pomp

noun cheap, pretentious display; ALSO ceremonial elegance and beauty

example sentences

Parades are often filled with **pomp**, from floats to costumes to music.

There is often a great deal of **pomp** involved in inauguration ceremonies.

The music, fireworks, and lightshow provided more **pomp** than the opening of the play warranted.

also written in this form **pompous**

words that are similar **affectation, grandeur, magnificence, vainglory, splendor, demonstration**

words that are opposite **dullness, plainness, simplicity**

Look up the full definition of "pomp" in the dictionary and use each definition in sentences of your own creation until you feel you fully understand the word and can use it in conversation.

Write five sentences using the noun "pomp":

_____

_____

_____

_____

_____

_____

_____

_____

entreat

verb **to earnestly ask for something**

example sentences

After the wreck he **entreated** his friend never to speak of the horrible night again.

They **entreated** her not to quit her job, but she did not listen.

June had to **entreat** her friend in order to try a bite of the dessert

also written in this form **entreating, entreated**

words that are similar **plead, ask, beg, beseech, petition, urge, wheedle, press, request**

words that are opposite **answer, command, demand**

Look up the full definition of "entreat" in the dictionary and use each definition in sentences of your own creation until you feel you fully understand the word and can use it in conversation.

Write five sentences using the verb "entreat":

_____

_____

_____

_____

_____

_____

_____

_____

Lesson 12.5
Vocabulary Review

As a review, **write one sentence using each of the words from this workbook.** Write a sentence that demonstrates your understanding of the word, not just its part of speech. For example, "It is substantial," is not a good demonstration of the word "substantial!" Try to create a sentence that you would provide as an example if you were helping someone else to understand the word. This will deepen your understanding of the vocabulary and help you remember it more easily.

If you don't remember the meaning of the word, have no fear! Look it up in your dictionary. This is an OPEN BOOK REVIEW! Look up what you need to help you make the sentences. It takes a lot of repetition to get this information down—nobody can remember it all just by looking at the vocabulary once.

accord

_____

_____

advocate

_____

_____

affect

_____

_____

afflict

_____

_____

allege

_____

_____

Lesson 12.5 - Vocabulary Review

apparent

appeal

appoint

approach

apt

ascertain

assail

assent

assert

_____

_____

attitude

_____

_____

attribute

_____

_____

bent

_____

_____

beseech

_____

_____

bestow

_____

_____

boast

_____

_____

bolt

_____

_____

Lesson 12.5 - Vocabulary Review

brook

---

campaign

---

canon

---

cardinal

---

cede

---

chamber

---

circumstances

---

cite

---

coast

commission

commit

compel

concept

concern

conduct

confer

consider

conspicuous

constant

constitute

contempt

contend

contract

contrive

convention

_____

_____

convince

_____

_____

court

_____

_____

cower

_____

_____

credible

_____

_____

crew

_____

_____

decree

_____

_____

delicacy

_____

_____

Lesson 12.5 - Vocabulary Review

dense

---

derived

---

despair

---

device

---

dispatch

---

disposition

---

distinction

---

dwell

---

earnest

elaborate

endow

engage

ensue

entertain

entreat

establish

Lesson 12.5 - Vocabulary Review

esteem

evident

exalt

exert

exertion

exploit

extravagant

facile

fancy

fare

financial

flag

flourish

formal

forsake

frontier

Lesson 12.5 - Vocabulary Review

frustrate

furnish

gale

generate

grant

gravity

grove

harried

heed

humble

humiliate

illustrious

impel

impose

inclined

indication

Lesson 12.5 - Vocabulary Review

insist

---

inspire

---

instance

---

institute

---

intimate

---

intrigue

---

issue

---

jet

---

justify

keen

kindle

knight

labor

latitude

league

level

liberal

lofty

majority

malice

manifest

merit

minute

mode

modest

multitude

muse

notion

notwithstanding

novel

obtain

oppress

Lesson 12.5 - Vocabulary Review

ordain

partial

passage

perish

perpetual

persist

philosophical

pious

plead

plus

policy

pomp

practice

predecessor

proceedings

project

property

provoke

purse

rail

range

reflect

render

resource

retort

rider

sanction

satire

scale

scarce

scheme

siege

Lesson 12.5 - Vocabulary Review

skill

_____

_____

slay

_____

_____

sob

_____

_____

stake

_____

_____

steep

_____

_____

steep

_____

_____

stock

_____

_____

straight

_____

_____

sublime

substantial

suffrage

suspended

temper

territory

theory

throng

Lesson 12.5 - Vocabulary Review

tide

---

toil

---

tour

---

tract

---

tread

---

undertake

---

undertaking

---

utter

---

vacate

vain

venerate

venture

vex

wander

warrant

wax

weigh

_____

_____

wont

_____

_____

yield

_____

_____

Lesson 13
Decoding Vocabulary

There are no vocabulary flash cards on the ACT. There is no moment when you'll need to recite the definitions of a word. That being said, chances are you'll encounter at least a couple questions which ask you for the meaning of a word or phrase as it is used in the passage. Even if you're familiar with the word, it might not be clear what its meaning is in the passage.

The key to solving this sort of question is to go find where the word or phrase is used, then use the information surrounding the word or phrase to eliminate the answer choices that don't work. Even if you don't understand what is being asked about, you can use the surrounding sentences to gain an insight into the meaning.

Transition words, like however, despite, and, therefore, and others can give you a hint about what the author is suggesting. These words tell you that the word or phrase either agrees or disagrees with what was said before.

Ask yourself these questions:

- How does this word relate to the rest of the sentence?
- The rest of the paragraph?
- Is it supposed to agree with what the author was already saying?
- Or is it supposed to disagree?
- Should it have a positive meaning?
- Or should it have a negative meaning?

Answer choices which don't fit what you expect can be eliminated. You'll be left with a simpler choice.

Another powerful technique you can use to answer even the most challenge vocab questions on the ACT Reading test is the substitution method. Replace the word being asked about with each of the answer choices. There will be at least a couple choices which simply do not fit the wording of the sentence or the meaning of the paragraph. Eliminating these choices will bring you much closer to a correct answer.

You can also use this method to weigh out two alternatives that look equally appealing to you. By using substitution, you might find that one choice is a better fit than another. Just looking at the answer choices, without plugging them into the passage as a whole, might not make this clear.

Keep in mind that you're not really being asked what a certain word means. You're really being asked: "Which of the following words or phrases could replace the word that we're asking you about?"

Let's practice solving questions of this type. Try using some of the techniques we have covered in this lesson.

Reading Mastery - Level 1

Passage

Instructions: Skim the passage in 3 minutes, then answer the 10 practice questions that appear below. Use a timer to keep track of when you should start answering the questions. Just like on the ACT, you are allowed to refer to the passage in order to find the correct answers.

NATURAL SCIENCE: This passage is adapted from *Cave Regions of the Ozarks and Black Hills* by Luella Agnes Owen, published by Editor Publishing Co.

Marble Cave, which is the finest yet explored in Missouri, is southeast of the center of Stone County, a short distance north of the picturesque White River.

Beyond the Wilderness is the Marble Cave
5 property and the entrance to the Cave is through a large sink-hole in the top of Roark Mountain. This hole is said to be about two hundred feet long, one hundred feet wide and thirty-five feet deep. It is shaped like a great oblong bowl with sloping sides, divided irregularly
10 near the middle, and having the bottom broken out in a jagged way that is very handsome and gives an ample support to the growth of ferns, wild roses, and other vegetation with which it is abundantly decorated. About half of the descent into the basin is accomplished
15 by scrambling down the roughly broken rocks, and the balance by a broad wooden stairway ending at a narrow platform that supports the locked gate.

Being the first visiting party of the season, certain disadvantages were encountered in a great
20 accumulation of wet clay and rubbish, washed in by the rains since the previous summer; but the gate was opened with considerable effort, and slowly and cautiously we descended the slippery, clay-banked stairs to the immense mound of debris forty-five feet
25 below the gate, to behold, at last, the grandeur of the Auditorium.

The magnificence of that one chamber should give to Marble Cave a world-wide fame even if there were nothing more beyond. The blue-gray limestone
30 walls have a greater charm than those of an open canyon, owing to the fact that they sweep away from any given point in long, true curves to form an elliptical chamber three hundred and fifty feet long by one hundred and twenty-five feet wide, with the vault above
35 showing absolute perfection of arch, and measuring, by the survey, from its lowest to its highest point, one hundred and ninety-five feet. In addition to the artistic superiority of architectural form, its acoustic properties having been tested, it is found to be truly an auditorium.
40 The curving walls and pure atmosphere combine to aid the voice, and carry its softest tones with marvelous distinctness to every portion of the immense enclosed space.

The chief ornament of the Auditorium is the White
45 Throne, a stalagmitic mass that when viewed from the stairway appears to rest solidly against the most distant wall, and looks so small an object in that vast space as to render a realization of its actual measurement impossible. The height of the Throne is sixty-five feet
50 and the girth two hundred. It is a mass of dripstone resting on a limestone base reserved from the ancient excavation to receive it, and on careful inspection the perpendicular lines, observed on the front, are found to be a set of rather large organ pipes. A fresh fracture
55 shows the Throne to be a most beautiful white and gold onyx. The outer surface has now received a thin coating of yellow clay which was, of course, regretted, but later observations on onyx building reveals the pleasing fact that if the crystal-bearing waters continue to drip, the
60 yellow clay will supply the coloring matter for a golden band of crystal.

In the vicinity of Marble Cave there are several choice varieties of onyx and marble, among them a rare and beautiful onyx in black and yellow. The
65 coloring, tinting and banding of onyx seem generally to be regarded as one of the unexplainable mysteries of nature, but is in reality an extremely simple process that can be easily studied in any active cave.

When the percolating acidulated water passes
70 slowly through a pure limestone it is filtered of impurities and deposits a crystal, either pure white or transparent; if it comes in contact with metallic bodies of any kind, it carries away more or less in solution to act as coloring matter; the beautiful pale green onyx in
75 several Missouri counties taking its tint from the copper; in South Dakota, manganese in various combinations produces black and many shades of brown; in both states an excessive flow of water often carries a quantity of red or yellow clay which temporarily destroys the
80 beauty of exposed surfaces, but in after years becomes a fine band of brilliant color.

Small wind caves are numerous in the Ozarks and being cold are frequently utilized for the preservation of domestic supplies. The entrance to one in the
85 neighborhood of Marble Cave is high up on the hillside south of Mr. Powell's house and being visible from the porch was too tempting to be ignored, and the walk up to it for a better view was rewarded with a most charming bit of scenery as well. All the quiet valley,
90 divided by a rushing little stream, lay before us in the shadow of early evening, while to the north and east the hills were brilliant in summer sunshine, with one small open glade gleaming vividly among the darker shades of forest green.

95 The cave was a very small room at the bottom of a steep, rocky, sloping passage, and contained no standing water, although there had been a heavy rainfall the night before and the opening is so situated as to especially favor the inflow, which naturally indicates a
100 greater cave beneath a hidden passage. Here, as in most of the caves of the region, is found a small lizard: it is totally blind but its ancestors evidently were not, as is shown by conspicuous protuberances where the eyes should be, but over which the skin is drawn without a
105 wrinkle or seam to indicate a former opening.

Those who love perfect Nature in a most smiling mood should hasten to visit Marble Cave while yet no railroad quite touches the county.

Lesson 13 - Decoding Vocabulary

1. As it is used in paragraph 4 (lines 27-43) the word acoustic most nearly means:

   A. related to sound
   B. related to sight
   C. artistic
   D. related to smell

2. As it is used in paragraph 3 (lines 18-26) the word grandeur most nearly means:

   F. impressive greatness.
   G. overwhelming sentimentality.
   H. overdone showmanship.
   J. understated beauty.

3. As it is used in paragraph 5 (lines 44-61) the word girth most nearly means:

   A. circumference.
   B. height.
   C. weight.
   D. angle.

4. As it is used in the second paragraph (lines 4-17), the word ample most nearly means:

   F. insufficient.
   G. parasitic.
   H. sufficient.
   J. minimal.

5. As it is used in the third paragraph (lines 18-26), the word accumulation most nearly means:

   A. a door or gate into another area.
   B. a mass that has gradually gathered.
   C. a small, cave-dwelling predator.
   D. the cause of erosion.

6. As it is used in paragraph 9 (lines 95-105), the word conspicuous most nearly means:

   F. standing out so as to be clearly visible.
   G. invisible to even the trained eye.
   H. hideous in appearance.
   J. of or related to lizards.

7. In the context of the passage, which of the following words best describes the Auditorium?

   A. Claustrophobic
   B. Infinite
   C. Infinitesimal
   D. Majestic

8. As it is used in paragraph 6 (lines 62-68), the word vicinity most nearly means:

   F. essence.
   G. area distant from.
   H. composition.
   J. area nearby.

9. According to the narrator, which of the following words does NOT describe the Marble Cave?

   A. Beautiful
   B. Striking
   C. Precarious
   D. Massive

10. As it is used in the last paragraph (lines 106-108), the phrase smiling mood most nearly means:

    F. cheerful countenance.
    G. positive aspect.
    H. sarcastic disposition.
    J. happy attitude.

Reading Mastery - Level 1

1. As it is used in paragraph 4 (lines 27-43) the word acoustic most nearly means:

   A. related to sound
   B. related to sight
   C. artistic
   D. related to smell

   First we find where the word "acoustic" is used in the paragraph. Since the sentence in which it is used states, "In addition to the artistic superiority of architectural form, its acoustic properties having been tested, it is found to be truly an auditorium," we can conclude that "acoustic properties" are different than "artistic superiority," so we can eliminate choice C. Additionally, the next sentence discusses sound: "The curving walls and pure atmosphere combine to aid the voice, and carry its softest tones with marvelous distinctness to every portion of the immense enclosed space." The way the sentence is written seems to support the previous statement, which gives us a clue that the word acoustic probably means "related to sound." Choice A is therefore our best answer. While much of the passage discusses what we see, this particular part of the passage is discussing what we hear.

2. As it is used in paragraph 3 (lines 18-26) the word grandeur most nearly means:

   F. impressive greatness.
   G. overwhelming sentimentality.
   H. overdone showmanship.
   J. understated beauty.

   Scan for where grandeur is used. It appears in the last sentence of the third paragraph, line 25. If we read on, we see that the word is being used to describe the auditorium, which receives further description in the next paragraph, in lines 27-29: "The magnificence of that one chamber should give to Marble Cave a world-wide fame even if there were nothing more beyond." The paragraph continues to describe a massive vault and its "artistic superiority." This description fits choice F, which is the best answer choice. We can eliminate G because "sentimentality" includes the idea of being emotional, and there is no mention of such emotions in the passage. Also, nothing in the passage indicates that the chamber is "overdone." The word "overdone" is usually used to describe something a person tried too hard to make look good, not something occurring in nature. The words "magnificence" and "artistic superiority," as well as the massive nature of what is being described, allow us to eliminate choice J. The chamber is anything but understated.

Lesson 13 - Decoding Vocabulary

3. As it is used in paragraph 5 (lines 44-61) the word girth most nearly means:

    A. **circumference.**
    B. height.
    C. weight.
    D. angle.

Scan for where the word girth is used in paragraph 5 (lines 44-61). It appears as part of this sentence, in lines 49 amd 50: "The height of the Throne is sixty-five feet and the girth two hundred." Since we can assume that "two hundred" is referring to a number of feet, we can eliminate weight and angle (choices C and D) as choices. We don't say someone weighs 200 feet, or that a line rises to a 200 feet angle. Since the throne has already been described in this sentence in terms of its height, our best guess is that girth is referring to the Throne's circumference, (choice A). Circumference, in this sense, means "the distance around something."

4. As it is used in the second paragraph (lines 4-17), the word ample most nearly means:

    F. insufficient.
    G. parasitic.
    H. **sufficient.**
    J. minimal.

Scan for where the word ample appears in the second paragraph (lines 4-17). It is found as part of the sentence which describes how the bottom of the sink-hole is broken in out in a jagged way and gives "an ample support to the growth of ferns, wild roses, and other vegetation with which it is abundantly decorated." If we aren't sure about the definition of ample, we are not able to make any definite decisions about eliminating any of the options, but we can look for the most likely answer. Since the bottom of the sinkhole is "abundantly decorated" with ferns, wild roses, and other vegetation, we can guess that these plants have enough support. If they had insufficient (not enough) support or minimal support, we might figure that they wouldn't be so abundant (having plenty of something.) Parasitic support would harm what is being supported, so this doesn't fit with abundant either. For those reasons, choice H is our best choice.

Reading Mastery - Level 1

5. As it is used in the third paragraph (lines 18-26), the word accumulation most nearly means:

   A. a door or gate into another area.
   B. **a mass that has gradually gathered.**
   C. a small, cave-dwelling predator.
   D. the cause of erosion.

Scan for where the word in question occurs. It appears in the first sentence of the third paragraph, in lines 18-21: "Being the first visiting party of the season, certain disadvantages were encountered in a great accumulation of wet clay and rubbish, washed in by the rains since the previous summer." This sentence tells us that the accumulation is composed of wet clay and rubbish, and that it was washed in by rains. This allows us to eliminate choices A and C (since wet clay and rubbish hardly make a gate or a living thing.) Choice B is a better fit to the sense of the sentence. If we substitute the answers in for where the word is used, it clicks: "Being the first visiting party of the season, certain disadvantages were encountered in a great mass that had gradually gathered of wet clay and rubbish, washed in by the rains since the previous summer" Therefore choice B is the best answer.

6. As it is used in paragraph 9 (lines 95-105), the word conspicuous most nearly means:

   F. **standing out so as to be clearly visible.**
   G. invisible to even the trained eye.
   H. hideous in appearance.
   J. of or related to lizards.

First find where the word conspicuous appears. It can be found in the last sentence of paragraph 9, in lines 100-105: "Here, as in most of the caves of the region, is found a small lizard: it is totally blind but its ancestors evidently were not, as is shown by conspicuous protuberances where the eyes should be, but over which the skin is drawn without a wrinkle or seam to indicate a former opening." Since these conspicuous protuberances are shown, we can eliminate choice G. An invisible feature would not be shown. We can also eliminate choice H, since this definition of the word would cause the sentence to have a tone that is completely inconsistent with the rest of the passage. Marble Cave is described as wonderful and beautiful, not hideous and scary. Of the two choices remaining, choice F clearly fits, while choice J might fit, but goes against our instincts. The sentence already mentions that we are talking about a lizard, so why would the author use another word to mention that the animal's protuberances are lizard-like? Choice F is the correct answer.

Lesson 13 - Decoding Vocabulary

7. In the context of the passage, which of the following words best describes the Auditorium?

    A. Claustrophobic
    B. Infinite
    C. Infinitesimal
    D. Majestic

The Auditorium is described in paragraph 4 (lines 27-43). The best choice is majestic, which in this sense means "showing impressive beauty." This is supported by the chamber and its characteristics being described with words like magnificence, charm, perfection, superiority, and marvelous. Infinite would mean that the Auditorium would never end, and infinitesimal would indicate that the Auditorium is exceedingly small. If the space were claustrophobic, it would feel closed in and too tight, but the room is described as massive. Therefore choice D is the best answer.

8. As it is used in paragraph 6 (lines 62-68), the word vicinity most nearly means:

    F. essence.
    G. area distant from.
    H. composition.
    J. area nearby.

Find where vicinity is used in paragraph 6 (lines 62-68). It appears in this sentence, in lines 62-64: "In the vicinity of Marble Cave there are several choice varieties of onyx and marble, among them a rare and beautiful onyx in black and yellow." Choices F and H can be eliminated because the words essence and composition don't fit seamlessly with the sentence. It doesn't make sense to say "In the essence of Marble Cave there are several choice varieties..." If we wanted to talk about the core properties or composition of the cave, we wouldn't phrase the sentence like that. Between choices G and J, we go with J. The reason for this is that the entire passage is talking about Marble Cave. Why would the author change his focus to an area far away from Marble Cave? It's more likely he's talking about the rocks near Marble Cave.

9. According to the narrator, which of the following words does NOT describe the Marble Cave?

    A. Beautiful
    B. Striking
    C. Precarious
    D. Massive

In the passage, the author provides details that support the description of the Marble Cave as beautiful, striking (meaning in this sense "attracting attention by being unusual or prominent"), and massive (meaning in this sense "large.") Even if we aren't sure about the definition of precarious, which means in this sense "dangerously likely to fall or collapse," we can eliminate all the other choices. There are no details in the passage which support the idea of the cave being likely to collapse, so choice C is the best answer.

10. As it is used in the last paragraph (lines 106-108), the phrase smiling mood most nearly means:

F. cheerful countenance.
G. positive aspect.
H. sarcastic disposition.
J. happy attitude.

Take a look at the last paragraph (lines 106-108). From the combination of the words smiling and mood we can tell that we are talking about a happy attitude, but this question is a bit tricky. This phrase, as it is used in the last paragraph, does not mean happy attitude. Nature, itself, cannot literally have an attitude. For that reason we eliminate choice J. Instead we can conclude that we are talking about a positive side, or positive aspect, of Nature. Choice G is therefore our best bet. Choice F is wrong for the same reason that choice J is. Nature does not have a countenance, which in this sense means "a person's face or facial expression." Choice H does work because sarcastic is a negative word meaning "showing contempt" which does not fit with the tone and concept of the paragraph it is used in.

Reading Mini-Practice Tests

In the next section, you'll work through a series of eight mini-tests. These mini-tests emulate what you might actually encounter on the ACT. They are a great opportunity to improve your ability to pace yourself through the test and answer the wide variety of content that the ACT can throw at you.

As you work through these practice tests, be sure to use a timer. You want to read the question and answer the ten questions that go with it within eight minutes. Using this guideline, you can finish the entire Reading test with three minutes to spare.

You'll get the maximum benefit from these mini-tests if you imagine that you are in an actual ACT test environment.

Don't just blow through these mini-tests. Answer one at a time, then examine the explanations to the answer choices that appear behind each test. Reviewing answer explanations improves your certainty and confidence in answering ACT Reading questions, and so this is an important step that you should not skip.

These mini-tests are presented in a sequence that emulates the actual ACT. You'll first answer a "Literary Narrative," or "Prose" segment. In this segment, the passages are based either on fictional short stories or novels, or on non-fiction personal essays or memoirs, which are "biographies written from personal knowledge." They read like stories.

The key to getting through the this first segment of the ACT reading test is to make yourself as interested as you possibly can in the story being discussed. Engage with the passage like you would read a story, and try to skim it with the attitude that you might turn around and tell someone else the story one day. You can actually trick your brain into caring what is being talked about, and when you do that, you'll find it's much easier to remember where to find the details you need in the passage.

Try this in the mini-test you're about to work through.

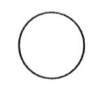

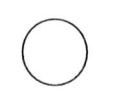

Reading Test
35 Minutes — 40 Questions

Directions: There are four passages in this portion of the test. Following each passage you will be given a variety of questions. Choose the best answer to each question, then color its corresponding bubble on your answer sheet. Refer to the passages as needed.

Passage I

PROSE FICTION: This passage is an excerpt from F. Scott Fitzgerald's short story, "The Jelly-Bean," published in 1922 as part of a collection of short stories called *Tales from the Jazz Age*.

Jim Powell was a Jelly-bean. Much as I desire to make him an appealing character, I feel that it would be unscrupulous to deceive you on that point. He was a bred-in-the-bone, dyed-in-the-
5 wool, ninety-nine three-quarters per cent Jelly-bean and he grew lazily all during Jelly-bean season, which is every season, down in the land of the Jelly-beans well below the Mason-Dixon line.

Now if you call a Memphis man a Jelly-bean he
10 will quite possibly pull a long sinewy rope from his hip pocket and hang you to a convenient telegraph-pole. If you call a New Orleans man a Jelly-bean he will probably grin and ask you who is taking your girl to the Mardi Gras ball. The particu-
15 lar Jelly-bean patch which produced the protagonist of this history lies somewhere between the two—a little city of forty thousand that has dozed sleepily for forty thousand years in southern Georgia occasionally stirring in its slumbers and muttering
20 something about a war that took place sometime, somewhere, and that everyone else has forgotten long ago.

Jim was a Jelly-bean. I write that again because it has such a pleasant sound—rather like the be-
25 ginning of a fairy story—as if Jim were nice. It somehow gives me a picture of him with a round, appetizing face and all sort of leaves and vegetables growing out of his cap. But Jim was long and thin and bent at the waist from stooping over pool
30 tables, and he was what might have been known in the indiscriminating North as a corner loafer. "Jelly-bean" is the name throughout the un-dissolved Confederacy for one who spends his life conjugating the verb to idle in the first person singular—I
35 am idling, I have idled, I will idle.

Jim was born in a white house on a green corner. It had four weather-beaten pillars in front and a great amount of lattice-work in the rear that made a cheerful crisscross background for a flowery sun-
40 drenched lawn. Originally the dwellers in the white house had owned the ground next door and next door to that and next door to that, but this had been so long ago that even Jim's father, scarcely remembered it. He had, in fact, thought it a matter
45 of so little moment that when he was dying from a pistol wound got in a brawl he neglected even to tell little Jim, who was five years old and miserably frightened. The white house became a boarding house run by a tight-lipped lady from Macon,
50 whom Jim called Aunt Mamie and detested with all his soul.

He became fifteen, went to high school, wore his hair in black snarls, and was afraid of girls. He hated his home where four women and one old man
55 prolonged an interminable chatter from summer to summer about what lots the Powell place had originally included and what sorts of flowers would be out next. Sometimes the parents of little girls in town, remembering Jim's mother and fancying a
60 resemblance in the dark eyes and hair, invited him to parties, but parties made him shy and he much preferred sitting on a disconnected axle in Tilly's Garage, rolling the bones or exploring his mouth endlessly with a long straw. For pocket money, he
65 picked up odd jobs, and it was due to this that he stopped going to parties. At his third party little Marjorie Haight had whispered indiscreetly and within hearing distance that he was a boy who brought the groceries sometimes. So instead of the
70 two-step and polka, Jim had learned to throw any number he desired on the dice and had listened to spicy tales of all the shootings that had occurred in the surrounding country during the past fifty years.

Reading Mini-Test 1

1. Based on the passage, the reader can infer that:
   A. Jim Powell was a good friend of F. Scott Fitzgerald throughout their lives.
   B. Jim Powell was a pleasant and amiable man.
   C. Jim Powell was a prominent figure during the '20s.
   D. Jim Powell was an odd and lazy man from the South.

2. This story takes place in which state?
   F. Tennessee
   G. Georgia
   H. Louisiana
   J. Virginia

3. In what way does the author use the term "Jelly-bean?"
   A. As a derogatory term used by a Northern man to insult a Southern man
   B. As a negative term for someone who does not put a lot of effort into anything
   C. As a term of endearment for a close friend
   D. As a nickname for someone with many amiable qualities

4. The fourth paragraph (lines 36-51) is used to detail:
   F. Jim Powell's beautiful home that set the scene for his childhood.
   G. Jim Powell's unfortunate childhood and untimely death of his father.
   H. Jim Powell's middle-class upbringing and how that affected him as a young boy.
   J. how Jim Powell was affected by his father's drinking habit.

5. Why does the main character get invited to parties?
   A. Because his looks remind people of his mother
   B. Because he is outgoing and friendly
   C. People pity him because his parents are dead
   D. Because he is shy and people want to help him with his social skills

6. Why is Jim Powell humiliated at the third party?
   F. Party-goers were gossiping about his lowly job
   G. Party-goers made him uncomfortable because they wanted him to dance
   H. Party-goers made fun of him for working at Tilly's Garage
   J. Party-goers made him eat straw

7. The passage portrays the South during the 1920's as:
   A. full of frivolous parties with drinking and dancing.
   B. a place where industry was booming and productivity was revered.
   C. inhabited by unemployed residents who passed the day sitting on their front porch.
   D. a place that Jim Powell could not quite fit in to.

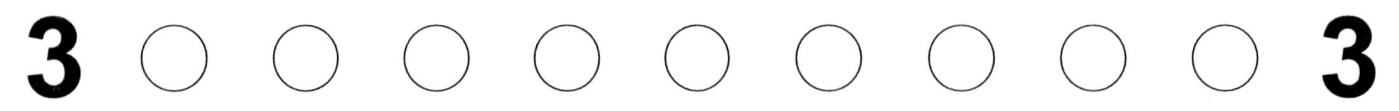

8. The narrator uses the term "Jelly-bean" rather than an alternative term because:

   F. it has a negative connotation and he intends to generalize southerners.
   G. he likes the way it sounds.
   H. the word evokes the imagery of candy.
   J. it is a common nickname that many readers can relate to.

9. In lines 69-73, it is implied that Jim Powell:

   A. becomes a social outcast with a bad reputation.
   B. develops a gambling problem.
   C. joins the military and goes off to war.
   D. makes a lot of money at the casino.

10. The overall tone of the passage is:

    F. comical and entertaining.
    G. cynical and patronizing.
    H. formal and didactic.
    J. descriptive and straightforward.

Reading Mastery - Level 1

Answer Explanations

1. **The correct answer is D.** The author frequently uses words like "idle" and "lazily" and describes Jim Powell as an outsider.

2. **The correct answer is G.** In lines 16-18 the author describes the location as "a little city of forty thousand that has dozed sleepily for forty thousand years in southern Georgia."

3. **The correct answer is B.** In lines 31-35 the author explains the term "Jelly-Bean" as someone who idles. Idle is another term for not moving or lazy.

4. **The correct answer is G.** The fourth paragraph explains the home life Jim Powell had as a child. Jim's father died when he was very young and then he was raised by a strict, harsh woman.

5. **The correct answer is A.** Lines 59-61 says that parents of little girls remembered Jim's mother and fancied a resemblance in his dark eyes and hair, so invited him to parties.

6. **The correct answer is F.** In lines 66-69 the author writes that Marjorie Haight was whispering about how Jim was a grocery boy.

7. **The correct answer is D.** It is evident throughout the passage that Jim is not able to fit in with the culture, people, and activities surrounding him.

8. **The correct answer is G.** In lines 23-24 the author writes that "[Jelly bean] has such a pleasant sound."

9. **The correct answer is A.** The last few lines of the passage explain how Jim Powell stops going to parties and becomes interested in gambling and fighting.

10. **The correct answer is J.** The passage is entirely devoted to introducing and describing Jim as a character. This choice better fits the passage than the other options.

Reading Mini-Test 2

The second passage in the ACT Reading test is always in the category of "Social Studies" or "Social Science."

Passages in this category might be about history, historical people and their stories, business, education, geography, politics, or psychology.

In other words, these passages are about people, either as individuals or groups, the things they do and the things they've done, and the way they think. They're about how people act and how they interact with the environment.

The human interest part of this passage type can help you stay engaged with the passage. While you are reading through the passage in the first three minutes of the segment, you want to stay as interested as possible. The more engaged you are with the passage, the less likely your brain will "skip tracks" or blank out.

Try to identify with the people being discussed, if there are people being discussed. Imagine what it would be like to be them. Imagine you're one of the people being described. You'd be amazed how much easier it is to remember what the passage is talking about using this trick.

I'm not saying to sit there and meditate for half an hour on what the passage is talking about. I'm just saying that as you are reading the passage, and without taking up any additional time, try to read it in a way that makes it interesting to you.

Try this technique with the passage that we'll work through in this lesson.

Remember to check your answers and read the explanations for the questions before you move on to the next mini-test.

Passage II

HUMANITIES: This passage is an excerpt from "Famous Men of the Middle Ages" written by John H. Haaren and A. B. Poland, two superintendents of schools in New York and New Jersey.

Pepin had two sons, Charles and Carloman. After the death of their father they ruled together, but in a few years Carloman died, and then Charles became sole king.

This Charles was the most famous of the kings of the Franks. He did so many great and wonderful things that he is called Charlemagne, which means Charles the Great.

He was a great soldier. For thirty years he carried on a war against the Saxons. Finally he conquered them, and their great chief, Wittekind, submitted to him. The Saxons were a people of Germany, who then lived near the land of the Franks. They spoke the same language and were of the same race as the Franks, but had not been civilized by contact with the Romans.

They were still pagans, just as the Franks had been before Clovis became a Christian. They actually offered human sacrifices.

After Charlemagne conquered them he made their lands part of his kingdom. A great number of them, among whom was Wittekind, then became Christians and were baptized; and soon they had churches and schools in many parts of their country.

Another of Charlemagne's wars was against the Lombards. Pepin, as you have read, had defeated the Lombards and given to the Pope part of the country held by them. The Lombard king now invaded the Pope's lands and threatened Rome itself; so the Pope sent to Charlemagne for help.

Charlemagne quickly marched across the Alps and attacked the Lombards. He drove them out of the Pope's lands and took possession of their country.

After he had conquered the Lombards he carried on war, in 778, in Spain. A large portion of Spain was then held by the Moorish Saracens. But a Mohammedan leader from Damascus had invaded their country, and the Moors invited Charlemagne to help them. He therefore led an army across the Pyrenees. He succeeded in putting his Moorish friends in possession of their lands in Spain and then set out on his return to his own country.

On the march his army was divided into two parts. The main body was led by Charlemagne himself. The rear guard was commanded by a famous warrior named Roland. While marching through the narrow pass of Roncesvalles, among the Pyrenees, Roland's division was attacked by a tribe called the Basques, who lived on the mountain slopes of the neighboring region.

High cliffs walled in the pass on either side. From the tops of these cliffs the Basques hurled down rocks and trunks of trees upon the Franks, and crushed many of them to death. Besides this, the wild mountaineers descended into the pass and attacked them with weapons. Roland fought bravely; but at last he was overpowered, and he and all his men were killed.

Roland had a friend and companion named Oliver, who was as brave as Roland. Many stories and songs have been written telling of the wonderful adventures they were said to have had and of their wonderful deeds in war.

The work of Charlemagne in Spain was quickly undone; for Abd-er-Rahman, the leader of the Mohammedans who had come from Damascus, soon conquered almost all the territory south of the Pyrenees.

11. The main purpose of this passage is to:
    A. give an elaborate detail of the history of France.
    B. inform the reader of a prominent figure in French history.
    C. provide a narrative for a famous French battle during medieval times.
    D. describe various battles in France during the Middle Ages.

12. Based on the passage, the reader can infer that the authors believe:
    F. Charlemagne was considered a great leader of the Franks.
    G. Charlemagne was a merciless and imperialist conqueror.
    H. the Lombards were a common enemy among all the regions of the Roman Empire.
    J. Charlemagne should have never wasted time invading Spain.

13. Lines 17-24 imply that:
    A. Paganism is a strange, but acceptable religion.
    B. Christianity is a better religion than Paganism.
    C. Charlemagne's people worked to convert the people they conquered to Christianity.
    D. people who practice paganism are Christian.

14. It can reasonably be inferred from lines 27-30 that many people of the Roman Empire believed Charlemagne to be:
    F. a fearless soldier who willingly killed any enemy.
    G. an invader of lands in the name of the Pope.
    H. a great friend and confidante of the Pope.
    J. an honorable and reliable aid in times of need.

15. In the author's description of the multiple wars of Charlemagne, it is apparent that:
    A. Charlemagne had many enemies who frequently threatened his land.
    B. Charlemagne went in search of battles everywhere he went because he was inherently violent.
    C. many of the wars were not actually Charlemagne's battles but rather wars he was fighting for other people.
    D. Charlemagne desperately wanted to instill Christianity throughout Europe and was willing to do so with force.

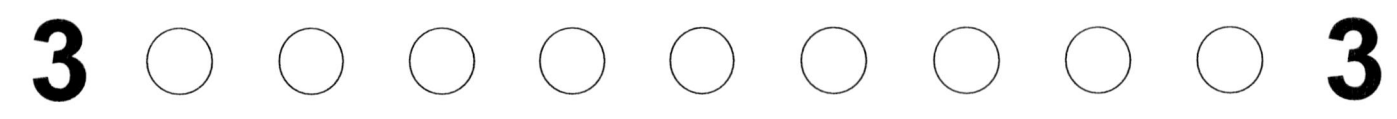

16. The main purpose of the fifth paragraph (lines 20-24) functioning as part of the entire passage is to:

   F. demonstrate the author's belief that Christianity is the superior religion.
   G. explain and justify Charlemagne's actions as an act of devotion.
   H. embody the main idea of the passage as an all-encompassing belief that Christianity improves the lives of many people.
   J. specify Charlemagne's actions as an expansion of Christianity throughout Europe.

17. Roland's death is described as:

   A. a valiant and honorable event that has been highlighted throughout French history.
   B. an unexpected but justified massacre because Roland and his men were invading foreign territory.
   C. a controversial way to die given the time period and circumstances.
   D. just another repercussion of war and battle.

18. From the passage, the reader can reasonably infer that Roland was:

   F. younger than Charlemagne.
   G. Charlemagne's son.
   H. a war hero who helped Charlemagne in all his conquests.
   J. Charlemagne's second in command and most trusted soldier.

19. In lines 6-8, the author's attitude towards Charlemagne can best be described as:

   A. admiring and reverential.
   B. sarcastic and mocking.
   C. appreciative and approving.
   D. marveling and deriding.

20. By including the failed acquisition of Spain, the author is:

   F. depicting an unbiased portrayal of an important time in French history.
   G. creating a well-rounded and thorough depiction of Charlemagne's conquests.
   H. revealing flaws in a historical figure who is commonly idolized and revered.
   J. introducing another one of Charlemagne's enemies.

Reading Mastery - Level 1

Answer Explanations

11. **The correct answer is B.** It is an educational passage giving detail about Charlemagne.

12. **The correct answer is F.** In lines 5-7 the author says "Charlemagne was the most famous king of the Franks. He did so many great and wonderful things…"

13. **The correct answer is C.** The author details how many Saxons converted to Christianity after being conquered.

14. **The correct answer is J.** The author tells about a time when the Pope called for Charlemagne's help and Charlemagne went right away.

15. **The correct answer is C.** The author tells of multiple wars that Charlemagne fought in and many of them were not started by Charlemagne.

16. **The correct answer is J.** The author writes about positive repercussions of Charlemagne conquering people and converting them to Christianity, setting up schools, etc.

17. **The correct answer is A.** The author writes, "Roland fought bravely" and that "many stories and songs have been written telling of the wonderful adventures."

18. **The correct answer is J.** The author writes that Roland commanded the rear guard and was a famous warrior.

19. **The correct answer is A.** The author makes a very positive description of Charlemagne throughout the passage.

20. **The correct answer is G.** The author could have only included Charlemagne's victories, but he also includes Charlemagne's defeats. The author, however, doesn't go so far as to depict a specific flaw of Charlemagne.

Reading Mini-Test 3

The third ACT Reading passage always concerns the "Humanities." By humanities, we mean things like architecture, art, film, language, music, literature, radio, theater, and philosophy.

To put it simply, the humanities passage is usually about some kind of art or philosophy.

While the second passage might talk about how Amazonians make violins out of environmentally sound wood, the third passage would be more concerned with the art of concert violinists.

Again, it's human interest that can increase your level of interest in this type of passage. You can trick your brain into being interested in this type of passage by telling yourself, "Wow, I always wanted to know more about _____ !" In the blank, insert what is being discussed. The more you can ignore the fact that you're being dragged through the ACT Reading passages kicking and screaming, the better you'll be able to perform on the ACT Reading test.

As you skim the passage in the first 3 minutes, associate what's being discussed with anything that you've personally experienced in your life to make it more memorable. Don't let unfamiliar words or concepts confuse you. If you don't know what a word or phrase is saying, take it as an opportunity. If that unfamiliar word shows up in the questions, you'll know exactly where you need to look!

We don't recommend an underlining strategy or note-taking tricks, because these things can slow you down, but one thing that can help you focus, if you are having difficulty with understanding a passage, is underlining words or phrases that you are unsure about. This can help you quickly diagnose where the comprehension problem is coming from. But the best thing to do is just move on! You only have three minutes for your skim.

Challenge yourself to answer the next set of questions as quickly and accurately as possible.

Passage III

SOCIAL SCIENCES: This passage is from Emmeline Pankhurst's "My Own Story" published in 1914. Emmeline Pankhurst was an activist during the Women's Suffrage Movement in Great Britain in the early 1900s.

When it came my turn to speak, realizing that the average man is profoundly ignorant of the history of the women's movement—because the press has never adequately or truthfully chronicled the movement—I told the jury, as briefly as I could, the story of the forty years' peaceful agitation before my daughters and I resolved that we would give our lives to the work of getting the vote for women, and that we should use whatever means of getting the vote that were necessary to success.

"We founded the Women's Social and Political Union," I said, "in 1903. Our first intention was to try and influence the particular political Party, which was then coming into power, to make this question of the enfranchisement of women their own question and to push it. It took some little time to convince us—and I need not weary you with the history of all that has happened—but it took some little time to convince us that that was no use; that we could not secure things in that way. Then in 1905 we faced the hard facts. We realized that there was a Press boycott against Women's Suffrage. Our speeches at public meetings were not reported, our letters to the editors, were not published, even if we implored the editors; even the things relating to Women's Suffrage in Parliament were not recorded. They said the subject was not of sufficient public interest to be reported in the Press, and they were not prepared to report it. Then with regard to the men politicians in 1905: we realized how shadowy were the fine phrases about democracy, about human equality, used by the gentlemen who were then coming into power. They meant to ignore the women—there was no doubt whatever about that. For in the official documents coming from the Liberal party on the eve of the 1905 election, there were sentences like this: 'What the country wants is a simple measure of Manhood Suffrage.' There was no room for the inclusion of women. We knew perfectly well that if there was to be franchise reform at all, the Liberal party which was then coming into power did not mean Votes for Women, in spite of all the pledges of members; in spite of the fact that a majority of the House of Commons, especially on the Liberal side, were pledged to it—it did not mean that they were going to put it into practice. And so we found some way of forcing their attention to this question.

Now I come to the facts with regard to militancy. We realized that the plans we had in our minds would involve great sacrifice on our part, that it might cost us all we had. We were at that time a little organization, composed in the main of working women, the wives and daughters of working men. And my daughters and I took a leading part, naturally, because we thought the thing out, and, to a certain extent, because we were of better social position than most of our members, and we felt a sense of responsibility."

I went over the whole matter of our peaceful deputations, and of the violence with which they were invariably met; of our arrests and the farcical police court trials, where the mere evidence of policemen's unsupported statements sent us to prison for long terms; of the falsehoods told of us in the House of Commons by responsible members of the Government—tales of women scratching and biting policemen and using hatpins—and I accused the Government of making these attacks against women who were powerless to defend themselves because they feared the women and desired to crush the agitation represented by our organization.

Reading Mini-Test 3

21. What is the context indicated by this passage?
    A. Emmeline Pankhurst is talking to her fellow women activists about the next course of action.
    B. Emmeline Pankhurst is on trial for leading women's rights protests.
    C. Emmeline Pankhurst is addressing a group of senators who support the Women's Suffrage Movement.
    D. Susan B. Anthony is persuading Emmeline Pankhurst to join the Women's Suffrage Movement.

22. What was the author trying to accomplish through her actions?
    F. Equal job opportunities
    G. Equal pay for men and women
    H. Women's right to vote
    J. Women's right to own property

23. Where was the author trying to succeed?
    A. The south of the United States
    B. All of the United States
    C. The United Kingdom
    D. Globally

24. According to the author, why is the general public oblivious to the Women's Suffrage Movement?
    F. The media dismissed all efforts of publicity made by women and never accurately portrayed the history of the movement.
    G. Society is run by men and men are ignorant of women's rights movements.
    H. No one showed up for all of the women's speeches.
    J. The media only portrayed women's rights protests in negative light by showing bouts of violence.

25. The author is implying with the word "shadowy" (line 31) that:
    A. the politicians do not really mean what they say about various topics.
    B. democracy is ignorant of women's rights.
    C. the government only protects certain members of society.
    D. democracy maintains a constitutional canopy over all members of society.

26. The author claims that most political support for women's rights comes from:
    F. the Liberal Party.
    G. the House of Commons.
    H. the newspapers and media outlets.
    J. none other than the Women's Social and Political Union.

27. According to the author, how does social status influence a woman's participation in the Women's Suffrage Movement?
    A. Women of higher social status were more likely to be involved in the movement because they had more time and resources.
    B. Working class women were most inclined to join the movement.
    C. Upper class women felt a sense of responsibility to society.
    D. The movement was comprised of only upper class women who felt entitled to a vote.

409

28. As a function of the entire passage, what is the purpose of lines 60-72?

    F. To evoke empathy from the jury for helpless women inaccurately portrayed
    G. To convince the reader that the women's rights movement is violent
    H. To explain that women were actually stronger than men when the movement erupted in violence
    J. To prove that the Women's Suffrage Movement was not actually violent, but only characterized that way

29. What is the author referring to when she mentions "militancy"?

    A. The adamant and aggressive pursuit of women's rights
    B. The use of weapons in the Women's Suffrage Movement
    C. The U.S. Military's interference in the women's rights movement
    D. The involvement of female soldiers in the Women's Suffrage Movement

30. The reader can interpret that the author believes men in general are:

    F. inherently to blame for inequality in society.
    G. comfortable the way things are and unwilling to reform to include women's right.
    H. uninformed about the women's movement, and so men in power were able largely block the women's suffrage movement.
    J. actively resisting all efforts made by women's suffrage movements as a way to maintain power and control in society.

410

Reading Mastery - Level 1

Answer Explanations

21. **The correct answer is B.** Emmeline Pankhurst is addressing a jury (line 5).

22. **The correct answer is H.** "Suffrage" is the right to vote.

23. **The correct answer is C.** Emmeline Pankhurst was from England, which is evident in line 26-27 when she mentions Parliament, and in the introduction which mentions "Great Britain."

24. **The correct answer is F.** In lines 22-29 she details the "press boycott against Women's Suffrage."

25. **The correct answer is A.** She is talking about the "fine phrases about democracy...used by the gentlemen," but on line 34 says that the politicians "meant to ignore women."

26. **The correct answer is J.** The author describes how the other organizations and political parties that are answer choices did not express any interest in women's equality.

27. **The correct answer is B.** The author writes in lines 52-54 that many working women or the wives of working men joined the movement.

28. **The correct answer is J.** The last paragraph refutes claims that "women were biting police officers," etc.

29. **The correct answer is A.** When the author refers to "militancy" she is talking about the efforts made by women as part of the movement. The definition of "militant" is "having a combative character; aggressive, especially in the service of a cause."

30. **The correct answer is H.** The author never directly attacks men in general for being intentionally ignorant, but rather they are ignorant as a result of their media and government, which neglects women.

Reading Mini-Test 4

The final reading passage always concerns "Natural Science." You could say that the science section of the ACT actually starts with the last reading passage. This passage could be about a wide number of science topics, including biology, chemistry, medicine, physics, technology, and zoology.

Tough vocab has the tendency of appearing in this section. The overall language of the passage will often be simpler, but the passage might use language specialized to the topic being talked about. The key to tough vocab in the Natural Science passage is to remember that most specialized science terms are just labels for objects or things that are observed. If they say fluorine, and you don't know what that is, keep in mind that they could have just said that chemical and the passage would still make sense. Use the strange words to help you stay oriented on where to find the details that you need in the passage.

Many Natural Science questions will ask you to find details, which can be the simplest of the question types. Do yourself a favor and actually get to this passage with at least eight minutes to spare. Several of the questions will be gimmies, if you can read past the strange terms and if you give yourself enough time.

Let's practice a Natural Science passage with its questions. Time yourself 8 minutes for this segment. Remember to review the answers and explanations when you're done.

Passage IV

NATURAL SCIENCE: This passage is adapted from George H. Carpenter's "The Life Story of Insects" published in 1913.

Insects as a whole are preeminently creatures of the land and the air. This is shown not only by the possession of wings by a vast majority of the class, but by the mode of breathing through a system of branching air tubes carrying atmospheric air with its combustion-supporting oxygen to all the insect's tissues. The air gains access to these tubes through a number of paired air holes or spiracles, arranged segmentally in series.

It is of great interest to find that, nevertheless, a number of insects spend much of their time under water. This is true of not a few in the perfect winged state, as for example aquatic beetles and water bugs ('boatmen' and 'scorpions') which have some way of protecting their spiracles when submerged, and, possessing usually the power of flight, can pass on occasion from pond or stream to upper air. But it is advisable in connection with our present subject to dwell especially on some insects that remain continually under water till they are ready to undergo their final molt and attain the winged state, which they pass entirely in the air. The preparatory instars of such insects are aquatic; the adult instar is aerial. All may flies, dragonflies, and caddis flies, many beetles and two-winged flies, and a few moths thus divide their life story between the water and the air. For the present we confine attention to the Stoneflies, the Mayflies, and the Dragon flies.

In the case of many insects that have aquatic larvae, the latter are provided with some arrangement for enabling them to reach atmospheric air through the surface film of the water. But the larva of a stonefly, a dragonfly, or a mayfly is adapted more completely than these for aquatic life; it can, by means of gills of some kind, breathe the air dissolved in water.

The aquatic young of a stonefly does not differ sufficiently in form from its parent to warrant us in calling it a larva; the life history is like that of a cockroach, all the instars however except the final one—the winged adult or imago—live in the water. The young of one of our large species, a Perla for example, has well-chitinized cuticle, broad head, powerful legs, long feelers and cerci like those of the imago; its wings arise from external rudiments, which are conspicuous in the later aquatic stages. But it lives completely submerged, usually clinging or walking beneath the stones that lie in the bed of a clear stream, and examination of the ventral aspect of the thorax reveals six pairs of tufted gills, by means of which it is able to breathe the air dissolved in the water wherein it lives. At the base of the tail-feelers or cerci also, there are little tufts of thread-like gills. An insect that is continually submerged and has no contact with the upper air cannot breathe through a series of paired spiracles, and during the aquatic life period of the stonefly these remain closed. Nevertheless, breathing is carried on by means of the ordinary system of branching air-tubes, the trunks of which are in connection with the tufted hollow gill-filaments, through whose delicate cuticle gaseous exchange can take place, though the method of this exchange is as yet very imperfectly understood. When the stonefly nymph is fully grown, it comes out of the water and climbs to some convenient eminence. The cuticle splits open along the back, and the imago, clothed in its new cuticle, as yet soft and flexible, creeps out. The spiracles are now open, and the stonefly breathes atmospheric air like other flying insects. But throughout its winged life, the stonefly bears memorials of its aquatic past in the little withered vestiges of gills that can still be distinguished beneath the thorax.

Reading Mini-Test 4

31. The author's purpose for writing this passage can best be explained as:
    A. to create a literary manifestation of his love for insects.
    B. to educate readers on the life story of insects.
    C. to compare and contrast the stonefly with the dragonfly.
    D. to convince the reader to conserve insect habitats.

32. From the passage, the reader can infer that "spiracles" are most similar to:
    F. fins.
    G. lungs.
    H. gills.
    J. snorkels.

33. The overall tone of the passage is:
    A. informative and insipid.
    B. fascinated and educational.
    C. scholastic and indifferent.
    D. objective and pensive.

34. Which of the following insects is NOT described in this passage as adapting physical features necessary for breathing underwater?
    F. Dragonfly
    G. Stonefly
    H. Beetle
    J. Mosquito

35. Given that "molt" is a verb meaning "to lose feathers, hair, or skin, to make way for new growth", the reader can infer that "instar" (lines 22-24) means:
    A. phase.
    B. scales.
    C. wings.
    D. life.

36. Lines 37-42 indicate that stoneflies:
    F. spend almost all of their instars underwater.
    G. prefer to lay their eggs underwater to protect them from non-aqueous prey.
    H. only spend the first half of their life phases underwater.
    J. hunt in the air but nest underwater.

37. The transformation of a stonefly from water insect to air insect is most like the transformation of:
    A. a human fetus to a grown adult.
    B. a caterpillar to a butterfly.
    C. a tadpole to a frog.
    D. a fish egg to a fish.

38. It can be reasonably inferred that the author "confines attention" to three species of flies in order to:
    F. provide examples of how typical flies go through some phases of their lives underwater.
    G. prove that some flies are named incorrectly.
    H. teach students about the larva of all insects.
    J. show that all insects fall into these three categories.

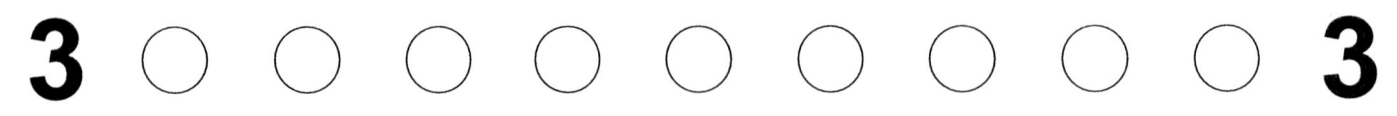

39. Based on the passage as a whole, it is implied that the author believes that:

    A. insects that can live in both the air and the water have a better chance of survival.
    B. insects that mature underwater are more likely to develop wings than insects born above water.
    C. insects who have the ability to lay eggs under water have higher offspring success rates.
    D. the dual environments of these insects make them exceptionally interesting.

40. In the first line of the passage, it can be inferred that the term "preeminently" is similar to all of the following definitions EXCEPT:

    F. mostly.
    G. primarily.
    H. greatly.
    J. predominantly.

Reading Mastery - Level 1

Answer Explanations

31. **The correct answer is B.** The title of the book is "The Life Story of Insects" and the passage details the life cycle of various insects.

32. **The correct answer is H.** In lines 4-9 the author details the spiracles on an insect, which function much like gills on a fish. Fins are not used for breathing, but for locomotion. Lungs are similar to "a system of branching air tubes" described in lines 4 and 5, not to the spiracles which are more like air holes. A gill is a more apt simile than a snorkel.

33. **The correct answer is B.** The passage is intended to teach the reader, but it is also clear in lines like 10 that the author is very interested in the subject.

34. **The correct answer is J.** The author mentions all of the answer choices except mosquitos in the passage.

35. **The correct answer is A.** This question is a little tricky because it is dealing with uncommon vocabulary. In lines 22-23 the author mentions a preparatory instar and then in line 23-24 the author mentions an adult instar. The two indicate that an "instar" most closely means a phase or stage in life.

36. **The correct answer is F.** This question is also a bit tricky because both F and H seem like reasonable answers. However, the correct answer is F because the author mentions in lines 37-42 that the insects being described remain continually underwater until achieving their final molt.

37. **The correct answer is C.** A tadpole lives and breathes underwater and eventually becomes a frog that breathes out of the water.

38. **The correct answer is F.** The author does not want to talk about every single species of insects all at once. These three are representative of the phenomena he is currently discussing.

39. **The correct answer is D.** The author writes about how the insects can live in both the water and the air and he uses the word "interesting" to describe it. The entire passage has a tone of strong interest and fascination. The other conclusions mentioned in the answer choices are not reached or discussed in the passage.

40. **The correct answer is H.** "Preeminently" is used in the first sentence saying that insects are "preeminently" creatures of the land and air. If you replace "preeminently" with any of the other options, the only one that does not make any sense in the sentence is H: "greatly." "Preeminently" means "above all; in particular."

Reading Mini-Test 5

Time yourself 8 minutes for the following mini-test. Start the timer when you flip this page.

Reading Mastery - Level 1

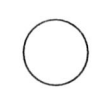

Reading Test
35 Minutes — 40 Questions

Directions: There are four passages in this portion of the test. Following each passage you will be given a variety of questions. Choose the best answer to each question, then color its corresponding bubble on your answer sheet. Refer to the passages as needed.

Passage I

PROSE FICTION: The following passage is an excerpt from J.M. Barrie's *Peter Pan*.

All children, except one, grow up. They soon know that they will grow up, and the way Wendy knew was this. One day when she was two years old she was playing in a garden, and she plucked another
5 flower and ran with it to her mother. I suppose she must have looked rather delightful, for Mrs. Darling put her hand to her heart and cried, "Oh, why can't you remain like this for ever!" This was all that passed between them on the subject, but
10 henceforth Wendy knew that she must grow up. You always know after you are two. Two is the beginning of the end.

Of course they lived at 14 [their house number on their street], and until Wendy came her mother
15 was the chief one. She was a lovely lady, with a romantic mind and such a sweet mocking mouth. Her romantic mind was like the tiny boxes, one within the other, that come from the puzzling East, however many you discover there is always one
20 more; and her sweet mocking mouth had one kiss on it that Wendy could never get, though there it was, perfectly conspicuous in the right-hand corner.

The way Mr. Darling won her was this: the many gentlemen who had been boys when she was a
25 girl discovered simultaneously that they loved her, and they all ran to her house to propose to her except Mr. Darling, who took a cab and nipped in first, and so he got her. He got all of her, except the innermost box and the kiss. He never knew about
30 the box, and in time he gave up trying for the kiss. Wendy thought Napoleon could have got it, but I can picture him trying, and then going off in a passion, slamming the door.

Mr. Darling used to boast to Wendy that her
35 mother not only loved him but respected him. He was one of those deep ones who know about stocks and shares. Of course no one really knows, but he quite seemed to know, and he often said stocks were up and shares were down in a way that
40 would have made any woman respect him.

Mrs. Darling was married in white, and at first she kept the books perfectly, almost gleefully, as if it were a game, not so much as a Brussels sprout was missing; but by and by whole cauliflowers dropped
45 out, and instead of them there were pictures of babies without faces. She drew them when she should have been totting up. They were Mrs. Darling's guesses.

Mrs. Darling loved to have everything just so,
50 and Mr. Darling had a passion for being exactly like his neighbors; so, of course, they had a nurse. As they were poor, owing to the amount of milk the children drank, this nurse was a prim Newfoundland dog, called Nana, who had belonged
55 to no one in particular until the Darlings engaged her. She had always thought children important, however, and the Darlings had become acquainted with her in Kensington Gardens, where she spent most of her spare time peeping into baby carriages,
60 and she was much hated by careless nursemaids, whom she followed to their homes and complained of to their mistresses. She proved to be quite a treasure of a nurse. How thorough she was at bathtime, and up at any moment of the night if one
65 of her charges made the slightest cry. Of course

her kennel was in the nursery. She had a genius for knowing when a cough is a thing to have no patience with and when it needs stocking around your throat. She believed to her last day in old-
70 fashioned remedies like rhubarb leaf, and made sounds of contempt over all this new-fangled talk about germs, and so on. It was a lesson in propriety to see her escorting the children to school, walking sedately by their side when they were well
75 behaved, and butting them back into line if they strayed.

No nursery could possibly have been conducted more correctly, and Mr. Darling knew it, yet he sometimes wondered uneasily whether the
80 neighbors talked.

1. What does the author mean when he writes that Mrs. Darling's mind was like tiny boxes?
    A. Mrs. Darling is a complex and secretive woman.
    B. Mrs. Darling is a deep and respectful woman.
    C. Mrs. Darling is a simple minded woman.
    D. Mrs. Darling has a very good memory.

2. Mr. Darling can best be described as:
    F. a bold, pretentious man.
    G. a family man of great character.
    H. a strict, authoritarian parent.
    J. a gentle and caring man.

3. Why did Mrs. Darling start slacking on the books?
    A. She started growing vegetables instead.
    B. Someone was stealing cauliflower from their garden.
    C. She wanted children and couldn't focus.
    D. Mr. Darling decided to do the books instead.

4. Nana does all of the following EXCEPT:
    F. bring the children to school.
    G. give the children baths.
    H. sleep at the foot of the children's bed.
    J. cure a child's sickness.

5. The narrator explains that women respect Mr. Darling because:
    A. he was rich and smart.
    B. he understood stocks and shares.
    C. he was a romantic.
    D. he demanded respect wherever he went.

6. It can be reasonably inferred from the passage that Wendy:
    F. is a center of attention in the house.
    G. is a neglected child.
    H. is adventurous and innocent.
    J. has been full of contempt since the age of two.

7. It is implied in lines 49-51 that:
   A. Mr. Darling valued reputation a great deal.
   B. Mr. Darling felt it was necessary for his children's health to have a nurse.
   C. the neighbors were of the same or lower social status as the Darlings.
   D. Mr. Darling's neighbors envied him.

8. The narrator claims the Darlings are poor because:
   F. Mrs. Darling does not work.
   G. Mr. Darling lost his job.
   H. Mr. Darling's job is based on an unreliable market.
   J. the children drink too much milk.

9. Why was Mr. Darling worried about what the neighbors think?
   A. Because they are poor.
   B. Because Mrs. Darling wears extravagant clothing.
   C. Because their nurse is a dog.
   D. Because their children drink too much milk.

10. What does the author imply by writing a description of Nana being compared to Mr. and Mrs. Darling?
    F. Nana is a more prominent character in the novel than the Darlings.
    G. Nana is going to be the main protagonist of the novel.
    H. Nana played a larger role in the children's lives than their parents did.
    J. Nana is more qualified to raise the Darling children than Mr. or Mrs. Darling.

Answer Explanations

1. **The correct answer is A**. The author writes that trying to figure out Mrs. Darling is like taking apart Eastern dolls where there is always another one inside and no one could ever unlock the last box (lines 17-20). This indicates that Mrs. Darling is complex and has secrets that no one knows.

2. **The correct answer is F**. It is evident in lines 49-51 that Mr. Darling believes he is worthy of praise and wants to impress people with his importance or value. He also *"had a passion for being exactly like his neighbors"* and worried if the neighbors talked about them.

3. **The correct answer is C**. In lines 41-48 the author writes about how Mrs. Darling kept the books, but began drawing babies instead. We can infer from this that she wanted children.

4. **The correct answer is H**. The author writes that she gives the children baths, walks with them to school, and *"she believed to her last day in old-fashioned remedies like rhubarb leaf."* Although the author writes that her kennel was in the nursery, he does not say that she slept at the feet of the children's beds (lines 63-76).

5. **The correct answer is B**. The author writes in lines 36-40 that Mr. Darling would talk about stocks and shares in a way that would make women respect him.

6. **The correct answer is F**. The narrator says in lines 13-15, *"...until Wendy came, she (Mrs. Darling) was the chief one."*

7. **The correct answer is A**. In lines 49-51 the author states, *"Mr. Darling had a passion for being exactly like his neighbors"* which shows that he cared a lot about what the people around him thought of him.

8. **The correct answer is J**. In lines 52-53 the author writes, *"As they were poor, owing to the amount of milk the children drank."*

9. **The correct answer is C**. In lines 77-80 the author writes that Mr. Darling knew no nursery could have been run as well as theirs, but he still worried about what his neighbors would say.

10. **The correct answer is H**. When the author describes Mr. and Mrs. Darling, he scarcely mentions them in regards to their parenting. However, he includes a lengthy, detailed paragraph (paragraph 6) on Nana as the caretaker.

Reading Mini-Test 6

Time yourself 8 minutes for the following mini-test. Start the timer when you flip this page.

Passage II

SOCIAL SCIENCE: The following passage is an excerpt from William T. Hornaday's *Our Vanishing Wild Life* published in 1913.

The preservation of animal and plant life, and of the general beauty of Nature, is one of the foremost duties of the men and women of today. It is an imperative duty, because it must be
5 performed at once, for otherwise it will be too late. Every possible means of preservation—sentimental, educational and legislative—must be employed.

The present warning issues with no uncertain sound, because this great battle for preservation
10 and conservation cannot be won by gentle tones, nor by appeals to the aesthetic instincts of those who have no sense of beauty, or enjoyment of Nature. It is necessary to sound a loud alarm, to present the facts in very strong language, backed
15 up by irrefutable statistics and by photographs which tell no lies, to establish the law and enforce it if needs be with a bludgeon.

This book is such an alarm call. Its forceful pages remind me of the sounding of the great bells in the
20 watchtowers of the cities of the Middle Ages, which called the citizens to arms to protect their homes, their liberties and their happiness. It is undeniable that the welfare and happiness of our own and of all future generations of Americans are at stake in
25 this battle for the preservation of Nature against the selfishness, the ignorance, or the cruelty of her destroyers.

We no longer destroy great works of art. They are treasured, and regarded as of priceless value;
30 but we have yet to attain the state of civilization where the destruction of a glorious work of Nature, whether it be a cliff, a forest, or a species of mammal or bird, is regarded with equal abhorrence. The whole earth is a poorer place to
35 live in when a colony of exquisite egrets or birds of paradise is destroyed in order that the plumes may decorate the hat of some lady of fashion, and ultimately find their way into the rubbish heap. The people of all the New England States are poorer
40 when the ignorant whites or foreigners destroy the robins and other songbirds of the North for a mess of pottage.

Travels through Europe, as well as over a large part of the North American continent, have convinced
45 me that nowhere is Nature being destroyed so rapidly as in the United States. Except within our conservation areas, an earthly paradise is being turned into an earthly hades; and it is neither savages nor primitive men who are doing this, but
50 men and women who boast of their civilization. Air and water are polluted, rivers and streams serve as sewers and dumping grounds, forests are swept away and fishes are driven from the streams. Many birds are becoming extinct, and certain
55 mammals are on the verge of extermination. Vulgar advertisements hide the landscape, and in all that disfigures the wonderful heritage of the beauty of Nature today, we Americans are in the lead.

Fortunately the tide of destruction is ebbing, and
60 the tide of conservation is coming in. Americans are practical. Like all other northern peoples, they love money and will sacrifice much for it, but they are also full of idealism, as well as of moral and spiritual energy. The influence of the splendid body
65 of Americans and Canadians, who have turned their best forces of mind and language into literature and into political power for the conservation movement, is becoming stronger every day. Yet we are far from the point where the momentum
70 of conservation is strong enough to arrest and roll back the tide of destruction; and this is especially true with regard to our fast vanishing animal life.

Reading Mini-Test 6

11. What does the writer intend to accomplish with this passage?
    A. He wants to shock the reader with gruesome facts about destruction of wildlife.
    B. He wants to introduce the reader to the concept of conserving wildlife.
    C. He wants to incite fear in the reader.
    D. He wants to provoke activism in the reader in order to conserve Nature.

12. Who does the author blame most for the destruction of wild life?
    F. People around the world
    G. Americans
    H. Southerners
    J. The reader

13. The author specifically mentions all of the following means of preservation EXCEPT:
    A. sentimental.
    B. legislative.
    C. economical.
    D. educational.

14. The author compares Nature to:
    F. fine jewelry.
    G. fine art.
    H. a feather for fashion-wear.
    J. a great battle.

15. It is implied throughout the entire passage that the author believes:
    A. Nature is not just a part of the world, but rather Nature is the world.
    B. living in harmony with Nature should be every living being's first priority.
    C. the main job of human beings should be to protect the world in which they live.
    D. human beings have no capacity for compassion when it comes to Nature.

16. The author says we must evoke action by:
    F. appealing directly to the opposition.
    G. emphasizing beautiful aspects of Nature that should not be destroyed.
    H. enforcing legislature about conservation and raising awareness.
    J. starting violent protests against people who destroy Nature.

17. The author uses lines 43-46 to:
    A. develop context for the rest of the paragraph.
    B. establish credibility and reliability in his passage.
    C. boast about all the places he has traveled to.
    D. encourage the reader to see places all over the world.

18. The overall tone of the passage can best be described as:
    F. angry and anxious.
    G. defensive and disdainful.
    H. honest and educational.
    J. determined and direct.

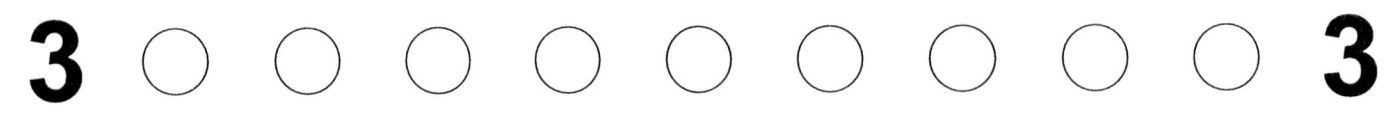

19. The final paragraph is vital to the passage because:
    A. it describes how conservationism is on the rise, yet emphasizes there is much work left to be done.
    B. it explains that humans are smart and innovative.
    C. it details how far humans still have to go in conservation efforts.
    D. it shows what efforts have already been made towards conserving Nature.

20. The author compares his call for action to:
    F. an alarm clock.
    G. the sounding of a medieval bell tower.
    H. a battle.
    J. an imperative duty.

Answer Explanations

11. **The correct answer is D.** The author is trying to encourage the reader to not only care about preservation, but also to *"turn their best forces of mind and language into literature and into political power for the conservation movement"* (lines 65-68). He describes his book as an *"alarm call"* in line 18.

12. **The correct answer is G.** In lines 43-46 the author claims *"nowhere is Nature being destroyed so rapidly as in the United States."*

13. **The correct answer is C.** In lines 6-7 the author mentions *"sentimental, educational, and legislative"* and not economical.

14. **The correct answer is G.** In line 28 the author writes that people no longer destroy great art, suggesting that, instead, we destroy Nature.

15. **The correct answer is C.** In the first sentence he says that preserving the plant should be the *"foremost duties of the men and women today"* (lines 1-3). This assumption is echoed throughout the passage.

16. **The correct answer is H.** The author says we must present facts with irrefutable statistics, and he says in line 16, *"to establish the law and enforce it."*

17. **The correct answer is B.** He tells the reader that he has been to many places in the world and therefore is establishing his credibility to say that people in the United States are destroying Nature the most rapidly.

18. **The correct answer is J.** He is straightforward with what he wants to say and also determined to argue his case to the reader about preservation and activism.

19. **The correct answer is A.** This is the most accurate description of the value of the last paragraph. The author writes that although some Americans are destroying Nature, others are changing and using their knowledge toward preserving the planet.

20. **The correct answer is G.** In lines 18-22 he writes that his book is like the sounding of the bells in watchtowers of the Middle Ages.

Reading Mini-Test 7

Time yourself 8 minutes for the following mini-test. Start the timer when you flip this page.

Passage III

HUMANITIES: The following passage is an excerpt from the introduction of E.M. Berens' *Myths and Legends of Ancient Greece and Rome*, which was originally published in 1880.

In appearance, the gods were supposed to resemble mortals, whom, however, they far surpassed in beauty, grandeur, and strength; they were also more commanding in stature, height
5   being considered by the Greeks an attribute of beauty in man or woman. They resembled human beings in their feelings and habits, intermarrying and having children, and requiring daily nourishment to recruit their strength, and
10 refreshing sleep to restore their energies. Their blood, a bright ethereal fluid called Ichor, never engendered disease, and, when shed, had the power of producing new life.

The Greeks believed that the mental qualifications
15 of their gods were of a much higher order than those of men, but nevertheless, as we shall see, they were not considered to be exempt from human passions, and we frequently behold them actuated by revenge, deceit, and jealousy. They,
20 however, always punish the evildoer, and visit with dire calamities any impious mortal who dares to neglect their worship or despise their rites. We often hear of them visiting mankind and partaking of their hospitality, and not infrequently both gods
25 and goddesses become attached to mortals, with whom they unite themselves, the offspring of these unions being called heroes or demi-gods, who were usually renowned for their great strength and courage. But although there were so many points
30 of resemblance between gods and men, there remained the one great characteristic distinction, which was that the gods enjoyed immortality. Still, they were not invulnerable, and we often hear of them being wounded, and suffering in
35 consequence such exquisite torture that they have earnestly prayed to be deprived of their privilege of immortality.

The gods knew no limitation of time or space, being able to transport themselves to incredible distances
40 with the speed of thought. They possessed the power of rendering themselves invisible at will, and could assume the forms of men or animals as it suited their convenience. They could also transform human beings into trees, stones, animals, etc.,
45 either as a punishment for their misdeeds, or as a means of protecting the individual, thus transformed, from impending danger.

Their robes were like those worn by mortals, but were perfect in form and much finer in texture.
50 Their weapons also resembled those used by mankind; we hear of spears, shields, helmets, bows and arrows, etc., being employed by the gods. Each deity possessed a beautiful chariot, which, drawn by horses or other animals of celestial breed,
55 conveyed them rapidly over land and sea according to their pleasure.

Most of these divinities lived on the summit of Mount Olympus, each possessing his or her individual habitation, and all meeting together on
60 festive occasions in the council-chamber of the gods, where their banquets were enlivened by the sweet strains of Apollo's lyre, whilst the beautiful voices of the Muses poured forth their rich melodies to his harmonious accompaniment.

65 Magnificent temples were erected to their honor, where they were worshiped with the greatest solemnity; rich gifts were presented to them, and animals, and indeed sometimes human beings, were sacrificed on their altars.

70 The most important of these divinities may have been something more than the mere creations of an active and poetical imagination. They were

possibly human beings who had so distinguished themselves in life by their preeminence over their
75 fellow-mortals that, after death, they were deified by the people among whom they lived, and the poets touched with their magic wand the details of lives, which, in more prosaic times, would simply have been recorded as illustrious.

21. The author's main purpose for writing this passage was to:
   A. educate the reader on the various gods of Greek and Roman mythology.
   B. portray the many benefits of polytheism.
   C. give the reader the background knowledge necessary for future reading on the subject of Greek gods.
   D. demonstrate the relation between the Greeks or Romans and their religion.

22. What does the author accomplish by showing the similarities between the gods and mortals?
   F. The author is able to demonstrate the relationship between the gods and the humans and quickly describe the gods.
   G. The author is able to show how the gods were superior to the humans.
   H. The author concludes how the gods were able to easily fool the mortals.
   J. The author determines that the gods were malicious because they looked like humans, but were more beautiful.

23. Lines 38-43 help the author demonstrate:
   A. how the gods accomplished everything through tricks and sleight of hand.
   B. some of the supernatural powers of the Greek gods.
   C. how the gods were able to be in two places at once.
   D. other ways that Greeks and their gods were similar.

24. The overall tone of the passage is:
   F. informative and straightforward.
   G. didactic and honest.
   H. critical and dramatic.
   J. informal and imaginative.

25. What hypothesis does the author propose concerning the gods?
   A. The myths could have come from legends of great and accomplished people.
   B. The gods were originally fellow mortals who had been granted immortality.
   C. Mortals did not really believe the gods existed, but rather that they were a figment of the imagination.
   D. The myths of the gods were just made up whole-cloth by ancient poets.

26. Lines 43-47 imply that the gods:
   F. were malevolent and vengeful.
   G. were wicked and cruel.
   H. cared about humans and shielded them.
   J. were both merciless and compassionate.

27. All of the following were mentioned as a part of a festive occasion of the gods EXCEPT:

   A. a feast.
   B. a god playing an instrument.
   C. singing.
   D. dancing.

28. The gods are similar to humans in that:

   F. they look exactly like any other mortal.
   G. they have human emotions.
   H. they can die from serious wounds.
   J. they could not have children.

29. From the lines 65-69 the reader can infer that:

   A. many Greeks were extremely devoted to the gods and would do anything for them.
   B. humans lived in fear of the wrath of the gods.
   C. ancient Greeks were very wealthy.
   D. the gods demanded that the mortals build them temples and give offerings.

30. It is implied in the passage that the word "divinities" means:

   F. religions.
   G. devotees.
   H. mythologies.
   J. gods.

Answer Explanations

21. **The correct answer is C**. The passage only builds background information and context for the reader, rather than providing information about specific gods, goddesses, or myths.

22. **The correct answer is F**. The comparisons drawn between Greeks and their gods provide information both about the gods and the relationship between them and their worshippers.

23. **The correct answer is B**. These lines (38-43) provide specifics about things that the gods were described as being able to do that were beyond natural, human abilities.

24. **The correct answer is F**. The author takes a factual, informative approach designed to directly supply his reader with interesting information.

25. **The correct answer is A**. In lines 72-73 the author writes that these gods *"were possibly human."*

26. **The correct answer is J**. In lines 43-47 the author talks about how the gods could transform humans in order to protect them (compassion) or to punish them (merciless).

27. **The correct answer is D**. In lines 57-64 the passage states that the gods would meet for festive occasions and have banquets (feasts), Apollo would play on the lyre (a musical instrument), and the Muses would sing. The author does not mention the gods dancing at these festive occasions.

28. **The correct answer is G**. In lines 14-19 the author writes about how the gods were superior to humans in many ways, but they still experienced human emotions.

29. **The correct answer is A**. The author writes that the mortals built temples, brought offerings, and would even offer sacrifices to the gods.

30. **The correct answer is J**. The author uses the word *"divinities"* when referring to the gods, as is evident in lines 57-58 when the author writes that the divinities lived on Mount Olympus.

Reading Mini-Test 8

Time yourself 8 minutes for the following mini-test. Start the timer when you flip this page.

Passage IV

NATURAL SCIENCE: The following is an excerpt from the first chapter of Charles Darwin's *The Origin of Species* published in 1859 after over 20 years of research that began with a five year journey throughout the world and to the infamous Galapagos Islands.

When on board H.M.S. Beagle as a naturalist, I was much struck with certain facts in the distribution of the organic beings inhabiting South America, and in the geographical relations of the present
5 to the past inhabitants of that continent. These facts seemed to throw some light on the origin of species—that mystery of mysteries, as it has been called by one of our greatest philosophers. On my return home, in 1837, it occurred to me that
10 something might perhaps be made out on this question by patiently accumulating and reflecting on all sorts of facts, which could possibly have any bearing on it. After five years' work, I allowed myself to speculate on the subject, and drew up
15 some short notes; these I enlarged in 1844 into a sketch of the conclusions, which then seemed to me probable. From that period to the present day I have steadily pursued the same object.

In considering the origin of species, it is quite
20 conceivable that a naturalist, reflecting on the mutual affinities of organic beings, on their embryological relations, their geographical distribution, geological succession, and other such facts, might come to the conclusion that
25 species had not been independently created, but had descended, like varieties, from other species. Nevertheless, such a conclusion, even if well founded, would be unsatisfactory, until it could be shown how the innumerable species inhabiting
30 this world have been modified so as to acquire that perfection of structure and co-adaptation, which justly excites our admiration.

Naturalists continually refer to external conditions, such as climate, food, etc., as the only possible
35 cause of variation. In one limited sense, as we shall hereafter see, this may be true; but it is preposterous to attribute to mere external conditions the structure, for instance, of the woodpecker, with its feet, tail, beak, and tongue, so
40 admirably adapted to catch insects under the bark of trees. In the case of the mistletoe, which draws its nourishment from certain trees, which has seeds that must be transported by certain birds, and which has flowers with separate sexes absolutely
45 requiring the agency of certain insects to bring pollen from one flower to the other, it is equally preposterous to account for the structure of the parasite, with its relations to several distinct organic beings, by the effects of external conditions, or of
50 habit, or of the volition of the plant itself.

It is, therefore, of the highest importance to gain a clear insight into the means of modification and co-adaptation. At the beginning of my observations it seemed to me probable that a careful study of
55 domesticated animals and of cultivated plants would offer the best chance of making out this obscure problem. Nor have I been disappointed; in this and in all other perplexing cases I have invariably found that our knowledge, imperfect
60 though it be, of variation under domestication, afforded the best and safest clue. I may venture to express my conviction of the high value of such studies, although they have been very commonly neglected by naturalists.

65 Although much remains obscure, and will long remain obscure, I can entertain no doubt, after the most deliberate study and dispassionate judgment of which I am capable, that the view which most naturalists until recently entertained, and which I
70 formerly entertained—namely, that each species has been independently created—is erroneous. I am fully convinced that species are not immutable,

but that those belonging to what are called the same genera are lineal descendants of some other
75 and generally extinct species; in the same manner as the acknowledged varieties of any one species are the descendants of that species. Furthermore, I am also convinced that Natural Selection has been the most important, but not the exclusive, means
80 of modification.

31. The author's main intention when writing this passage was:
    A. to explain the theory of evolution.
    B. to introduce his scientific findings.
    C. to introduce his findings and hypothesis in an objective manner.
    D. to construct a hypothetical analysis of scientific observations.

32. By "naturalist" the author most likely means:
    F. someone who writes about Nature.
    G. someone who studies natural history.
    H. someone who supports the theory of evolution.
    J. someone who has natural explanations for events.

33. Darwin studied all of the following aspects of the history of species EXCEPT:
    A. where in the world they are located.
    B. the offspring of different animals.
    C. ancestry of different animals.
    D. the food that different animals eat.

34. It can be inferred from the passage that the author believes naturalists have:
    F. had great ideas, but not much evidence to back them up.
    G. been idealists rather than scientists.
    H. only been looking at the origin of species in one way.
    J. seen similarities among animals, but made no attempt to connect them.

35. Which of the following does the author NOT accomplish by using the words "probable" and "likely"?
    A. He makes the passage open for discussion by avoiding taking an absolute stance.
    B. He is able to remain objective and inconclusive.
    C. He maintains an informality that makes the reader feel more comfortable.
    D. He is able to reassure the reader that his findings are not absolute.

36. Darwin decided to investigate "the origin of the species" with:
    F. woodpeckers.
    G. domesticated animals.
    H. wild plants.
    J. mistletoe.

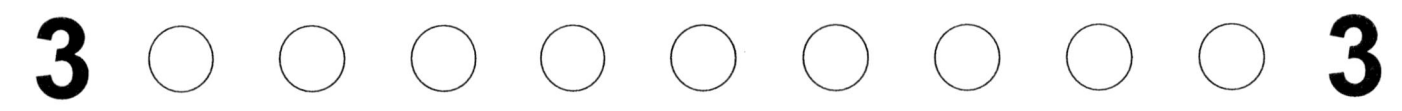

37. Why does Darwin write that his conclusion could possibly be "unsatisfactory" (Line 28)?

    A. He did not have nearly enough evidence to support his hypothesis.
    B. His conclusions could not be accepted unless they accounted for how species were modified for the perfection of their structure.
    C. His conclusion could never account for humans.
    D. His conclusion would never be accepted by other scientists.

38. The overall tone of the passage can best be described as:

    F. hopeful and nervous.
    G. respectful and didactic.
    H. confident and proud.
    J. careful and introductory.

39. The reader can infer from the passage that "Natural Selection" most likely means:

    A. the process by which Naturalists chose scientific observations.
    B. a process of modification and co-adaptation.
    C. the process by which species today have been modified.
    D. how species are independently created.

40. Darwin believes that mistletoe could not have been created independently because:

    F. its survival requires sophisticated relationships with many other species.
    G. it is a parasite that attaches to a tree.
    H. it must be pollinated by insects.
    J. it is a cousin to the woodpecker.

Reading Mastery - Level 1

Answer Explanations

31. **The correct answer is C**. This is the beginning of Charles Darwin's first chapter of his book *The Origin of Species*. He is only intending to introduce his findings and in a scientific manner, which would require him to be objective.

32. **The correct answer is G**. This question is a little tricky because Darwin does not explicitly explain the term *"naturalist,"* but he uses it frequently. The reader can figure it out, however, by the context of the passage. In line 1, Darwin refers to himself as a *"naturalist"* and then later he explains that naturalists (line 20) in the past have only looked at environmental causes of modification. This can lead the reader to conclude that a *"naturalist"* is someone who studies the history of a species, as Darwin is writing about the genetics, adaptation, and modification of a species over time.

33. **The correct answer is D**. Darwin mentions the first three options in lines 19-26.

34. **The correct answer is H**. In lines 33-35 Darwin writes, *"Naturalists continually refer to external conditions, such as climate, food, etc., as the only possible cause of variation."*

35. **The correct answer is C**. With the use of words like *"probably"* or *"likely,"* Darwin is able to avoid making a definite claim. Because he is drawing a conclusion from a limited set of observations and data, he uses words that only indicate the likelihood of his conclusion in order to maintain objectivity. These terms, however, are formal and do not create a tone of informality.

36. **The correct answer is G**. In lines 53-57 Darwin writes, *"a careful study of domesticated animals and of cultivated plants"* would make the best subjects.

37. **The correct answer is B**. In lines 27-32 Darwin explains why his conclusion would be unsatisfactory, writing, *"until it could be shown how the innumerable species inhabiting this world have been modified."*

38. **The correct answer is J**. The tone is introductory because this is the beginning of the book and he's simply setting up context. It is also careful because his word choice indicates that he has no intention of drawing definite conclusions or making absolute claims.

39. **The correct answer is C**. In lines 75-77 when Darwin writes, *"the acknowledged varieties of any one species are the descendants of that species,"* he is basically saying that traits from species get passed down to their offspring resulting in genetic variation. Lines 77-80 indicate that *"Natural Selection"* is referred to as *"a means of modification."*

40. **The correct answer is F**. Lines 41-50 detail the parasitic mistletoe's relationship with so many other species on the planet. In order for mistletoe to survive, so many other species must make it possible. Thus, Darwin concludes that mistletoe cannot have been created independent from all of these other organisms.

About the Author

Craig Gehring has helped thousands of students work toward their higher educational dreams since 2003, his junior year in high school when he earned perfect scores on both the ACT and the SAT. That year, parents started calling the school and asking for Craig to tutor their children. Ten years later, he has written the books—literally—on mastering the ACT and leads an effort to improve preparation for standardized tests. His *ACT Mastery* program averages more than a three point improvement in only six weeks, four times better than the national test prep average.

Contact Craig by email, on his blog, or on Facebook:

craig@actmastery.org
www.actmastery.org
http://www.facebook.com/CraigGehringACT

Further Study

For more information, and to find an ACT prep course in your area or online, visit WWW.ACTMASTERY.ORG

Classroom discounts available upon request.

Other Craig Gehring Titles:

SAT ACT Mastery
ACT English Mastery, Level 1
ACT Math Mastery, Level 1
ACT Science Mastery, Level 1
ACT Writing Mastery, Level 1